A HARD MAN TO BEAT

An Oral History by Howard White

A HARD MAN TO BEAT

THE STORY OF BILL WHITE,
Labour Leader, Historian, Shipyard Worker, Raconteur

HARBOUR PUBLISHING

First published in 1983 by Pulp Press Book Publishers
Reprinted by Harbour Publishing in 2011, copyright © Howard White

1 2 3 4 5 — 15 14 13 12 11

Harbour Publishing Co. Ltd.
P.O. Box 219, Madeira Park, BC, V0N 2H0
www.harbourpublishing.com

Cover photograph: Launching of the Kootenay Park (Hull #104), West Coast
Shipbuilders, June 11, 1944, courtesy of Allied Shipbuilders Ltd.
Cover design by Teresa Karbashewski
Text design by Mary White
Printed and bound in Canada

Harbour Publishing acknowledges financial support from the Government of
Canada through the Canada Book Fund and the Canada Council for the Arts,
and from the Province of British Columbia through the BC Arts Council and
the Book Publishing Tax Credit.

Library and Archives Canada Cataloguing in Publication

White, Howard, 1945–
    A hard man to beat : the story of Bill White, labour leader / Howard White.

Includes index.
"A Vancouver 125 legacy book".
ISBN 978-1-55017-551-6

    1. White, Bill, 1905–2001. 2. Labor leaders—British Columbia—
Biography. 3. Labor unions—British Columbia—History. I. Title.

HD6525.W43W45 2011   331.88092   C2011-904635-0

*Dedicated to all the good trade unionists I met
during my time in the labour movement.*

Illegitimus non Carborundum
(Don't let the bastards grind you down.)
—BILL WHITE

CONTENTS

Introduction

I t was typical of Bill White, feisty ex-trapper, ex-Arctic traveller, ex-Royal Canadian Mounted Policeman, and ex-communist union boss, that he remembered Senator Gerry McGeer as the reactionary double-crossing Vancouver mayor who turned mounted policemen loose on jobless demonstrators in 1935. Most people remember McGeer as one of the city's great mayors, a flamboyant Depression-era populist responsible for such renowned monuments as the City Hall and the fountain in Lost Lagoon. When twenty thousand residents turned out to see McGeer's funeral procession in 1947, Bill White, as a leading labour spokesman, was asked to comment on the "wonderful tribute."

"That was no tribute," White replied. "Them people just come out to make sure the old bugger was dead."

The anecdote says much about Bill White and the reason I chose to do this book with him.

Although some of the forty-thousand-odd Canadians who took part in the wartime shipbuilding program in British Columbia may remember "Bareknuckle Bill" as the bruising, outspoken union boss of Vancouver's teeming shipyards, and the *Vancouver Province* reported his 1955 retirement as head of the Boilermakers Union in a front-page box, his place in history is certainly not as prominent as that of Senator McGeer, longtime BC premier W.A.C. Bennett, or a host of industrialists, jurists, politicians and fellow labour leaders whom Bill, in this book, "tears hide off by the yard."

One reason Bill's story interested me was, of course, the wartime shipbuilding program, which from a standing start in 1941 trained green help and produced over three hundred ships by the war's end. Considering the province's yards don't produce one seagoing hull a year today, I had always thought the wartime effort something of an industrial miracle.

A memoir of this period would be fascinating enough, but Bill's story has more to it than that. Looking back now I realize that as I composed this book from Bill's vast and rambling conversation, the real subject I tried to bring into focus was the man himself—his personality and his language no less than his experience.

This is a crooked old world and the bendable types have the best time of it, but their histories are uninstructive and dull. Bill was different. He had a type of genius we haven't invented a word for yet; he was a straight arrow who couldn't go far without giving someone a poke. His principled stubbornness cost him a comfortable career with the RCMP when he refused to be used to intimidate the unemployed during the Great Depression. The same unbending insistence on fair play as he perceived it propelled him to the forefront of organized labour in the shipyards, as it propelled him out of the labour movement thirteen years later.

The experiences of such a man provide us with a view of familiar historical landmarks and of society as a whole that is refreshingly in contrast to the version normally presented. Bill was an adventurer whose wayward singleness of purpose led him to experience a kind of socio-political netherword. It is a world that stands back-to-back with our own familiar one, in many ways making it possible, but one which most of us live and die without ever knowing. Bill White's account of the violent side society turns upon those who seriously challenge its prevailing order adds an important dimension to our understanding of the world we occupy.

The effect of starting this book is a bit like dropping in on a heated conversation between two old campaigners who have already been carrying on all night. The air is thick with strange names, technical language and a familiarity with the intricacies of the labour movement you can't at first make whole sense of. But you don't need to know exactly how to burn the tubes of an old boiler in order get the point of what Bill says about them, namely that it was a very tricky task, and he is not afraid to say he got damn good at it. And all you need to know about the way the labour world fitted together in the 1940s and '50s you will know by the end of the story. I have tried to make this book accessible to readers who might not have given much thought to labour history before by dropping into Bill's narration all that's necessary to follow the story, and the obligatory chapter of facts and dates has been held until about halfway through where I thought most people would be ready for it. Several who read the manuscript expressed the concern that Bill sometimes voiced "incorrect" thinking or displayed unattractive sides of his personality. Most of the suggestions made for airbrushing out these faults I respectfully declined to implement because I felt they represented a misunderstanding of the book's aim, which is to reflect the real world through the real language of a real person. I would ask readers to judge the tenor of Bill's assertions here against the kind of thing they themselves might utter in private conversation, and not against the kind of considered statements that are normally prepared for public consumption.

I make no claim to present the story told here as a history in the formal sense. I would rather have it taken as a story, a yarn by a man who has come back from the wars, who makes a clean breast of his bias and whose rightness or wrongness he was happy to have the reader judge on its own merits.

—H.W., Pender Harbour, 1983, 2011

Note to the 2011 Edition:

As my first prose book, *A Hard Man to Beat* has always held a special place in my affections and I was honoured to have the Legacy Books Project select it as one of the books to be republished for Vancouver's 125th Anniversary.

A Hard Man to Beat was an experiment. Bill White was a neighbour in Pender Harbour where I grew up and still live (our shared surnames were coincidental; there was no family connection) and he wanted me to write a book about his stint in the Canadian Arctic with the RCMP during the 1930s. I was interested because Bill was a good talker and I was looking for a subject for a book-length oral history. I had been doing a number of short oral pieces in my journal *Raincoast Chronicles*, but now I wanted to try something different. There had been plenty of oral histories appearing in the wake of Studs Terkel's groundbreaking *Hard Times: An Oral History of the Great Depression* (1970) and even a few book-length efforts in the voice of a single narrator but I felt none of these went far enough in replicating the way their subjects spoke.

I believed then as I do now that vernacular speech is one of nature's great wonders and an under-utilized literary resource. I go Professor Henry Higgins one better and hold that people's natural speaking style not only contains the keys to their class but their world view and their personality. Speech patterns are as unique to individual speakers as their palmprints, but I felt that most oral history writers failed to preserve these complex and delicate structures intact and thereby squandered much of the form's potential. I wanted to do a book that would go further than anyone had before in capturing the exact way one effective but untutored speaker reflected his whole world view and his whole being in the way he used language.

Bill seemed like the perfect partner in such an enterprise, but we had a problem. Every time he started out talking about his days in the Arctic he would get sidetracked and start talking about his more recent days in the labour movement. I liked the labour stuff better. Bill's yarns about the Arctic were knowledgeable and funny but I had read plenty of good books about the Arctic. On the other hand, I had never read anything remotely entertaining or informed about BC labour, and Bill's stories were both. We made a deal. We'd do two books, and start with the one on labour.

Of course it's not easy to transpose vigorous conversation into equally gripping prose. You can't simply transcribe the tape word-for-word, stumble for stumble. Literal transcriptions are mostly unreadable and have the effect of making even a Churchill come across as an inarticulate oaf. The challenge and the art is in making a Churchill read like a Churchill sounds. The speech has to be reconstructed, but in such a way that retains what is characteristic about his vocabulary, his syntax, his mannerisms—and his habits of mind as well as tongue. The skills it calls upon are those of a good dialogue writer, something that is generally considered a god-given talent possessed by only the best dramatists and novelists, although I set out to show it could be acquired by a very determined tyro with a tape recorder.

Re-reading the book three decades later, it is no surprise to find the results uneven. The more surprising discovery is that so much of the time I did succeed in making Bill come across in print very much the way he did in person. The best parts are where I allowed his meaning to remain implicit in the way he spoke. The characteristic failings are where I pushed him to be explicit and intruded too much with my own book-learned knowledge of his era. I did this by comparing his accounts with such scattered written records as I could find, then asking him to explain any discrepancies and blending his replies into his original versions. I thought as long as I used his words in the way he spoke them I could stay true to my aim, but the fact is that I pushed him to say things he would not normally have said, and it breaks the spell. It made the book more defensible in historical terms, but made him seem a more abstract thinker than he was.

I had the notion people would respond to natural-sounding speech in a more visceral and emotionally-involved way than they did to more formal writing and I was curious to see how *A Hard Man to Beat* would be received.

It didn't quite go as I expected. The book was popular, going through several printings and generating much comment in Vancouver media. Jack Webster, who had covered Bill's wartime activities as a cub reporter and had since graduated to prime-time TV, had Bill on his show for several lengthy sessions that got the whole town talking. Columnist Denny Boyd called the book "crude, vulgar, slanted, vindictive and utterly delightful." You couldn't ask for better than that. Bill gave great interviews and for a time in the early 1980s he became a media fixture, much as he'd been back in his days as Vancouver's favourite union bad guy.

Nobody commented on the style of the book. Nobody that is, except Bill's wife Ivy, who complained that it made her husband sound like some street ruffian.

"He has never once used such dreadful language around this house," she said. "The Bill I know doesn't sound like that at all. He always speaks like a gentleman."

In fact we'd done most of the taping within Ivy's hearing and I had thirty-two hours of cassettes to prove it. I chalked up her undoubtedly sincere opinion as further proof of the invisible divide between what we hear and what we read.

I am not sure what Bill thought. Whatever misgivings he might have had about appearing in public with his psyche stripped naked were soon overtaken by his enjoyment of the celebrity it brought, along with the chance to really bog it to his old enemies, which provided a nice break from monotonous retirement. Only many years later, when he was in his nineties and finally losing his iron grip, he surprised me by saying we should do another book on his union days, only this time "tell it straight and not all phonied up so a man doesn't even recognize his own words." I was so taken aback by this utterance I forgot to ask whether this would mean making him sound more like a gentleman, or less.

Whatever he truly felt all those years, it never seemed to diminish his enthusiasm for spreading the book far and wide. His great ambition was to get a condensed version into *Reader's Digest*. Needless to say, that never happened, though he did manage to cultivate a substantial following around Mesa, Arizona, where he spent his winters. Nor did his experience with the first book do anything but increase his desire to carry on with the second part of our collaboration, the book on the Arctic. By this time I was caught up in a publishing job that left me little time to write, but we did manage to get together occasionally and eventually accumulated another thirty-plus hours of tape which unfortunately was still gathering dust in my closet in 2001 when Bill wobbled off to that great igloo in the sky at the age of 96.

I had hoped to make a breakthrough with *A Hard Man to Beat* that would allow me and a host of others who would surely seize the initiative to publish an endless stream of life stories featuring the many BC pioneers I came to know about through *Raincoast Chronicles*, and I did manage two more, *Spilsbury's Coast* and *The Accidental Airline*. Both are still in print, having generated much favourable comment and sold some 50,000 copies combined, which is about as much endorsement of the method as I could have asked for, but somehow that great stream of oral history I once envisaged never quite materialized. Fate and mortgage payments ordained that I would spend my productive years serving as midwife to some 600 books of other kinds by other hands and raising two fine sons who are now finding their own way in the literary world.

Silas, the elder son, co-authored his first book when he was in grade 11, but Patrick, the younger, betrayed no interest in things literary until he was completing a history degree at the University of Victoria and suddenly decided to become a reporter. I couldn't scare him out of it by talking about all the derelict ex-newspapermen I knew so I decided to do the next best thing and encourage him to be the best reporter he could. That meant applying to the godhead of journalism, Columbia University in New York. He had excellent credentials and references, but was turned down. Columbia had a limited quota for foreign students and weren't about to waste it on middleclass WASP males, of which they already had an oversupply. Patrick could apply again, but unless he did something to set himself apart, another rejection could be expected. What could he do?

He could publish a book. He had the right publishing connections, but how could a young whelp fresh out of college write a credible book that we could get onto store shelves inside of one year?

Patrick was just getting born about the time Bill and I were wrapping up the interviewing for this book, but he knew about the box of dusty Arctic tapes and asked me if I would consider turning that long-deferred project over to him. Here was a chance to settle an old debt and help my son at one go, and I jumped at it. We got the blessing of Bill's daughters, I gave Patrick a seminar on my patented oral history technique, he set up in the basement and spent a gruelling summer getting Bill's Arctic adventures down on paper. *Mountie in Mukluks* finally saw print in the fall of 2004 and sold out two printings—the ultimate vindication. The dons of Columbia were impressed enough to accept Patrick in the next round and as I write this he rejoices in the title of national correspondent with the Toronto *Globe and Mail.*

Chalk another one up for Boilermaker Bill and the power of the spoken word.

Part One

THE SHIPYARDS

The RCMP patrol vessel *St. Roch* under construction at Burrard Drydocks in 1928. Bill White would later sail on the *St. Roch* and head Burrard's main union. NORTH VANCOUVER MUSEUM AND ARCHIVES, 27-2457

1

They Never Admitted It was a Depression

For a labour leader, I guess I had a pretty unusual background. I was a cop—a Mountie up in the Arctic. I sailed in there with Henry Larsen on the *St. Roch,* and spent the first half of the Depression at Cambridge Bay, Victoria Land. That's funny when you think about it because we couldn't help becoming heroes up there, even when all we did most of the time was sit around the post and play crib. I made a 1,200-mile dogsled trip on a murder case there one time, and Jesus, a reporter come up all the way from Chicago to write about it. Big doll of a blonde she was too, and the story went all over the continent. Reporters all over me when I came out, I could have quit the force and went into competition with Nelson Eddy.

Instead, I went into union work and joined the Communist Party, where I was really busting my ass to make things better for the average Joe, and that's when I found out I was a public enemy. This was during the great wartime shipyard boom, and I got to be head of the Boilermakers and Marine Workers Union, which at that time was the largest local union in Canada. The newspapers took a new view of me then and from that time on I couldn't do anything but I come out looking like a villain. This is the way they work it you see, the establishment. They control the people's minds without them ever realizing it.

You see, my sympathies were always on the side of the working stiff, long before I got into the union. I come off a homestead on the prairies and I knew what a hard time was. I was born in Ontario, but we moved out to the town of Yellowgrass, Saskatchewan, in 1908; I remember moving out there, you know—we moved out in a hayrack and four horses, all our gear piled up. Dad had been out and built a little shack not as big as my living room now. There was quite a rise of land about half a mile off and as we come up over this Dad said, "Well there it is!" Just this little tiny shack setting in a square of green, surrounded as far as you could see by brown prairie wool. He'd took and ploughed a fireguard around the edge, then burnt the place off as a safeguard, and it was all coming up green. You could just see this one square of green in that bloody sea of dry prairie, I can remember it so well.

It was a damn good thing he done that, too. We hadn't been there long before a fire come through. The smoke was coming over for about two days. Kept getting worse till finally it blotted the sun, thick yellow smoke. You talk about being hard on the nerves, now. Dad went and ploughed extra fireguards, got everything ready, but all you could do was wait. We had a little pothole of a lake there in front of us, and we put all our faith in that. One Saturday morning Dad said, "It's close now," and bygosh, inside of a half an hour it came. Just a damn wall of flame. Rolling—it seemed the flames were rolling in a ball up off the ground, roaring like a blowtorch and scorching the grass ten feet off. It passed by us on both sides but the lake stopped it in the middle. In no time it was gone.

We looked out and it was like we'd opened our eyes on a different world. Everything jet black, just ashes and little spirals of smoke here and there where a dry cow turd was smouldering.

We were forty miles from the railroad. That was a three-day trip. In the wintertime Dad would have to go in to get coal. He'd get in there and maybe there'd be twenty sleighs all waiting. You'd have to wait your turn, and sometimes the coal wouldn't be in and you'd have to sleep in the box of the sleigh—in the dead of winter when thirty below was considered not too bad. There was times they had to wait a week like that.

I put in quite a stretch banging around working at one thing or another. It wasn't until I was over twenty-five I got in the RCMP. As early as 1924 my cousin Mike Allewell and I went to work in a logging camp at Big River in northern Saskatchewan. The pay was twenty dollars a month. The grub consisted mostly of beans and prunes. You were out in the woods when it was still pitch dark and you stayed out till it was pitch dark at night. Lunchtime they'd make a fire and the cook would bring out a pot of beans all wrapped up, it was supposed to've been kept hot, but what with the thirty and forty below—it'd be half ice. You'd eat this and go back to work. Come quitting time you'd go in, eat more beans, and go to the bunkhouse. The bunkhouse was about forty feet long and sixteen feet wide with muzzle-loading bunks three tiers high all down both sides. These were about thirty inches wide and you crawled in from the end so you had forty guys packed in there just like pigeons in a coop. When everybody got their gear off it'd be piled up on the floor almost as high as the bunks, and what with that and the beans and prunes, the air was so rank you'd think you were going to choke. Everybody cut spruce boughs for a mattress, so there was a continuous hail of dry needles on the guys in the lower bunks. The logs in the wall had inch-wide gaps between them so you'd get covered with snow if a blizzard come up, and by the second day you were lousy as a pet coon. And anyone who kicked about anything was fired out of hand. The working man had no rights whatsoever in those days.

Another time I went working for the CPR on a construction gang laying new steel on the Weyburn-Assiniboine line into Crane Valley. Laying ties and steel and tamping ties, we were about four miles out of camp and we had to pump out on these handcars, a dozen or so guys to a car. You'd work up til noon and then you'd have to run to beat hell down a quarter-mile to where you ditched the handcars, get them up on the rail and pump to beat hell to get back out before one o'clock. They had several Italian bosses there, loud, mouthy bastards, and they carried bloody clubs like baseball bats to poke at these guys, mostly Italians, and just like a herd of cattle they'd get them running down the track to work. Merv Dickens and me were the only Anglos in this gang and we'd just let them all go running past us and take our time you see—fucked if we were going to be herded around like sheep. Well, they'd have to wait for us then and oh Jesus, they didn't like that. This old boss would come up to us waving his club, "Why you no run? Why you no run?" He wouldn't poke us though, he wouldn't dare.

Finally he fired us. We were way down the track carrying our shovels back to the handcars, and soon as he fired us we just dropped our shovels on the grade. The silly bugger, he thought he could make us pick them back and carry them in, even after he'd fired us. We had the pleasure of telling him where to put these shovels—crossways, we told him—and he had to walk back and get them himself with us laughing at him. He got the last laugh on me though: I never got paid. Merv was smart, he went in and charged up a bunch of stuff at the company store so he got that much out of it, but me, I never got a cent. The CPR still owes me.

I'd done a lot of trapping on RCMP time while I was in the Arctic and I come out with ten thousand bucks, but with everybody I knew broke and two years of· travelling around it wasn't long before I found myself in the job line-ups with the rest of them. Another fella I'd met up north, Rudolph Johnson, who later was engineer on the *St. Roch* trip through the Northwest Passage, did even worse. He came out with a twenty-thousand-dollar stake in the fall and blew it all by spring. He had expert help though—he hooked up with a dame in Vancouver they called the Danish Queen who had a lot of experience at helping guys blow in their stakes. She'd been over the road before they rolled the rocks off, that one. Anyways, just before she got interested in Rudolph she'd been cavorting with a fella named Tom Kelley, and one way or another I got to meet Kelley and he got me my first job in the shipyards. In the course of my travels I'd stopped off in Chicago and took a welding course, so Kelley put me to work converting this steel sailing ship into a log barge.

There was a hell of a man, old Tom Kelley. There was nothing phoney about him like so many guys, working stiffs that no sooner they get a few bucks than they turn into the very worst type of labour-hating reactionaries. Tom, he was one of the biggest operators on the West Coast in the thirties but if you didn't know you'd have took him for some old hooktender who didn't have a dime. He proved it you don't have to be a prick to be rich.

He got his start on the Klondike, Kelley. He had a claim on El Dorado that he said wasn't a very good claim, so he sold it for twenty thousand dollars. Which gives you an idea what real estate was like up there, when a poor claim went for twenty thousand. Twenty grand bought a lot of cigars in 1901.

I'm not sure where it was we did that barge conversion on the old *Monangahila*. It might have been BC Marine—it was down toward the Second Narrows end of Vancouver Harbour. They started work on the Lions Gate Bridge about the same time, and you know, by the time we were done in 1938 they had that damn bridge almost open. They really slammed that thing together once they made their mind up—I think it was fourteen months start to finish.

There was nothing else going on the waterfront when we finished the barge so I took a job drilling. Kelley had a prospect up in the Omineca and I went up for him and drilled til winter on Quartz Creek, then I came back to town and hit the bricks again. You'd just go the rounds, all over the city, you'd go into one outfit after another:

"Whaddayou want?"

"Have you got any work?"

"Leave your name at the door. We'll call you if we need you." Real snotty.

I'll tell you another thing about the Depression. We hear about how tough it was—about the Okies starving and babies born dead from malnutrition, and all the people out of work and all this kind of thing. We hear about this now, and people say well, that was "The Depression." Things like that could only happen during "The Depression" and there'll never be another "Depression." Well let me tell you, during the Depression they never admitted there was a depression on. It was always things are a little slow right now, but we expect an upturn by the next quarter, just the same as we hear now. And as far as unemployment goes, they were still giving out this line that any guy who really wanted to find a job could go out and get one. Right in the blackest depths of the Depression! Sure! "These bastards in the hobo jungle, in the relief camps, they're just lazy. If they wanted work they'd find work!" I tell you now, it was heartless!

And don't you think for a minute that people didn't fall for this. People ate this up. You'd see them in these little towns putting up signs, "No Transients", "Clean up Duckburg, Ban the Bums." They herded all the unemployed men off into camps and made them serve at hard labour for twenty cents a day, and people thought this was just fine.

Pattullo was elected premier in '36 or '37 on a programme of work and wages. He'd find work for us and pay us all decent wages. Pattullo was another veteran from the Klondike, but he was no miner. If I'm not mistaken he'd been a gold commissioner. His work and wages program produced no work and less wages.

I was keeping my eye on the shipyards but I don't think they had a hundred guys on steady altogether in those days. Guys all over town would be watching for a boat to come in, for repairs or a shave-and-a-haircut, and by the time she docked there'd be a crowd gathered at the gate over at Burrard Drydock in North Vancouver. If they needed twenty-five or thirty men the foreman would take twenty-five or thirty brass tags and just scatter them into the crowd. There'd be fights and scuffling and if you got a tag you could go up to the office and get hired. There was a crowd of steady guys they called "The Chosen" because they were always chosen to work ahead of everybody else, and they weren't the best men either, they were company brown-nosers. There was no fairness to it at all, the men were treated like dogs. In fact if you treated dogs like that nowadays, the SPCA would put you in court.

I mention this for a reason, because during the Depression this kind of treatment was the rule rather than the exception. With an unlimited supply of labour and no unions to stand up for the rights of the worker, the boss pushed his advantage right to the hilt.

I guess I should mention here that after I came down from the Yukon, I got married. I'd met Ivy when I first came down from the Arctic and the subject of marriage had raised its ugly head at that time but I figured out some dodge, I forget just what. But she kept working at it and after five or so years she wore me down. I got a job up in the Yukon for ten months and maybe that put me at a disadvantage. We'd been writing and she was going to meet my boat but I got waylaid and she ended up meeting empty boats for a week or so. By the time I finally got in she'd gave up so I had to go up to Woodward's where she was working and look her up. I guess she'd been doing quite a propaganda job on the other salesgirls because I remember getting looked over pretty careful. I'm afraid I didn't measure up too good because it just turned out I was wearing a hell of a big purple-and-yellow shiner. I'd got tangling with some bastard before I left Dawson and I'd zigged when I should have zagged. Ivy I guess was pretty embarrassed, but she got used to that. I used to get in on a few rhubarbs in those days.

I wasn't on the bricks too long that time before I got a chance to go back to welding, up at Ocean Falls. I wasn't too happy to be getting away from Ivy so soon but welding was what I was trained for so I decided to take a crack at it.

Tom Kelley was on the boat going up there and I helped him kill a bottle up in his stateroom.

"You won't stay at Ocean Falls long," he tells me.

"Why is that?" I says.

"Just remember I said it," he says.

Well, Tom couldn't have been righter. That was one of the worst holes I ever got into. The cockroaches were everywhere—baked in the bread, they were in the mashed potatoes—you'd get to the bottom of a cup of tea and there'd be a soggy-looking cockroach looking up at you. Walking into the cookhouse—the floor'd be just moving with them and in the bunkhouses you'd see them running around the cracks between the boards in the walls. At night you'd hear them dropping on the guys sleeping in their beds. I woke up one time with one of the goddamn things on my face. I must have woke the whole goddamn shift up cursing. Goddammit that made me mad!

They sent me down to weld inside one of these liquor tanks and the air was so bad, you'd run a bead and while it was cooling it'd be just sparkling—blue-green-yellow-blue—from the sulphur settling down out of the air. This is what you were trying to breathe. And of course you were inside this tank and the more you welded the more she heated up, til you were just roasting yourself alive in there. I'd go as long as I could, then go up the ladder to get some air, just hang over the edge with my tongue out, but they didn't like to see too much of that either. You'd get dirty looks from the strawboss—like you were shirking, you see. Just no thought of anything like ventilation, no thought of spending a buck on something that wouldn't give two bucks back. And what for? The comfort of the men? If you stood up in a place like that and said they should spend some money to insure the safety or comfort of the men they'd treat you as being insane, criminally insane, and so would the men. It was unthinkable, you see. It's hard to picture now the way it was.

That place really got me down. I got one of these what they call a sulphur cold. Boy, you talk about a cold now, there's a cold. Worst I ever had in all my life. Whether the sulphur weakens your resistance, opens your pores, feeds the germs, I don't know, but it's well known to anyone who works around sulphur.

What made you feel worst in them days is you were just so goddamn powerless to help yourself. Especially up against a corporation situation like there, they managed to get you feeling you and the cockroaches were about on the same level. A lot of guys, you'd see them kind of cave in. Good men, family men who'd never missed a day's work in their life before, you'd see them wandering around all sick and lousy and broken down. They've turned the Depression into an adventure now, but I tell you, it was no adventure. It was—*depressing*.

What scared hell out of me at Ocean Falls was the talk going around that with the war starting men were going to be froze on their jobs. They were going to set it up so you couldn't change jobs for the duration of the war. I sure as hell didn't want to get nailed down in that sinkhole, especially thinking how it would get once they knew you couldn't quit on them.

The first boat south I was on the dock waiting. And walking up the gangway, who should I see leaning over the railing but old Tom Kelley, grinning like hell.

"Don't get mad at Pacific Mills," he told me. "Get mad at the men. The company wouldn't do it unless the men let them."

I could see he was right.

I was figuring to enlist as a tailgunner in the RCAF. I'd heard stories about the gunners being hosed out at the end of their bombing missions, but I figured it couldn't be much worse than getting froze on the job in Ocean Falls. Besides, I wasn't a half bad shot and I kind of thought I'd be good at it. But I was thirty-five and married and they wouldn't have me.

2

Raining Red-Hot Rivets

There was talk of a big boom in shipbuilding when the war broke out but there was very little sign of it happening through 1939 and '40. I guess it took them a while to realize what was going on. Allied shipping losses in 1939 was some eight hundred thousand tons. In 1940 it was some four million tons. It was the fall of 1940 before they realized that they were going to lose the war not because they were short of warships, but because they were short of cargo ships. All of a sudden the war hinged on building freighters.

In Vancouver there were only three yards working in steel—Burrard Drydock and Norvan Ship Repairs in North Vancouver, and BC Marine down by the north foot of Victoria Drive—and none of these were ready to build ten-thousand-ton freighters. BC Marine never did get into the big stuff, but two more yards got started up later—South Burrard, owned by the same family as North Burrard, the Wallaces—and West Coast Shipbuilders, which was started down on False Creek by a tough old Scotchman named W.D. McLaren. Norvan, which later became Pacific Drydock and still later a part of Burrard, was owned by the Burdicks.

It was a real good time to be in the shipyard business, especially if you had connections with the Liberal Party. The government paid you all the costs of getting set up, then they gave you all the work you could handle at a guaranteed profit. All the war work as far as I know was basically cost plus ten percent but the smart ones made a lot more than ten percent.

We were living in North Vancouver and I could see they were getting busy down at Norvan Ship Repairs, they'd bought the lot next over and they were filling the harbour in and putting in four big building berths for these ten-thousand-ton freighters. I kept dropping around the Union Hall to see the business agent, Lush Campbell—he come by that name honestly too—but always it was this 'no work, no work'. I sat around the hall for days on end. Guys told me if I started off by slipping Lush a fiver my luck would improve, but I didn't have one extra. Finally I went directly over to the shipyard and they took me on the spot. Hired on as a burner. I figured to go as welder but burners was what they were hiring that day so I took it. It was all the same pay—ninety cents an hour. Welders and burners and platers, drillers

Women workers at Burrard Drydock, August 1945. Women made up a large part of the shipyard workforce during the war years. NORTH VANCOUVER MUSEUM AND ARCHIVES, 1421

and riggers were all classified as mechanics and all mechanics got ninety cents an hour. Erector specialists, bolters up, helpers, labourers were all on lower classifications and lower rates—sixty cents, forty-five cents. There were more classifications than you could shake a stick at. After they hired me on, the Lush came around wanting me to join the union, which I was glad to do. They didn't have checkoff in those days, didn't have the company timekeeper take the union dues off your paycheque automatically, so the shop stewards had to tag around after the guys on the jobs hitting them up and the business agent had to tag around after the shop stewards. It worked okay as long as there was only a handful of guys, but when things started to build up it got to be just a hopeless mess. Some guys would claim they paid twice, other guys wouldn't pay month in and month out. It was too much for Old Lush. Dues days you'd see him passed out there on the apron of the old North Van ferry with money sticking out of every pocket, flapping in the breeze. It was a bloody poor excuse for a union in those days.

It was the spring of '41 when I started work at Norvan. They weren't in high gear yet by any means. They had a contract they were working on for a couple Corvettes and they were just getting underway on that. I remember the first one, when they went to launch it, it hung up on the ways and they had to push the damn thing into the water with jacks—along with everybody pushing like hell.

I think there was one other burner besides myself on the second shift and we got used mainly on specialty work. Welding and burning hadn't come in at this time the way they did later on. The old shipbuilding techniques were still being used much the way they'd been since the nineteenth century—steel was cut mostly by shearing and joined mostly by riveting. I guess in the two years that followed there was more progress in shipbuilding than the fifty years before that.

Blowing rivets was one of the big burning jobs. Every rivet was inspected and any one didn't look good they'd chalk it to be done over. I blowed thousands and thousands of rivets. There was quite a knack to it. What I done, I'd use quite a big tip on the torch because it was fast, you know. Lots of pressure. I'd get the rivet pretty damn hot before I give her any air, I'd put a quick X on it, just in maybe a quarter of an inch, then I'd put that torch in the center, open her up, and soon as she started to blow I'd drag the tip back, just give it to her, whoof! She'd just blow right out—WHOOF!

Another pretty tricky job was burning the stay-bolts out of boilers. The bolts are screwed into the boiler plate and you have to take all the bolt threads out, but not touch the threads in the parent metal. It's pretty doggone tricky. You take a thread comes right up to a knife edge, and you've got to singe that out of there, the one without touching the other.

And burning portholes. All the portholes in the hull had to be burnt out by the burners, and it was quite a ticklish business too, mainly just because it involved making a hole in the hull of the ship— you don't want some clown cutting a bay window in the side of the ship, or putting a hole where there isn't supposed to be one. So they had a real rigamarole worked out for doing this, you see. First of all the shipwright came along and located where the porthole was going to be. He had to measure it all up and put a centre pop for the centre. Then the driller come along and he'd put his drill on the pop mark and make a hole through. Then there was a fella come along and threaded that. The burner come along with a burning outfit mounted on an arm and he screwed this into the threads and burnt out the right size of a hole. It done a nice job, too, but it sometimes took days.

One of these tin cans, one of the Corvettes—the shipwrights had it all laid out and popped and I was supposed to do the burning but as usual it was taking a hell of a long time for the drillers and threaders to get around to their part of it, so I got thinking how I could do it without them.

What I come up with was a rig something like a drawing compass. I took a straight piece of rod and braised a bearing out of a car generator on one end to take the tip of the torch and rigged a kind of a pointed leg so it could slide along the rod and you could clamp it at whatever radius you needed. To use it you just held the point of the leg in the pop mark, set it at the right radius and swung your torch around in an arc. I burnt the whole damn works of these portholes out without anybody noticing and just left the cut-out plates lying there when I went off at the end of the shift. Well, this presented them with

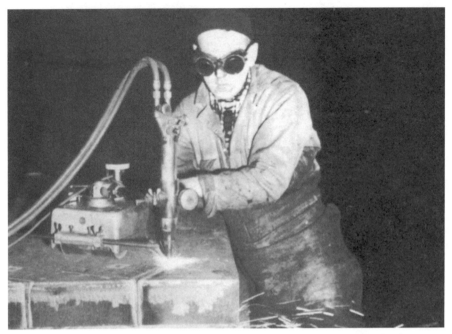

A burner at work cutting a heavy plate. This was Bill's job when he first went into the wartime shipyards.

a mystery, you see. Nobody had ever seen a porthole cut-out without a hole in the centre before.

It was interesting to see the reaction of the bosses. You could see they didn't like it, having a guy in their charge go ahead on his own hook and do something like that, but the thing worked so damn good and there was so much propaganda about speeding up war-work they couldn't say much. In no time at all every burner in the yard had one of these gadgets. Different guys told me I ought to patent it and I took a caveat out on it but I never pushed it further than that.

II

The thing to realize about the establishment is that they can turn anything to their own advantage. When the economy fell on its ass in '29 Herbert Hoover said, well, the solution is for workers to tighten their belts, work hard, and give business everything it likes so it can get back on its feet and save the country. Later on the experts decided that what had caused the Great Crash in the first place was business having *too* free a hand and not being controlled enough, but that didn't make no difference. When the war come along they said, well, the solution here is for workers to work extra hard, peg wages down, and give business a free hand so it can produce a lot of war goods and save the country. And today that's what they're saying again, telling *us* to lower our expectations and big business to raise theirs. They call this the new conservatism, but they should call it the New Hooverism. Boom or bust, their answer is always the same: take less for yourself and give us more! And the working stiff, he gets taken in every time by the same damn line.

One of the big hoaxes they had going during the war was the Dollar-A-Year Men. These big shots that went to work for the government for a dollar a year to help save the country. They didn't quit their regular jobs mind you, they did them both at the same time so you had a real hand-in-glove thing going on between the war administration and big business. A lot of guys in the course of serving the country managed to set themselves up pretty good, like H.R. MacMillan. He lent himself to the government for a dollar a year and by the end of the war MacMillan Export Company had BC's share of the world export market in wood products sewed up and locked in a box. And there were hundreds of others, waving the flag and filling their boots for all they were worth. E.P. Taylor was another one.

But it took them a while to realize what they had hold of, I think. They started off the war kind of cautious, doing things just the regular way. For example, when I first went into the yards, there were only two burners doing the work of about six. Christ, at first there we didn't even have helpers, and these big dollies on small iron wheels with all the tanks and hoses and torches and tools, you'd be dragging them all over the yard by yourself, pulling your guts out trying to plough through this goddamn loose gravel they'd put down . . .

Well, somebody put their thinking cap on somewhere along the way and decided that the wartime situation with its cost-plus called for a different method of doing business—that there should be six guys doing the work of two—and Jesus, before we knew it that place was jammed with bodies. Over seven thousand at the peak, in a yard half the size of a city block. Just like an anthill.

They'd take guys and give them four bolts, and their day's work would be to put in those four bolts. The guys would put these bolts in, tighten them up, undo them, put them in upside down, take them out and shine them up, try them in different holes, see if they could bust them off . . . It's worse than being overworked, having to look busy when you've got nothing to do, you know. They'd have whole gangs of men hiding in behind bulkheads, doing nothing for weeks at a time but playing cards and telling stories.

And the stuff that went out of that yard—just something terrific! They didn't give a damn. The bosses themselves were the worst. Old Don Service the general manager built a whole house with shipyard

Burrard workers surge toward the ferry terminal at shift change. The wartime yards employed 30,000 at their peak. NORTH VANCOUVER MUSEUM AND ARCHIVES, 27-678

materials *and* shipyard help. The guys would go out and work on it and they'd be charged up to the shipyard.

The streetcars used to run in North Van during the war and they had these wicker seats, with a crack at the back you see, you'd sit there and put your feet up under the next seat. One fella was pinching paint, carrying it out of the yard in an empty whisky bottle. He'd pack the bottle in and out under his coat and he was getting away with a quart of paint every time he went off shift. It was a screw cap on this bottle and the silly bugger, he filled it too full. He had it in his hip pocket, and on the streetcar going home it happened that the guy sitting behind him with his feet up under his seat was the night superintendent. It was warm and stuffy there inside the streetcar and what with the guy's body heat, the paint expanded and broke the bottle. The paint ran through the crack of the seat all over the super's boots.

Well, management tried to look the other way as much as they

The end of a work day at Burrard Drydock's shipyard, September 1945.
NORTH VANCOUVER MUSEUM AND ARCHIVES, 27-679

could, but here were the super's boots all covered with bright yellow paint! They felt they had to do something about it and tried to can the guy. But when we started muttering about the stuff the bosses were getting out, they dropped it.

The deal was, you see, the shipyard got ten percent on every dollar that was spent, so the more waste there was, the richer they got. The more cost the more plus.

III

What made me so damn mad was that while these guys were plundering the country from inside, us working stiffs were frozen on the job, our wages were pegged and we were forced to work under conditions that were inhuman.

You picture it now. You've got a ship going up. You've got your riveting gangs. Firepots, coke firepots, like a forge, you've got these all over inside the hull, and the heater is there with his rivets in a line, turning them over in the heat, like a man roasting chestnuts, moving the line along, and when he's got one just right, he takes it in his tongs and—phttt—he flings it up to where they're riveting and the passer catches it—often the passer was a woman—this red-hot rivet comes just like a bullet and she's to catch it in this thing like a funnel with a handle then quick pick it out and pop it into its hole with tongs. Then the bucker-up gets his dolly on it, the riveter gets his airgun and batters it down, and the caulker comes along with another airgun and hammers the hell out of the plate to work the metal up around the rivet and cinch it tight. Well just picture all this—you can't see the guy next to you because of the smoke from the goddamn pots, there's red-hot rivets raining through the air on all sides of you, there's three-ton plates swinging around overhead, it's so noisy from the guns you couldn't hear a warning even if the guy was shouting it in your goddamn ear, you've got all these goddamn people swarming around, who don't know the sharp end from the blunt end . . .

I remember one incident there, they had a fella welding at an outfitting dock. They launched each hull as soon as she'd float and finished working on her tied up at an outfitting dock. This fella was down over the side on swing-staging like a window washer, but the hull sheered in and the staging hung straight so he was dangling out about six feet from the work. One of the foremen—a real company stooge he was, too—decided to pull the staging in against the hull with a rope through one of the portholes, but instead of going and getting a good piece of rope he took a broken-off end that was lying there. It was a big heavy piece of manilla rope that had broken off at one end, and the other end had been seized with cord to keep it from ravelling. It wasn't long enough, so what this foreman did was he split it, unwound a strand out of it and tied that to the staging, and led the other two strands in the porthole and around a stanchion. This doubled the length, but all that was holding the rope together in the middle was this cord seizing.

The welder hardly got started before the damn thing parted and the staging swung out. He was leaning forward, all loaded up with his gear, and he just dropped into the chuck.

Lawrence Shorter was the diver that brought him up, he said you could see where his two feet hit the mud and he took one step and that was all. Lawrence found him resting on about a forty-five degree angle with his heels on the bottom and a crab setting on his face, starting in to work on him.

I was there just after it happened and here this foreman was trying to get rid of the staging and rope, but I wouldn't let him. I grabbed it, and when the cops came I demanded they impound it. I could see what the hell had happened right away. This damned old piece of un-ravelled rope had come apart just where you'd expect and this foreman was guilty of criminal negligence. But nothing come of it. The coroner ruled it death by misadventure, no blame attached.

This was par for the course, you see. Fellas would drop into holds, plates fell on them, they'd get burnt up or asphyxiated working in a confined space, and people took this as normal. It didn't occur to them it was all unnecessary. I did a lot of preaching about it but all that come of it was that I became shop steward for the burners and welders.

The shop stewards we had at that time were mostly no good, but even if they were they couldn't get backing from higher up in the union. Some beef would come up and The Lush or Matt Mills, the president, would go into the company office and get a shot of whisky and a pat on the back and then come out and tell us that the company was trying to do the best it could under difficult conditions and that we were all in this together or some phoney line like that.

The fellas weren't union-conscious, they'd put you up to beef about some deal but then when the heat come on they'd wilt. Then *you* got shit, you see. The foreman got it in for you. He'd ride you to beat hell, give you all the dirty rotten jobs. Like one time he put me way off in "purgatory" by myself so I wouldn't have contact with the other guys.

But in spite of the miserable conditions, the thing that got a guy most was the attitude of the bosses. The minute some gutless sad-sack got appointed strawboss he became an iron-fisted tyrant that figured he had the power of life and death over his former workmates. The tone of voice they used to give orders was like the voice cops use on you when you're in jail, there's a rasp to it that tells you you're nothing, you're shit on their boots. Ever since that run-in with the gang foreman at Weyburn, I had been unable to bear that tone of voice. It made me just about frantic. This son-of-a-bitch of a welding foreman—even when I was on the second shift, he'd leave word I was to be sent out on some goddamn make-work job out in the scrap yard, off by myself, doing beginner's work. He never seen me but he'd bark some goddamn insult.

One day when he'd been riding me more than usual I was working on a scaffold up around the superstructure. He'd sent me up there to do some stupid damn thing and I was holding a piece of cable across the scaffold, working on it when he came along. He started to raise his arm to beckon me out of his road, but he caught himself. He must have seen the look on my face and he got down on his knees and crawled past. I was so close to being a murderer there I still shiver to think about it. I think if he'd even parted his lips to say "hi" I'd have let fly at him. And that would've been it for both of us, he'd have gone fifty feet straight down and I'd probably still be in jail today. I was so frustrated, I was just desperate for some way to get back at those bastards.

This was where the reds come in, you see. Different guys would come up to me and say, you know the Communist Party has a programme to take care of all this. The CCF had men in the yards talking too, but the CCF was kind of a pie-in-the-sky deal—join us, work to join up others, eventually we'll have enough to vote in CCF members in the government, and then maybe years from now they'll make the laws softer on labour. But to a guy in the yard with a beef on the go this is all too far away. The appeal the Communist Party had was that they were for taking up the battle with the boss right there on the job, not in the future in parliament. They'd say we should all get organized and demand action. And they'd have it worked out, just what the demand should be. This was Party policy, you see. One of the founding planks of the Worker's Party of Canada was "To lead in the fight for the immediate needs of the workers; broaden and deepen their demands, organize and develop out of their every day struggles a force for the abolition of capitalism."

Up to this time I'd thought, like most people, that a communist was a guy with long whiskers and a bomb in his pocket. But if you come on a job and start putting up a fight for conditions, the men don't give a shit whether you're a communist or an episcopolian. And in the yards there during the war a guy was just so goddamn *frustrated,* it seemed like it was just you standing against the whole goddamn world. But the Party—you knew it had some clout. Not only was it world-wide and running Russia, it controlled most of the big unions in Western Canada—the IWA, the Mine, Mill and Smelter Workers, the United Fishermen's Union. And those unions were the ones putting up a fight in the struggle for worker's rights.

There weren't many Party guys in the yards when I first started, but there were some, and we kept finding ourselves on the same side of the fence. So when a welder named Charlie Caron come up to me and said look, we'd like to have you in the Party, I was really ripe and I said, "Fine. You bet."

It made a hell of a difference being in the Party. One guy alone can't do much, but five or six guys working together can have a hell of an influence. For example, before a union meeting the Party would go round and rustle up as much support amongst the rank and file as they could, they'd caucus outside the hall and line up speakers for questions they knew were coming up—you lead off, you follow him and you follow him—they'd even tell you where to sit. Now, that's very effective, especially if you've got a chairman who'll recognize you. After that, when I had some problem I wanted to get action on, there was a way to go about it.

3

Dirty Work and Dirty Money

The first big thing that woke that yard up arose over a kind of a silly thing, the spotters. The company had hired all these guys who had no job of their own, they were just supposed to hang around and spy on everyone else. It was a ridiculous thing because these spotters weren't shipyard people, they didn't know their ass from their elbow, yet they were supposed to watch us and report to the office if they saw anything that wasn't right. Really all it was was another way of loading the payroll you see—more plus for the boss.

These fellas would come around and stand behind you and watch and take notes. Never say anything. Never talk to anybody. Walk around, watch this guy and that guy. Well, if there's anything gets a guy's goat, its some son-of-a-bitch standing around watching, you see. You don't know what he's doing, you don't know why he's there, and he's in your way. Guys in the yard got hotter about these goddamn spotters than just about any other thing that come up. Everybody was squawking, "Here comes that son-of-a-bitch again. What does he want?" Every time the spotter turned his back a rivet would zing past his ear.

I was working on an outfitting dock, on a boat that was launched and tied up, so I went around and said, "Hell with this bullshit. Let's do something about it. Get rid of this bastard."

"What'll we do?" they said.

"When he comes on the boat, we walk off," I said.

Well, be goddamned if they didn't go for it. This spotter come on board the ship and we all walked off, every single worker. So off he come too. So we went back on. He turns around and comes back on again, and off we go again. So he beats it and after a while he comes back with the superintendent, Don Service. Old Don stands at the foot of the gangplank and sends the guy aboard. Well sir, soon as he got aboard, guys started to pour off again. Old Don spread his arms out like he was going to block the way—he was quite fussed up—and when the guys pushed by he grabbed the first one and told him he's fired.

They had barrels of rivets there on the dock and I jumps up on a barrel and yells, "Okay guys, they just fired Wally. Let's plug her."

Inside of fifteen minutes the bloody yard was down. Plunk. Not just that ship, but all the ships. Just like that. And then a confab. Matt Mills, the Union president, comes over and tells us, "The company has the right to have these fellas there on the job—they're efficiency experts."

So I said, "That's fine—let the efficiency experts build the goddamn ships then. We're not going back till the sons-of-bitches are gone."

After a couple of hours they gave in. They got rid of them. No more spotters.

This was the breakthrough, you see. It wasn't an important issue, but it got the whole yard involved and we won it clear and quick. It proved that by standing together we could make a dent after all. The guys that were thinking union, it gave them confidence. And it gave me confidence, too. That was the first time I'd really waded into it, and it worked out all right.

Around this time while I was still a shop steward there was an upheaval going on amongst the union executive. There was an election in December 1942 and quite a few Party guys got in. Bill Stewart beat out Matt Mills for president and Malcolm MacLeod took over as secretary from Bobby Stephens. This set off one of the real bad cases of inter-union wrangling in Canadian labour history. Old Aaron Mosher, a right-wing son-of-a-bitch who was head of the Canadian Congress of Labour, took it on himself to stem the red tide by declaring the election void, suspending the union charter and appointing the old union officers back to their positions. Him and Alex McAuslane, the representative of the CCL in BC, did everything they possibly could do to antagonize the rank and file members of the union. The old officers would come over and get booed right out of the meeting. The Party played the thing up all they could and it ended up Stewart was re-elected by a huge majority, and on November 3, 1943, the BC Supreme Court ruled Mosher's actions illegal. As settlement Mosher had to give the Boilermakers their independence, give it full status as a national union instead of keeping it a Congress local, and reduce our per-capita tax for membership in Congress from twenty-five cents to three cents. It was a great victory for the Party.

When the election come up they had to have a business agent for the burners and welders. This was a paid position, a full-time union position. I had first been a shop steward, then later was elected as a trustee when Stewart got in as president. Now, a few months later, a bunch of the guys put me up and I was elected business agent. This was quite a switch—I wasn't working in the yard any more, I was a union official. I'd never figured on it, but I wasn't backing away, either. I'd spent a lot of time on jobs where a man just didn't have any goddamn rights at all, and I was good and ready to get some licks on the other side. Most of my time was taken up dealing with working conditions in the yard. That was what got me into the union and that was what I was interested in.

The first thing I found out was you had to have good reliable men at the grassroots level to act as contacts and to carry out union policy. The most likely people to do this work were the shop stewards. So I saw that the first step to getting anywhere with job conditions was to build up a strong backbone of shop stewards. I went around to the yards picking out the progressive, active individuals and setting them up as shop stewards and then, as a second step, seeing to it they got involved. I had meetings of stewards' councils going on all over the city regularly, and I gave them lots to do. I did all my dealings through them. This built it up, you see. Pretty soon I had a real army there I could send in to do battle when I needed it.

At Norvan there was Dave Clark, Art Lanou, Tony Beck—I can't remember who all. Burrard had Jack O'Kane and Bill Schwartz, who was chairman of the shop stewards for a time. Bill Gee was chairman of the joint shop stewards and one of the solidest trade unionists I ever knew. Walt Jacobs, who was later secretary of the union, was shop steward for the welders and could always be depended on to take a good position, as could Bill McGaw and Lou Noveski. Another one who always put up a great fight for the men was Harold Long, who was for the burners. Jack Klemola was shop steward at both Norvan and Burrard and was a real battler. Klemola was the man I generally sent when a coroner's inquest arose from a shipyard accident. He was very fiery. They didn't get anything past him without knowing they'd been in a fight.

Two guys who played a key role organizing Western Bridge and later policing the contract there were Eli LeChance and Johnny Yurichuck. Bruce Johnstone was a key man there too. I almost hate to start naming guys because I'm bound to leave so many out. There are others I know and who know themselves that they should be mentioned but I'll have to ask them to bear with me. They say there's three sure signs of old age. One is you can't remember things and the other two I forget. It was over thirty-five years ago now, but I still get a touch of pride thinking of that bunch of guys, and what a good feeling it was to know we had men like that going for us.

A guy doesn't want to make it seem too cut and dried, mind. Remember, we were frozen on the job and our wages were frozen. We could occasionally pull off a sitdown but we were under tremendous pressure not to interrupt war production. Conditions was the only issue left, and these old time bosses, oh Jesus, they wouldn't budge an inch on conditions. "You're building ships here, you're not at some goddamn pink tea," they'd scream at us. "Shipbuilding is dirty and rough, it's been that way for a hundred years and we ain't gonna change it because a bunch of pantywaists comes in off the street and don't find it to their

Workers grease the skids for the launch of another 10,000-ton freighter at
Burrard South. NORTH VANCOUVER MUSEUM AND ARCHIVES, 27-348

taste!" The sight of a union man would just make those old-time bosses spit. Nobody was going to tell *them* what to do.

I saw that we were going to have to really plan our moves carefully and concentrate our efforts one place at a time. We were strongest amongst the welders and burners and that was the area I understood best, so I decided the issue we'd start off on would be 'dirty money'. The idea was, extra money for dirty jobs. Any of these goddamn filthy places they'd send you into where you couldn't breathe clean air or you were lying in water or mud or tar or you didn't have room, you'd penalize the company for it by charging higher wages—time-and-a-quarter, say, or time-and-a-half. As it was you'd see men down in a hole with their wives' vacuum cleaners trying to get air, and the company didn't give a damn. Dirty money was something the guys on the job could see, for two reasons. Number one, they hated to work in these goddamn places, and number two, it increased their take. A guy sometimes hates to fight for nothing, but he doesn't mind if it puts a dollar in his pocket, you see—the monetary angle. We made a list of what we considered dirty money situations, typed it out and presented it to management at all the yards. They laughed at us.

The showdown came on February 27, 1944, the day of the founding convention of the Shipyard General Workers Federation. They sent a guy to do some welding between the double bottoms of a liberty ship—he wouldn't go in without dirty money, and it come to a goddamn rhubarb. Old Lewis was general manager and he called me into his office.

"I understand you've told the men not to go down in the double bottom unless they get extra money," he said.

"Yeah, that's right," I said. "We agreed on that."

He called in his super, Jimmy Martinez and told him, "The first man that refuses to go in there, fire 'im." So I said, "Okay, and the first guy that you fire, we're going to plug 'er."

"Alright," he said, "That's just fine. You go right ahead, but the ashes will be on your head."

That was the term he used—"the ashes will be on your head." He could see that I wasn't very big in the union—I was just business agent for burners and welders, I wasn't a table officer like Stewart, and Malcolm MacLeod was head business agent over me. I went down, told the stewards what was in the wind, they said, "Yup, we're ready." Martinez fired the guy and bang, the welders and burners sat down.

Well, then there was hell to pay. Some of the guys weren't sure what the hell was going on, and there was this one stooge who refused to stop work. I went over and tapped him on the shoulder—"We're all plugging 'er Mac!" And he threw off his bloody helmet and put his dukes up—he was going to clean my clock. Well, imagine how that would look—the business agent fighting with an employee because he wouldn't go on strike. So I went up to the shop steward, a real husky bugger and a good guy too. I said, "There's a prick down there still welding."

"Just leave him to me," he said. I don't know what happened but the welding sure stopped in a hurry.

The yard was down, and this was serious business. I got hold of Stewart. He was presiding at the convention, but he said he'd get down as soon as he could. This was two o'clock, and after waiting til five o'clock with all these men standing around I phoned again.

"Isn't Stewart down there?"

"He left here hours ago," they told me.

The day shift finally went home, the second shift came in and we explained it all over again to them—they continued to plug. At ten o'clock a goddamn taxi pulls up at the gate, and out gets Stewart and MacLeod and a couple of other guys who weren't even in the union. MacLeod is so drunk he can't stand up. The guard won't even let him in the yard. Stewart was really high too, but they let him in and we call a meeting in the lunchroom.

One of the guys makes a motion that we give management twenty-four hours to settle up or we pull the rest of the workers out in sympathy with the burners and welders.

"Twenty-four hours, nothing," Stewart yodels in his full convention howl, "By eight o'clock tomorrow morning if they haven't agreed to all of our demands, down comes the whole yard!"

"Yaaayyy!"

Big cheer goes up.

At eight o'clock the next morning Stewart was still sleeping it off. I had to go in there with another business agent I worked with a lot, Ed Simpson, a real solid guy, and we managed to hold the welders although we had no authority to call the others out.

Well by God, we were lucky. The company caved. It went against their grain to beat hell, but they were in such a panic for production they just couldn't stand to be held up.

That was the first showdown, and once we got the dirty money program established there we really put on a drive in the other yards. We had sitdowns there too, and it was easier going because we could always point to South Burrard. "We've got it there, why can't we have it here?" This was very hard to answer, you see. Eventually we got them all to accept dirty money in principle.

The double bottoms became a popular place to work—guys would try to get down there to get the extra money. No doubt a lot of them didn't understand the principle behind dirty money, but that didn't matter. It was one of those ideas that couldn't help but succeed. Alice Kruzic has a story about when she first went to work in Burrard South as a sweeper, a guy come up to her and asked her how she'd like to go down in the double bottoms and earn some dirty money. Well she hadn't heard about it before and she took it the wrong way. She gave the guy a good scolding. "I came here to earn honest money and help the war effort!" she said.

In the course of the dirty money campaign we come to the notice of the papers—labour trouble in the yards! We drew a lot of editorial fire. The government appointed an investigation by this Mr. Justice Ivan Rand, the famous labour conciliator who later invented the "Rand Formula." I logged quite a few hours in front of Mr. Justice Ivan Rand, and you know that fella, he ate cigarettes. He'd sit there and put a fresh tailor-made in his mouth and as proceedings wore on that cigarette would get shorter and shorter til there was just a stub about a quarter of an inch left.

The outcome was that certain standards as to clean working conditions were laid down in law and the Department of Industrial Hygiene was brought in to enforce them. The guy they put on there was not a bad fella, quite a young fella name of Ellstrom. And here is where you see how the old-school employers were stupid, because they reacted to government inspectors and so on the same way they did to union guys and anybody else who stood in the way of their desire to operate their businesses like feudal kings. "Who's this goddamn white-collared bastard gonna tell me how to run my shipyard?" So they antagonized him as well.

Many's the time I just walked them into a damn confrontation—I remember this one time we had a dirty money beef up before an arbitration board and the company was represented by a lawyer named Walter Owens—the same fella who was later Lieutenant Governor of BC—and Owens wouldn't go along with us on dirty money one inch. I was doing what I could to break through and one of the things I tossed out was that I'd bring this Ellstrom in to straighten Owens out. Owens wasn't good at taking a rub so he says, who's this Ellstrom, what's he got to do with this kind of thing. That gave me an idea, so I kept coming back to Ellstrom and Owens kept getting more and more disparaging about him, I guess without really stopping to think who Ellstrom was. On the third day I brought Ellstrom in, but before he took the stand I said, "I think there has been some confusion about the authority of my next witness which I would like to clear up," and I repeated all the goddamn lousy things Owens had been saying about him. You could see Ellstrom kind of squirming in his chair, and by the time his turn came he could hardly hold himself down.

"Mr. Owens, I would like you to understand this," he started out, shaking a finger in Walter's direction, "I am an employee of the Federal Department of Labour and I have authority to go into any plant in this province and issue orders which are binding under the authority of the Canadian parliament . . ." Oh, his neck was pulled. He went right down the line with us and the board had no choice but to find in our favour.

I had a lot of fun with that fella Ellstrom. He'd come and take samples of the air and until such times as the company came and put in proper ventilation we got our dirty money. Oh Jesus, this hurt them, and they'd get into the damndest fights with this guy, and I could just sit back and enjoy the show. As far as I was concerned the government was phoney, and the boss was phoney, and any time you can get two phonies fighting each other, well that's good business.

Winning the dirty money fight gave us a toehold and from there we went after other issues.

Up to a point we had to fight them every inch, and then things began to get easier. I think the turning point was when we went after seniority firing in Pacific Drydock. The idea behind seniority firing was to protect the employee from the whims of ornery bosses who might fire him without reason, or for some phoney reason. It was in the contract but we were having a hard time getting them to take heed of it. We were having a lot of goddamn trouble with the foremen and superintendents.

What come up was, they laid off one of the oldest riveters in the yard, Johnny Maxamento. Just because the foreman didn't like him. I didn't like the bastard either, but that didn't make any difference—he was a good riveter. I took it up with the super, then with the personnel manager, Tommy Thompson, but they weren't going to budge on it. Alright, I said, what we're going to do is stop working overtime. Work-to-rule wasn't a term that was in use then, but that's what it would've been called today. They had a rush repair job in and the guys were all working overtime to get it out on schedule, you see. The general manager at that time was old Bill Jordan, a rough bugger who had come up the hard way, and he was on the phone to me first thing in the morning.

"What the hell's coming off here?" he says. So I told him.

"You better get over here," he says, and hangs up the phone. So I walk into his office primed to argue it out, but he just cuts me off.

"I know Maxamento," he says. "I know he's as good a riveter as we got. I'm going to straighten this out my way." So he calls in Tommy Thompson, and Tommy—you know he could blush like a boy when he was getting in the grease—he says to Tommy, "You git down there and you git every super and foreman in the yard and you bring them in here, pronto." And he says to me, "You git your head shop stewards too, I want them up here." There were only three of them—Tony Beck, Dave Clark and Art Lanou—and we were back long before

Tommy and his bunch. I have to laugh when I think of it—we had the only chairs, and when these foremen and supers started coming in they had to line up along the walls like a bunch of schoolboys—they had to sidestep over each other to get in, and oh Jesus, they were so all a-jitter, these hard-nosed yard bosses who'd been giving us such a rough time outside.

Jordan just roasted them. "We have a contract with the Boilermakers Union," he said. "And when this company signs a contract it doesn't matter who that contract is with, my duty is to make sure it's lived up to. If there's a violation of this here contract, it's the union we'd expect to be guilty, not ourselves. Today I find this is not the case." So he bawled the Jesus out of them for firing Maxamento and told them it was the last time he wanted to hear of anything like that happening in his yard. "Do you guys understand that, now?" "Yes, Mr. Jordan, yes Mr. Jordan." Then he turned to the shop stewards. "Now if a case like this does come up again, I want you to report it directly to me, and I'll see that there's some fast management changes around here."

From that time forward the stewards pretty well called the shots in that yard, and it spread out from there to the other yards. That's when the shop stewards movement really come into its own.

Things weren't going near so good for Stewart, but he didn't know it at the time. You'd have to know Stewart a bit to see what the problem was. I think Bill Stewart was the most useless man I ever run into. He couldn't drive a nail. He used to make a joke of it. "Anything that needs to be done around our house, my wife has to do it," he used to say. "She won't even let me change a lightbulb." He actually had contempt for guys who all they could do was work. I remember

Bill Stewart was president of the Vancouver Boilermakers Union.

seeing him in the yards when he was supposed to be working, the men'd be carrying a heavy piece of plate and there'd be Bill, following along just holding on with a limp hand and that wiseguy look on his face. Being smart to him was everything, and he was smart too but maybe not so much as he thought.

He got quite a kick out of it if he thought he was pulling a fast one on anybody. Often him and I would be at some meeting and he'd get up and string the guys a line of just absolute crap and when he come to sit down I'd lean over and say, "What a bunch of pure, unadulterated bullshit."

"Yeah but it sounded good, didn't it? They'll never know the difference," he'd say. This was his attitude.

You see, Stewart wasn't like Harold Pritchett or Ernie Dalskog or Harvey Murphy or any of those who came into labour from a long working career. The only work experience he'd had was as a busboy in the old Vancouver Hotel. He got elected business agent for the Hotel and Restaurant Workers when he was twenty-two. It's getting more common nowadays for labour leaders not to be workers themselves, but I always figured that type lacked the gut feeling of guys who'd suffered real abuse on the job.

Stewart had problems keeping union money and his own from getting mixed up and got bounced out of the Restaurant Workers, so the Party parachuted him into the IWA. The fact he'd never had caulk boots on in his life didn't bother them. They made him a business agent in a New Westminster local. Then when they needed someone to carry their flag in the Boilermakers they pulled him out and set him up as leader of the shipyard workers, where again, he didn't know a rivet from a davit.

Stewart told me once that he never got into a fix he couldn't talk his way out of. And it was true. Bill Stewart could get a meeting eating out of his hand in no time and at a convention there wasn't anyone in the country could touch him. He was a wonderful orator.

He was a fair analyst, too. He could look at a situation and figure out whose chain was being pulled by who. He liked to set people up, but sometimes his tactics backfired. One of the fellas there, Cliff Worthington, a carpenter, was served with a warrant for an infraction just as he was due to go back to a convention in Regina. Stewart advised him to ignore this court order and go to the convention. He said, "It'll be the finest thing that ever happened to you if you're arrested on the floor of the convention." It might have been, but the police aren't totally stupid—they just waited til he came back and they nailed him. So then he was in double trouble for skipping out on this warrant. Stewart was great at figuring things out like that, and he was in his glory campaigning against the Congress or heading up delegations to Ottawa or rearranging the world at Party drinking sessions.

On the other hand, the day-to-day problems of men on the jobs were foreign to Bill. He didn't have the feel for it and he wasn't interested—he tended to brush it off as small-time stuff. This didn't go over with the workers because their day-to-day working conditions were a damnsight more important than arms agreements with Russia or who was vice-president of the Congress way out in Ottawa. They wanted union officers who would come around and talk to them and back them up with their beefs, and Stewart was hopeless on a beef. One time a guy got fired for ploughing a foreman. It went to arbitration, and Stewart sat on the board. I went to watch and I was absolutely appalled at the position Stewart took. They had Walter Owens there for the company and Stewart let Owens walk all over him. I never seen a guy on a beef look more hopeless. He acted like he was embarrassed. I couldn't understand it—he wasn't a timid sort of guy, he had more damn gall than a Mexican bandit, but here all he did was sit and listen while Owens put the screws to him. So the guy stayed fired.

This was where his background let him down, you see. Stewart didn't know what it was like to be at the mercy of some power-drunk pinhead of a foreman and wanting to tear his head off. The men soon sensed this about him and they resented it.

We were coming up to the executive elections at the end of 1944 when Stewart asked me how I thought he was going to do. "Well, I'll tell you something, Bill," I said. "I think you're going right out the goddamn window." He thought that was a real joke. "Well, we're all going to be out of work next week," he told Malcolm MacLeod, grinning all over. "That's what Bill White here tells me." He figured because he'd been cutting a swath on the national labour scene he was untouchable, but I was around on the job and I listened to fellas talk.

"You just damn well remember I said it, now," I told them.

"Bill, I'll bet you twenty to one I win this election," Stewart said.

"Okay," I said, "I'll take twenty bucks worth of that."

"Ah, I don't want to take your money." He was just *so* cocksure.

The day of the election the two of them come in and voted, then five o'clock they come back. MacLeod was so damn drunk we had to take him home. Stewart beat it for awhile and came back while we were counting ballots, about ten, real gassed up.

"How's she going," he says, cocky as hell.

"Just like I said," I says, "right out the window."

"Bullshit!"

"Go and look." He went over to the chalkboard, and Jesus, he just about flaked out. It was running five or six to one against the Party slate.

"We gotta do something," he says. "We can't let them have it."

"It's too goddamn late *now*," I says.

Well it wasn't too late for Stewart. He went and got a bunch of helpers and together they marked over a thousand ballots and stuffed them into the boxes. But even at that they underestimated how bad it had gone. They saved some of the Party guys—Caron got back as secretary—but Stewart lost by a hundred and some-odd. I couldn't believe it when I seen what they were doing but I couldn't do anything. Gordon Farrington was the returning officer in charge of the election and he'd been helping Stewart do the stuffing. After it was over Ed Simpson and I went down to the Kremlin—the Party headquarters on Pender Street—and put in a report on what'd happened. They hauled Stewart up on the carpet and he got sentenced to work in the yard for two years without holding any union office. I think the Party was madder at him for losing the election than slugging the ballots, though. The guys who held onto their seats weren't disciplined in any way.

I had to laugh reading this little book the union put out by Ben Swankey, *Shipbuilding in BC*. Farrington has a piece about Stewart's defeat saying as how "this was perhaps his finest hour" and he could have undoubtedly been re-elected but instead chose to become a humble plate hanger and be in closer touch with the men on the job. Stewart would rather have done anything else if he'd had a choice.

The new executive was hopeless. The fella who'd defeated Stewart, name of Henderson, hadn't the first idea of unionism. He'd been a farm implement salesman. He didn't represent anybody—the CCF, the Congress or the companies—his election was a protest against Stewart pure and simple. Union meetings became complete bedlam. Guys standing up on chairs screaming curses at each other across the room—we had to turn the lights out at times or there'd have been a bloody riot. After two meetings Henderson resigned and we had a by-election. I was one of five guys who ran for president and I got more votes than the rest of them combined. So, in 1944 I became president of the Marine Workers and Boilermakers Union. And I was on the Party ticket. Stewart is on record as saying he was defeated because of a "widespread campaign against militancy"—red-baiting in other words—but it's damn odd how it worked against him and not me.

I was as nervous going into my first meeting as a long-tailed tomcat in a room full of rocking-chairs. We had to bring things under control or I'd be down the road right on Henderson's heels. I told them, "Okay now fellas, we're going to have a new deal here. You can get up and say what you damn well want to say and nobody'll interrupt you. And if anyone does, he'll be called to order once and if he don't come to order he'll be called to order once more and if that don't do it he'll be thrown to hell and gone out of this hall." And I said, "To make sure the orders of the chair are carried out—stand up fellas." I had thirty-two shop stewards sat right in the centre of the hall in a block. And I said ,"Now, they're going to enforce the rulings of the chair. You can say whatever you want but we're going to have some order here."

Well hell, the meeting wasn't five minutes old when some guy gets up and starts yelling across the floor and he won't come to order—he has to try it out. We threw out about six or eight guys at that first meeting. At the next meeting there were less, and finally you couldn't have wanted better conducted meetings. We'd have huge meetings there and never a guy speak out of turn.

Once we got things worked out that union hummed. The shop

stewards were the key to it. Jesus, that was a good shop stewards' movement.

There was one time there after the war, we had a strike at Pacific Drydock—we were out I think three weeks or more and we were winding up negotiations with the company reps, Tommy Thompson of Pacific Drydock and Bill Wardle of Burrard. We had an agreement pretty well hammered out except for one demand—holidays with pay, which at that time was a new item being pioneered by our union. This was the last thing, it came up late in the day and they said, okay, don't worry about that one—we haven't discussed it with the owners but we'll recommend acceptance and we can assure you there will be no trouble. That gave us everything we wanted so we went back and put notices on radio and in the papers telling the men to report for work in the morning. About nine o'clock that night I got a phone call from Thompson—holiday pay had been rejected.

Well, this was a double-cross pure and simple. They figured once the men were back at work we'd never be able to get them out again just for this one controversial demand. It was impossible to reach the membership, so I phoned Jack Lawson, who was the chairman of the shop stewards in Pacific Drydock. The reason I chose Pacific Drydock was because it was the yard where our shop stewards were the most militant and disciplined. I told Jack, "You contact your stewards coming over on the ferry and you plug that yard as soon as you get into it."

They plugged her, not a wheel turned. The company was sure surprised that we could pull back that quick. Thompson was there making a racket. "Forget about that BS," I said, "either you come clean or inside of an hour the other yards'll be just like this one." That did it—they had a hurry-up employer's conference and decided they could afford paid holidays after all. But if we hadn't caught it fast they'd have had us. We couldn't have done it without a strong shop stewards' movement. I've always maintained and I still do today—a strong shop stewards' movement is the lifeblood of any union.

4

Beefs

I

A good shop stewards' movement is no substitute for strong membership support, and the one would be useless without the other. You have to have your shop stewards, but you have to make sure they have the strong backing of the rank and file. And how you do that is, you service the membership well. You take care of beefs. A guy gets fired, or beat out of his dirty money, or he gets shorted on his holidays—you go and take it up right away. Then you've converted that guy. The union is something he can understand. Our grievance record was second to none and I made sure it stayed that way.

Often when I went on a beef I had no idea how I was going to make anything out of it, and many's the time I failed to. But you couldn't win any of them unless you started by putting up a fight, and often by putting up a fight you'd win where you didn't expect to.

There was another time a guy ploughed a foreman—quite an old guy, Mac Kendrick. He was working with the fitters and the bull gang boss was a guy named Sargent, a loud-mouthed red-faced bugger always whooping and hollering. There was a hose laying on the deck and Sargent hollered to Kendrick, "Hey, move that hose!" Well Mac didn't like that, he wasn't a labourer on the bloody bull gang, so he

Cafeteria, Burrard Drydock, North Vancouver.

didn't do it. "You son-of-a-bitch," Sargent hollers again, "I told you to move that hose!" Old Mac just walked over and ploughed him. Sargent jumped up and Mac knocked him down again. And he got up a second time and Mac decked him a third time, and Sargent stayed decked. So Sargent laid charges against Mac in court.

It was clear-cut assault, but Mac come to me about it. So I said well, at least we can put up a fight for it. I went and got the union lawyer, Johnny Burton, and I told him, "We want to get this goddamn foreman." Burton said, "Well, we'll see what we can do but I'm warning you, it doesn't look hopeful."

When Sargent gave his evidence he decided to play the role of an innocent party. "I really don't know what happened," he said. "I asked this guy to move a hose, and I woke up in the hospital."

"You mean to say, you didn't see the accused make a move to strike you?" Burton asked.

"No sir, I didn't even see him."

"Well why did you lay charges against him then?"

"He hit me!"

"But you just told the court you didn't know what happened."

"Well I know because people told me."

"That's hearsay evidence," Burton said. So they were stuck. The judge had no choice but to dismiss the case, and we got Mac back.

There were run-ins like that coming up constantly. One involved Louis Van Dale, who held a black belt in judo. He was having trouble with one of these real bastardly foremen and he told me, "You know one of these times that guy's giving me shit I'm going to take him apart."

"Don't do it," I said. "Next time he goes after you see if you can get him to take a swing at you, and if he does, phone me. Don't hit him back." Well, the foreman slapped Louis, and Louis phoned me. I went over to the office and demanded Willie Wardle fire the guy.

"Come now, we can't have the union saying who's going to be our foremen," Wardle said.

"Alright, then, if you won't fire a foreman for hitting a man then you can't fire a man for hitting a foreman. There's about a dozen guys

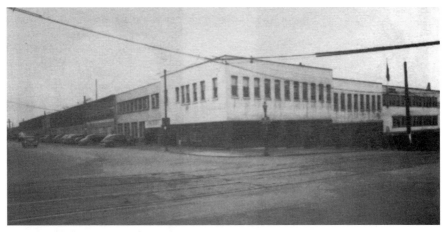

Burrard Drydock in the war years with a view of head offices in North Vancouver and shops in the background.

in here that're ripe for it and we'll just declare an open season, starting with this case here. Louis will just tear that son-of-a-bitch apart."

He was sitting in a swivel chair and he swung around with his back to me, stroking his chin and looking out the window. I didn't trust him altogether, but there'd been worse managers come to Burrard Drydock than Willie Wardle. He was a two-quart-a-day man. Every day two quarts of whisky but you know, you never seen that man when he showed liquor. His colour would be a bit high but other than that you'd never suspect. The only reason it got around the yard was he had a hell of a time getting whisky during the war—he'd buy up the permits of all the guys that didn't drink. He stayed there as general manager up to the time Claude Thicke was brought in.

After a good minute-and-a-half he swung his chair around with his head down. "Okay," he said. "I'll let him go." So we got rid of the bastard.

The best incident involved Pug Hayden. Pug had been in the pro ring for years but he wasn't the defensive type of fighter. He could deliver a punch like a Holstein bull can deliver a kick but when it came to stopping a punch often as not he wound up stopping it with his head. It left him a bit jumpy. The fellas all knew Pug, he was a hell of a good guy.

Pug worked on the second shift and the super was a fella named Steeves who didn't mind having a laugh at Pug's expense. Every time he run into Pug he'd square off, put up his dukes, and have a big laugh. It wasn't funny to the rest of us but Steeves was a superintendent and I guess he figured that made it alright for him to be laughing when no one else was. The only one who'd grin for him was Pug, because Pug was as good-natured as a Newfoundland pup.

One day Steeves come busting around a corner and run slam into Pug. He jumped back and squared off as usual but it happened a bit too quick for Pug and he drove the guy so hard it took a bunch of his teeth out. It was just a reflex, you see. The next minute Pug was down on his knees begging Steeves to forgive him and picking up teeth, and Steeves was meowing, "Eesus Chris' Bug, I wuv jus' kidding ya . . ."

I know there's not much chance of it but I always like to think Pug did that secretly on purpose.

Sometimes you pull tricks that you're not proud of, but it might be the only way to handle a particular situation. They had a superintendent of welders in Burrard Drydock, Eric Dunnett. He was a kind of anemic guy, he wasn't aggressive or anything, but one morning for no reason at all he up and fired two burners. One of them come to me and kicked on it, "Dunnett won't say why he fired me." I knew Dunnett very well so I said I'd go over and find out what the score was. I went in and said, "What the hell was wrong with you this morning, Eric? Did you get out the wrong side of the bed?"

"No, why?"

I said, "Well you fired those guys and one of them come to me on it—why'd you do it?"

"We-ell," he said, "I didn't think he was doing a job . . ."

"What, did he pull a boner?"

"Naw, I just—just didn't like the way he was going at his work . . ."

"Christ, he's been here for years!"

"Yeah . . ."

"Ah, what the hell's wrong with you," I said. "Put the guy back to work."

He said he'd think about it and tell me after lunch. So I left him. Now, the procedure with beefs, the grievance procedure as we had it laid out in our contract, said as a first step you had to take it up with the personnel manager, then higher management, then if you still weren't satisfied, you'd apply to the LRB to go before a board of arbitration. Tommy Thompson was personnel manager, so on my way out I stopped to see him. I said, "I got a beef, Tommy."

"Oh? What?" as if he didn't know. I told him what it was and he said, "Oh, I don't think you got a beef there, Bill."

"Well I expected that from you, Tommy," I said. "After all, you gotta do something to justify that salary of yours. You know I only come in here because I have to before I can get to somebody who can do something."

"Bill," he says, "I think you're forgetting that a superintendent does have the authority to fire men under him. He can fire whoever he likes."

"Yeah," I said, "with *cause*. They didn't give this fella any reason why he was fired."

"Oh there was cause," he said. "No one is fired in this yard without cause."

"Bullshit!" I said. "If that was true Dunnett himself would be out on his ass."

"What do you mean?"

"I know all about that seven-thousand-dollar bulkhead he fucked up," I said.

"Oh, is that so!"

"Yes, that's so," I said.

Dunnett had introduced a new method of welding and they'd tried it out on this bulkhead. Well, the damn thing warped and twisted so bad they had to get the heat gang in, but even they couldn't straighten it out. They had to chuck it, and it was worth seven thousand dollars.

"For your information," Tommy said in his very precise way, "Dunnett didn't do it."

"Oh yeah? Who did, then?"

"Geordie Matthews. Geordie takes full responsibility for that bulkhead error."

Well Geordie was the bloody yard superintendent, the boss over all of them, and I knew him better than that. I left then, and during lunch hour Tommy called Dunnett in and told him not to put the guy back. I came over after to get the verdict and he said, "Nope! I was talking to Tommy about this and I decided, when I fire a guy he stays fired. I'm not taking him back."

"Okay," I said. So I wandered in to see Geordie Matthews.

"How's she going, Geordie?"

"Oh not so bad, Bill. How's you?"

"Alright. Jesus Geordie, I hear you're skating on thin ice around here."

"Oh? Why?"

"Tommy Thompson was just telling me you fucked up a seven-thousand-dollar bulkhead."

"I never did no such thing!"

"Well I thought it was Dunnett who'd done it, but Tommy tells me you take full responsibility."

Jesus, Geordie's jaw dropped. He stood bolt upright.

"Will you come up there with me?" he said.

"You're damn right!" I said.

"C'mon, c'mon." He grabbed my arm and up we went. Thompson wasn't in his office, but Matthews wouldn't leave. He made me sit there and wait. In a few minutes, in come Tommy. He stuck his head in the door and soon as he saw us his face turned fiery red.

"Come on in, Tommy," I sang out. His own office. He slunk in very slowly and sat down. I said, "Tommy, somebody's been selling you a bill of goods."

"Oh?"

"You remember you were telling me it was Geordie here who fucked up that seven-thousand-dollar bulkhead? And I told you I thought it was Dunnett—"

That's as far as I got. Geordie cut me off.

"You sons-a-bitches aren't hanging that thing on me! I tried to tell that stupid bastard it wouldn't work." And on and on. Tommy shrivelled up like a piece of bacon. When he got through, I said, "Well, how this come up, Geordie—Dunnett fired old Joe this morning without giving cause, so I came in here—"

"Is that right? Is that right?" He was boiling mad.

"Well . . ." Tommy said.

"Put him back! Put him back, goddammit, put him back!"

I hated to pull that on Tommy, but he'd gone out of his way to fuck me up. I could have handled Dunnett by myself.

One of the best tactics was to get the brass down for an on-site inspection and argue a beef on the job. They could see then what the problem was, they didn't have to take your word for it. I used to just love to get some of those big shots in their pinstripe suits crawling around a bunch of rusty pipes and walking through bunker oil in their white shoes. And when the bosses were on the jobsite looking the guys in the face, the same guys they were trying to screw—it took some of the fight out of them. Watching the workers jump around, lifting weights that'd break their backs put the brass more in a frame of mind to give the men credit. You could often talk them into going to the job easily, but once they got there and got this uncomfortable feeling, they'd be in quite a sweat to get away. I'd try to hold them there and get them arguing in the men's hearing, because I knew they'd get tough again pretty quick as soon as they got back in their leather chairs.

Old Jock Dalrymple really wasn't in the white-shoe class, he was an old-time shipbuilder and a hell of a nice fella. He was manager of South Burrard after Lewis. One time I had a beef with him over dirty money. There was a repair job in and the men were steaming bunker oil out of the double-bottom tanks. There was no question on dirty money for the steaming gang but the welders were working in the hold directly over these tanks and the beef was from them. The hold was like a sauna with all this steam and the floor was so hot it'd just about burn a guy's feet off. They wanted either a stop on the steaming while they were there or else extra money.

Old Jock wouldn't go for it, so I said, "There's only one way we can settle this and that's if you come down and see for yourself," and he agreed.

"That deck is nae hot," he blustered, "there's no part of it I couldn't sit on with me bare arrrse.' He was verrry Scotch, you know. We went in and I felt around til I found a spot where they had the steam on, and Jesus, you could have fried eggs on the damn thing. I couldn't hold my hand on it.

"Okay Jock," I says, "down with your pants. I want to see you plank your ass right there!"

He put his hand down. "Oooh!" he says, "'tis a bit warrrm alright!"

"Your damn rights it's warm, but if it's this hot here what do you think it's like up under the deckhead where those guys are?"

There was a long plank running up on a slope for the guys to walk up, so I said, "Go up there and try it." He walked up til his head was up under the bottom of the deckhead where all the steam was collecting, and I walked up behind him. Jesus, it was really scalding, and I stood behind him blocking the way down. I was lower on the plank where it was cooler, and that's where I did my talking. Pretty soon the beads of sweat come out on his forehead and run down his nose. Finally he says, "Alright you boogerrr. You win. Let me doon."

II

You couldn't get a fair shake through the regular channels so you were forced to resort to anything that would increase your chances. You'd try to settle with management if you could, because when a beef went to arbitration the chances of getting a favourable settlement were just about nil. Boards of arbitration were set up under the Labour Relations Board and they consisted, like other industrial relations tribunals, of one labour rep, one company rep and one chairman who was supposed to be neutral. The thing was, the LRB itself wasn't neutral so it was incapable of setting up anything else that was neutral. Chairmen were appointed who were so employer-oriented they'd often make the company rep look neutral in comparison.

Burrard Shipyards, as I mentioned earlier, was owned by the Wallace family. It had been started by Andrew Wallace who began building Columbia River fishing skiffs on False Creek where Burrard Bridge is now. He had two sons, Clary and Hubie, who took over from him, and Clary had four sons, who come in with him. They were Dave, Blake, and Phil and Dick, the twins.

Young Phil Wallace was the one who liked to fire guys. One time we had a real top-flight burner named Wally who was working on the deck of a ship just outside the burner's shack. He had to make a cut through heavy plate and he needed a bigger tip for his torch so he went to the burner's shack. The tips were in a drawer of a desk there and while he was bent over looking for a tip in this drawer, Phil happened to stroll by outside the window. Apparently there was a newspaper lying on top of this desk and it looked to Phil like a guy was in there reading a newspaper so he dashed up to the office and had Wally fired. We wrangled it through the grievance process but we couldn't get anywhere with the company so the case went to arbitration. The chairman for this board was a lawyer named A.J. Cowan who we knew all too well and regarded as an out-and-out company stooge. The guys who Wally had been working with, including the guy who sent him in to get the tip, were with us, and they all swore he hadn't been gone more than a minute—he'd just stepped in there, grabbed a tip and come out as quick as possible, and he was completely unaware of Phil Wallace standing outside the window. He hadn't been aware of the newspaper lying on the desk either. Cowan found some cockeyed excuse for ignoring all this evidence and ruled that the dismissal was warranted.

When I'm getting shafted I like it at least to be done with class, and I was a bit piqued at the boldness of this lawyer, so I stood up and objected. There's an act some of those lawyers put on when they're trying to give the impression of authority—they kind of puff themselves up like a bullfrog, and deepen their voices, you know. He cut me off with his gavel and said, "We'll have none of your nonsense on this board, Mr. White. Do you understand?"

Well, I'd had enough of that, so I stood up and hammered the desk with my fist and told him this was once he was going to sit and listen to what the workers thought of his brand of justice.

"You think your authority is so goddamn great because you got yourself appointed to this kangaroo-court of a board that you can take and twist the law any damn way you want and not even give a decent excuse for doing it, but you're sadly mistaken. Working men of this province are more than willing to abide by any decision they respect, whether it's for them or against them, but the only thing you earn from our working men with the kind of travesty you just put on here is contempt, and labour will never be bound by a decision it holds in contempt!" I laid into that bastard at the top of my lungs for about two minutes, and all he could do was sit there and take it. It kind of undoes those pompous buggers when you throw their authority back in their faces like that. They act like God himself until somebody refuses to go along with it, and then they don't know what to do. Very few of them have any contingency plans in case someone refuses to buy their authority, and they're just kind of helpless when it happens.

The injustice was so goddamned blatant that Tommy Thompson come up to me as we were leaving the hearing and said, "You tell Wally to go back to work." This guy was too much even for the company to stomach. But this was the problem of the neutral chairman, and it was present anywhere you had government supervision of labour-management relations.

Once in a rare while you'd get a chairman you could get to. One such time arose over a dispute at Pacific Drydock where they had a man polishing stainless steel. This was the first polisher they ever had and we couldn't agree on his rate of pay. The union took the position that he was a mechanic, entitled to mechanic's rate, while the company took the position he was a helper and would have to take helper's pay. It was haywire insofar as helpers are not allowed to use tools except under supervision of a mechanic, but here they wanted to put this guy in charge of his polishing tools. The argument knocked around between the various company offices for a long time and finally we took it to arbitration.

I heard we were getting a fella named Percy McDiarmid for chairman. He was very well connected, being a brother of the McDiarmid, McDiarmid, Miller and Coe brokerage firm of McDiarmids, but poor old Percy was a lush. I'd heard about his drinking habits, so the day of the case I told our nominee to the board, Lawrence Anderson, to go pick Percy up and throw a few drinks into him to get him in a good humour. Old Percy had a wooden leg and didn't drive, so he was glad for the offer of a ride and agreeable enough to the idea of a drink before the hearing, but Lawrence got a bit overeager. When they arrived Percy was stiff. He was reeling around on top of this wooden leg, pounding his chest and sniffing the fresh air. The company rep come up with a proposal that they drive down and view the work before they went into session.

"I don't think that'll be necessary," Percy says, gazing off into the distance. "My mind is already made up!"

Well sir, he was so damn boiled we had to adjourn the hearing for a week. We kept the same game plan for the next session, but I said to Lawrence, "Go a little easy on the guy, don't feed so many into him." It come off fine this time—he got Percy there still more or less in possession of his faculties and he came right down the line with us.

"That man is a mechanic, there's no doubt about that!" he said.

So the fella got about a year's back pay, but Percy never got another arbitration board.

Another time we had a beef over at Western Bridge, which had some kind of business tie-in with West Coast Ship Builders, McLaren's yard down on False Creek. Old W.D. McLaren was handling it and he was just as tough as nails. He had no give at all when it come to unions. This time he'd put the riveting gangs on piece work, paying them so much a rivet instead of by the hour with production bonuses and so on. We didn't like piecework because it was a sweat-shop technique, and since it amounted to a change in pay rate, and we were the men's certified bargaining agent, we demanded a consultation. McLaren gave us the cold shoulder, so we pulled the men out. McLaren promptly fired all forty-seven of them. He was just so goddamn arbitrary, you know, he was right out of the Stone Age.

We took it to the National Employment Service and they held a hearing. McLaren got in old Alan Thomas, the Western Bridge personnel manager, for his main witness. He was a hell of a good guy too, Alan, but he had a nervous stomach and couldn't stand any excitement. I liked the old guy, but you can't afford to like a guy too much when he's standing between you and the jobs of forty-seven men. I had the right to cross-examine and I really went for him. He got so excited he had to run out to heave up.

They'd been counting on Thomas, and when he bombed McLaren decided he better leap into the breech himself, so he took the stand. He didn't have a presentation worked out, and when he talked about how he'd been on the Clyde as a small boy and all this sort of stuff, I objected.

"Mr. McLaren isn't giving evidence pertaining to the question," I said. "Whether he's the world's greatest shipbuilder or not is not relevant here." He *was* a good shipbuilder, too. There was no denying it. But this really made him bristle.

So he said, "Mr. Chairman! May I have the temerity to ask Mr. White a question?"

"Mr. White," old McLaren said, "How long have you been engaged in shipbuilding?"

"Oh, about seven years," I said.

"Seven years. I will ask you another question then. Who do you think is in a better position to judge, a man who's been in the business seven years, or a man who's been in the business forty years?"

"Come, come, Mr. McLaren," I said. "Surely with all your experience you know that what one man learns in forty years another man can learn in seven!"

Well sir, that old bugger pretty near took a fit. They had to rest their case. I used to do that quite a bit—try to get their bloody goats—and it worked quite good on the stiff-necked ones. The board found in our favour and the guys were reinstated with full pay for the two weeks they were off.

Jack Whitehead at Norvan Ship was another one I didn't mind giving a good rub. We had a kind of running battle going over there about quitting time. They wanted the men to stay on the job til the whistle went and put their tools away on their own time, and we wouldn't have it. Jack called me into his office one day just at quitting time and he said, "Now I want you to see this with your own eyes. Look out there." I looked out his window and saw the guys bunching in front of the gate waiting for the whistle to go. They'd start collecting about five minutes before quitting time and by the time the whistle blew, there might be several thousand standing there ready to bolt. And by Jesus now, you didn't want to fall down in front of that crowd. Somebody dropped a lunchbucket once and it come out flatter than piss on a platter. The bosses spiked it down and painted a big yellow ring around it as a warning.

"You see that?" Whitehead said. "That's five thousand dollars an hour worth of manpower standing around going to waste and they do it every day. I demand you do something about it. I don't want to see that again."

"I can fix that but quick," I said.

"You can?"

"Sure."

"Well I wish you would."

So I went over and jerked down the blind.

"If you keep this here blind pulled down you'll never see them again," I said.

The battle with the employer is never over. The minute you get thinking that, your usefulness to labour is finished. The employer keeps a steady pressure on and the minute you weaken they crush you. I remember one time there was a ship, the *Robert Dollar*, in at Pacific Drydock for repairs. I was going down to see about some beef—I forget even what it was—and they had a guard at the head of the drydock so you had to sign in. I told him what I was there for and he said, "I've got orders not to let you in."

"Who gave those orders?" I said. "RCMP," he says. He had a phone there so I picked it up and called the RCMP and told them the score, and they said, "Somebody's pulling your leg, Buster, we never issued any such orders."

"What'd they say?" the guard said.

"They said you was a damn liar."

"Well that's what the company told me."

I said, "Well, you get ahold of the company then." There wasn't a company rep to be found anywhere. Everyone of them was "out".

Just then the shipping agent for the Dollar Company come walking off so I asked him to let me in. He looked at me as though I was something that crawled out from under a board, took the pipe he was smoking out of his mouth, pursed up his lips and shook his head.

"That, my good man, is one thing I can't do," he says.

"Well who the hell can do it, then?" I says.

"Head office of the company."

"Where's that?"

"Seattle."

"Alright," I said. "I've had about enough of this crap. You had better make up your mind right now whether you want me to go aboard and see the men, or if you want the men to come off and see me."

"Suit yourself, my friend," he said, and put his pipe back into his mouth and strode away. I got up on the edge of the drydock and motioned to one of the stewards to come out. I told him to get all the stewards, and ten minutes later down they come.

"That Yankee bastard says I can't come aboard," I told them. "Call the men off." Back they went, and I could hear the noise of the riveting guns dying down, dying down. Pretty soon she was still as a grave. And within ten minutes every company official in the yard was not only "in," they were down there all wanting to talk to me at the same time. "What's coming off here, what's coming off?"

"Damned if I know," I said. "I just come down to check on a beef and somebody gave an order I can't go aboard, but nobody seems to know who it was."

This was about two o'clock in the afternoon. At four-thirty, in come the second shift. I told them the score, and they sat down. Along about six the company men come down and said, "Okay, go aboard."

"Well it's not very damned important," I said. "I'll go in the morning and see about it." I sent words to the stewards it was over and went home. They were testing all the time you see, but when you had a group that worked together as well as that, it was pretty hard for the bosses to catch you off stride.

5

The Battleground of the Bargaining Table

I

The big test a union has to face on a regular basis is negotiations. Generally contracts come up once a year, but it can be every two or three years, depending on what was agreed on at the last negotiations. Negotiating the contract can be the making of a union if it comes out well, and it can just as easy be the union's downfall if it comes out bad. Negotiations time is an exciting and dangerous time, a time when the union suddenly emerges from the shadows and pits its strength against the combined power of the company and its establishment allies. It's like the test of battle to the army, and like war, it's total, it's an all-out struggle where your success depends as much on your preparation and the position you've worked yourself into beforehand as your action during the battle.

The most common mistake of an inexperienced unionist is to put too much emphasis on negotiations alone, and to find that once they begin, he hasn't laid enough groundwork to make a strong stand. This can result in a strike which breaks or cripples the union and loses the confidence of the membership. It doesn't matter how fancy a talker you are, if the company sees you're in a weak position, you won't get anything from them. You have to have your troops right there in a solid line at all times—you don't want to get too far out ahead of them or you'll get cut off. And if you don't get out far enough you'll likely get trampled. It calls for careful judgement.

The pressure job at contract time is that of the negotiator. No union is complete without an effective negotiator who can carry the organizational work through to the final payoff and secure all the gains the union has been working towards in a written contract with the employer. Sometimes the negotiator will be the union president but often as not it's someone from down in the ranks who specializes in it. From the time I took over as president I did all the negotiating for our union and as I became more experienced I did it for other unions as well.

I haven't kept up on all the changes in the labour code lately but when I was doing negotiations it was set up so as to put as many stumbling blocks in the union's way as possible. First, you were required to give the company so much notice that contract negotiations were coming up, so they had several months' warning. Then you had to make an effort to reach an agreement through direct negotiations with the employer, and if that failed you then had to go to a conciliation board hearing with an LRB-appointed conciliator. The conciliation board would give a recommendation, but it wasn't binding. You could go to arbitration where a mutually-agreed arbitrator would make a binding settlement, but nobody ever did that. Only after a conciliation board report was voted on and rejected by the union membership could strike action be considered. A strike vote would then

William (Bill) White, president Marine Workers and Boilermakers Industrial Union of Canada Local No. 1 from 1944 to 1955.

have to be called and strike notice served at least seventy-two hours before any stoppage of work took place.

This is always what made me so mad, you see, because it was so damned unfair. Anytime the boss wants more for his service, he just ups the price—he doesn't have to ask anybody—and either you pay or you don't get the service. But if the worker tries the same thing, says you give me more or I'll withdraw *my* service, well hell, that's illegal. He has to go through months of red tape before he can withdraw his service. This is class discrimination at the heart of our labour-relations outlook, and the fact so many people accept it as normal shows how far we are from having or even expecting equal treatment of the classes in this country.

I've been asked, what do the negotiators talk about all the time they're in there with the door closed—after you say you want a dollar and the company says all you can have is a quarter, what is there left to talk about?

Sometimes that is a problem and talks break off, or they never begin, and it takes a long strike before real bargaining can get going. I used to say to the company negotiator, there must be something wrong with us if we can't sit down at the table and work out a solution right now, because if we go out on a strike, no matter how long it is, we're eventually going to have to come back to this same table. I would generally have some concession ready to drop at such a time, but you had to be careful. If you were too reasonable, you'd see the wheels start going around: Aha! The bastards are afraid to strike, this is the time to hang tough. So then instead of creating an opening you'd end up with the company negotiator announcing he'd said his last word and daring you to strike.

Generally, finding enough to talk about was no trouble. Negotiations start off with the union establishing its policy committees, and the company or employer's association you're dealing with does the same. (The shop stewards were at all times the policy committee for the union, but policy had to be endorsed by the general meetings.) Then a meeting is arranged, and you go about preparing your list of demands. You try to dig up any information that might help your case—wage rate in comparable lines of work, cost-of-living increase statistics—and anything you can find out about the financial state of the company. Early on we had to do our own research but later the Trade Union Research Bureau was set up under two independent left-wing economists, Bert Marcuse and Emil Bjarnason, and boy, they were really good. We'd sometimes go into negotiations knowing more about company finances than the company reps themselves, and always we'd know a lot more than they wanted us to.

All this information would be figured into the brief which you'd present to the company negotiating team. They would counter with a brief of their own, and this would form the basis of discussions. You would go through the briefs clause by clause.

You'd hammer away to beat hell, but there would be an undercurrent running all through the argument that really what you were doing was putting on a show, and the thing you were trying to settle was who had the stronger position, who would come out of a strike the winner.

Sometimes there was so much damn talking it got me down. We were up before a conciliation board this one time and I was the union's nominee to the board. The thing with these boards was that they were often loaded with lawyers and hired professionals who made a hundred bucks a sitting, so they liked to draw them out over as many sittings as they could. Stewart was presenting our brief this time, so I said to him, "Just read our list of demands and sit down." No argument or nothing.

So he did. And they were very surprised, "Is that all?" The employers had a long bloody brief, it took them damn near an hour to read all the reasons they couldn't do anything for us.

"Alright," the chairman said, "We will now proceed with cross-examination by the union. You may start, Mr. Stewart."

"No cross-examination," Stewart said.

That was all there was to it. In a couple of hours it was all over.

"I've never seen a board like this here," the chairman said. "There's no argument from the union, they've done nothing to support their position at all."

"Yes, I'm aware of that," I said. "There's nothing to do now but get onto our report. What do you recommend?"

"Well," the employer's rep said, "our position is that we can't exceed our last year's offer, and I've heard nothing here to make me change my . . ."

"Fine!" I said, and turned to the chairman. "What's your position?"

"I'm inclined to agree with the company representative . . ."

"That's settled then," I said. "You two put in your majority report and I'll submit a minority one."

The chairman started to meow then, they could see they were hooked, you see. They knew damn fine they'd never get away with a position like that. The employer's rep said, "We're prepared to talk this over, you know."

"There's nothing to talk over," I said. "You said last year's contract and the chairman agrees. You got your majority, what more do you want?"

They had to go through with a recommendation for no increase, and when the fellas heard it they just went wild. We got a near hundred-per-cent strike vote, which scared the company off completely. That's what you want you see, you either want to come out of negotiations with all your demands or none at all. It's when you've got almost everything you want that you have a hard time getting a good strike vote.

Often the companies would hire a lawyer or a labour-faker to represent them in negotiations. Guys like Med McFarlane and Walter Owens or Terry Watts. I was always pleased when the company hired a lawyer to represent them. They were duck soup. All they knew was what the company told them. You can't fill a guy in on all the details, and even if you did he couldn't remember them all. So it didn't take very doggone long before you found out where his information fell short, and you had him at your mercy. The companies never seemed to get wise, they figured if they were paying big money, they were getting good service. Of course it didn't matter if you did back them against the wall, when it came down to it they'd just shake their heads and say no, no, no. But a lot of the foremen could have done far better—they knew more than the hired lawyers.

Walter Owens used to be one of the favourites. They'd get him on arbitration boards, conciliation boards, negotiations and anywhere they felt they needed his great expertise at dealing with us union types. He'd been the city prosecutor one time and he'd go after witnesses in his best courtroom style and really beat the poor bastards up, but much as he loved to dish it out, if you gave it back he'd blow up on a short fuse. It was very easy to get him to lose his temper.

The first time I run into him had to do with the wooden yards. We'd got our contract in the steel yards, so Malcolm MacLeod and George Brown were trying to get the same contract in the wooden yards, but the owners wouldn't go for it. We took a strike vote and it was carried, but not by too damn much. We were on new ground in the wooden yards and the men were edgy about going all out for the union. We held a meeting just before the final negotiating session to reaffirm our list of demands and there was a hell of a bunch of dissidents. Company stooges were standing up and saying they knew for a fact the companies would never settle—they'd close down or move out first. It was a rough meeting and I took quite a beating in the chair.

We had to meet the shipyard owners committee at the top of the Marine building that afternoon for the final negotiating attempt. There was Jack MacDonald, Kenny MacKenzie and Art Mercer with Owens acting as their spokesman. Malcolm MacLeod and George Brown had been acting for the union but they weren't making any headway, so I just took over. The owners were really putting up a fight against being lumped in with the steel shipyards, saying their economics was all different and we should recognize this, but I hung tough. The deadline for a settlement was six o'clock that night or we'd go on strike the next morning.

The meeting was in one of those real handsome panelled rooms that had a big window looking out over the harbour. You could see MacDonald's Shipyard down there on Coal Harbour, it's all part of the Bayshore complex now. Old Jack MacDonald would hear a motor start up down at his yard and stand up to take a look.

"There goes another goddamn boat!" he'd grumble.

"You can't blame them, Jack," I'd say. "They sure as hell don't want to be caught behind a picket line."

We'd talk for a while more and there'd be another boat start up—boats that were tied up at the shipyard for repairs pulling out before the strike.

"They're all going to be gone pretty soon," I told MacDonald. "And you know what they're going to do. They're going to take their work somewheres else and find out how you been rooking them all these years—you'll never see them again!"

Owens loosened his tie, then took it off completely. He ran his fingers through his hair—he was quite good-looking, we used to call him Pretty Boy Owens. The deadline was damn near up and he was very agitated.

These boats continued to flock away. I said "Look at them go, eh?"

I had kind of a technique I used to use, I'd really rip into a guy, then before he could collect himself I'd crack a joke—make him think the pressure was off so he'd get his guard down—then I'd rip into him again. It was pretty effective if you did it right. It kept them off balance.

The six o'clock deadline came and they really started talking fast. I could sense they would bolt so I looked around.

"It's time we were packing our bags, boys," and I started scooping up my papers.

"No, wait," they said. They had their heads together there—buzz, buzz, buzz.

"You guys better make it pretty damn quick," I said.

So they settled. They swallowed our package whole. We didn't have the contract there to sign so I wrote out a memorandum in longhand with all the terms on it and got them to sign that. There was a final union meeting that night and we barely had time to grab a bite before it started.

The union hall was jammed with all these guys expecting to get the strike announcement. I brought the meeting to order without letting on there was any change in plans.

"Before we go any further I've got a memorandum here I think you might want to hear," I said, "so I'll just read it out."

I read the list of our demands one by one and then at the bottom "these terms agreed to such and such date, for the union—W.L. White, for the company—J. MacDonald, K. MacKenzie, A. Mercer."

There was a few seconds silence and the whole hall just stood up and cheered.

"It would appear the majority of the members favour this offer," I said. "However, you will recall from the previous meeting there were several members who opposed your committee's position and in fairness they must be given a chance to register their opposition by a formal vote if they so desire. I would call on any of those dissenting members to indicate whether or not they wish a formal vote to be taken so they can register their opposition to this offer."

I could see the bastards squirming around in their chairs hoping no one would say anything, but as soon as I drew attention to them, the whole meeting pounced.

"Yeah, what about it you guys? What was that horsecock you were feeding us about the companies closing down?"

"Come on you bastards, get up and tell us what you got to say now!"

"Tell us the latest bullshit from the boss, you yellow bastards!"

I'm telling you, those fellas really caught shit. The guys just turned them on the spit for a while, and I let them go to it.

Company guys would sometimes ask me, "Why in the hell, when you guys go to negotiate, when you want four bits you'll ask for a dollar? Why don't you come out and say you want four bits and stick to it?"

"Well," I said, "if we did that we'd just be committing hari-kari. You'd come out with a ten-cent offer, and we'd say no, we want fifty. You'd come up to twenty cents, and we'd say no, we won't meet you. You'd come to twenty-five. Well, Christ, then you'd go to the bloody press and say look at that goddamn union—here we're negotiating in good faith and they won't budge!"

So I said, "When you match us, we've got to be able to match you. You offer us twenty-five and we can come down to eighty. Eventually we meet somewhere in the middle and that's where we want to be in the first place."

You see, you can't afford to ignore public opinion. You can't afford to ignore anything. If you let the bosses get the public against you, then the politicians won't be afraid to hit you with the police, or a cabinet order, or a phoney LRB ruling. You've got to cover your flank.

One of the things they love to throw at you is the old line that your demands are just something the union leadership is trying to push, you're not speaking for the men. I ran into that one time when I was up before a conciliation board negotiating a contract in the wooden boatyards. The board was, as usual, one labour man, one company man and one neutral chairman who was neutral as hell on the side of the boss. I couldn't shake them through persuasion, so I thought, by God now, here's a chance. I contacted the wooden stewards and told them, now there's another board meeting tomorrow in the courthouse on Georgia Street and here's what you do—and I told them what I wanted. Well sir, by the Gods of war, by ten o'clock there we are assembled in the courtroom just getting ready to go, comes a bunch of muttering and shuffling in the hall, and they start to pour in. Old caulkers smelling of tar and oakum, shipwrights smoking their pipes, apprentices all covered head to foot with copper paint, mechanics in their greasy coveralls—they crowded in, they packed up against the walls, in behind the chairman's desk, the corridors were plugged, oh it was a sight to be seen.

I had told the men that likely they would be ordered out of the courthouse by the police but to refuse to go on the ground they were present as witnesses. Lawyers and judges on the way to various courtrooms in their gowns had to squeeze through the men, and they were packed tight. They were ordered out but they refused to go, which was their legal right, and the police were stymied. This was a great morale booster as the men felt they were taking part in negotiations—as they were. That was the last time we ever used the courthouse for negotiations—it was not our idea in the first place but the company representative's, who possibly thought he could do better in more impressive settings.

Right away the employer's rep sets up a howl—"This is a strike. An illegal strike. You've called these men off in an illegal strike and made a travesty of this board."

"No, no, no," I said. "Mr. Chairman, you will recall our friend here has been stating that the demands before this board are just a pipedream of union leadership and I have been unable to cure him of this delusion. This left us with no alternative but to call the men here to speak for themselves. These men are here as witnesses to this board and I intend to call every one up and ask him if he endorses these demands."

Well that would have taken about two weeks. They didn't know what the hell to do with these workers crowded up against them—they couldn't wait to get shut of them. Finally the company rep says, "Well, to save time we'll concede the point and agree, your demands have the support of the men." That shook them. They couldn't get their argument back on the track after that.

After that, I run into old Fred Smelts, the employer nominee on the Labour Relations Board. Fred was just about the hardest-nosed guy I ever had to come up against, he and I used to tear each other to pieces. He'd heard about this caper and he kind of enjoyed the idea. "You're the only son-of-a-bitch I know who could've pulled off a thing like that!" he said.

I was doing so much negotiating I just got so I'd try anything. I had all the legal moves down by heart. I was right up on what was going on in government and industry and all that. I read all the business papers and if some company that said they'd go broke meeting our wage demands had a good quarter, I'd make a note of it.

I'd save up any little bits of information that might come in handy. I heard some guys talking about something they did at one of the yards one time—there was a repair job in and they hid a bunch of guys. The guys would come in in the morning, go up on the staging, play cards all day and go home. They hid two riveting gangs for several weeks and then they charged it up to this job, you see. Well some time after this I was negotiating with the boss of this yard, and he come out with a long lecture on the cost of shipbuilding, and how they couldn't compete the way wages were. So I come out with this story of the two riveting gangs and said, "It can't be too damn competitive when you can pad your bills up like that and get away with it." Oh Jesus, was he furious! To think I'd have the temerity to bring out something like this, you see.

Things like this built up your confidence. You got so you could walk in on anything and meet whoever you came up against head on. You got to know all the personalities you had to deal with by where the chinks were in their armour. A fella like Tommy Thompson, the personnel manager at Pacific and later Burrard. They used Tommy as a negotiator a lot, he liked to save face. You get the bulge on Tommy and right away he'd want to find an honourable way out. He'd be more worried about that than going on with the fight.

II

After the war ended in 1945 and the shipyard shrinkage took place, we spread out into the small welding shops and machine shops where a lot of our members had gone for work. These shops'd have maybe eight or ten men up to anywhere from twenty-five to thirty and they formed their own group and negotiated in a block, which simplified things for us. They'd get one guy to act as spokesman for all the shop owners and this one particular time the spokesman was Walter Depford who owned The Welding Shop at 1600 Main.

If you settled for two bits and various conditions in the shipyards, this became what was known as "the pattern" for throughout the industry. We'd already settled in the shipyards and it was more or less a formality for the shops to follow suit, but this time they wouldn't agree. I saw these fellas individually and I said, "What the hell's wrong with you guys? You know you've got to sign that contract."

"Well, you better just talk to Walter," they said. "He's our spokesman."

I knew Walter was very anti-union and I suspected right away that he was putting these other guys up to it. He hadn't been very happy about being unionized himself and he was going to carry on his battle with us, using his competitors' troops. So I called for a strike vote, but instead of holding it in all eight shops we singled out Walter's place and held it just there. We got a real thumping majority and Walter started to get nervous.

"What about these other shops?" he said.

"Oh well, we'll get around to them," I said. I went down and talked to his workers at lunchtime and there was a stoolie there. I talked up a fight, but I purposely never mentioned anything about a strike date. Just as I was leaving this stoolie come up.

"Are we going to go out on strike?" he whispered.

"Yeah!" I whispered back.

"When?"

"Next Tuesday, but don't tell anybody."

I knew I wouldn't be out of there five minutes before he was in to tell Walter. Monday, Walter sent all the work he was doing out to other shops to be finished off because he figured he was going to be shut down. Come Tuesday, all his men show up for work and there's no work to do. He had to send the trucks out to bring it all back in again.

"I thought you guys were going on strike," he said to me.

"First I heard about it," I said. He cussed to beat hell, and I gave him a big smile. A couple days later I came down to talk to the guys again, and as I was leaving this doggone stoolie came up again.

"What happened?" he said. You could see he'd taken a beating over this foulup he'd got Walter into. "Aw, some other thing come up. We had to put it off til next Tuesday."

The next week Walter sends his work all out again. Tuesday morning he has to haul it all back in again. I went down that noon for another talk to the fellas and Walter stopped me as I was going through the office.

"Are you guys going on strike or aren't you?" he said.

"That depends on whether you come to your senses, Walter."

"I wish you'd make up your damn mind so we can get it done with and get on with our work."

"Do you really want to know?"

"Waalll," he said, "I'd appreciate a bit of warning, yeah."

"Well I'll tell you, then," I said. "Just as soon as you get right in the middle of a big juicy contract with your pants down, that's when we'll pull the plug. You'll have about five minutes notice. That's when we'll go on strike. Now you can't say I didn't tell you."

"What the hell's the idea of picking on me, anyway," he said.

"You're the bloody one that wants to fight," I said. "The other guys don't give a damn. They'll be glad to take care of all your customers while you're out of business, too."

I never told any of the guys beforehand when we'd go out, I just kept them ready. We didn't want to strike really, there was nothing to be gained by it. We had come down a nickel on our demand but Walter still wouldn't move. I let him go till he kind of eased off worrying about it, then I walked into his shop at ten o'clock in the morning. The machines were really humming you know, they were real busy, and I said, "This is it, boys. Down she goes." We had a picket line up within minutes and Walter was caught.

He called a meeting of the other shop owners, but they were all still working, you see. All he got from them was sympathy, because all along he'd been the guy who was pushing to fight the union. He called us in then, he said, "Now I understand the other day you agreed to reduce your demands by five cents."

"That's quite right, Walter," I said. "The other day we did do that. But today we're asking a nickel more. You had your bloody opportunity for a deal and you wouldn't take it. You deal on our terms now."

The poor bugger could hardly stand it, but he could stand even less to lose all his business to his competitors, so he signed. I talked to the other owners later and they laughed about it—how Walter boxed himself in that time. But I knew what Walter was like, you see, and I knew all along it was him who had his foot on the brakes.

There were bosses whose word you could take and never worry about and others you couldn't believe on a deck of bibles edged with prayer books—their word was worthless and you had to keep a constant watch that they didn't violate the contract or evade their commitments. Old W.D. McLaren was one who was always looking for a dodge, and another was Willie Wardle who pulled that double cross that time on the paid holidays. At the other end of the scale was Claude Thicke, the general manager at Burrard. He was generally disliked by the union representatives because he was tough to deal with—he was a real no-nonsense guy and he would just as soon peel the hide off one of his foremen as anyone else if he thought they needed it. But when old Claude gave his word it was as good as his bond. He expected the union to live up to the letter of its agreement, but he made sure the company did too. I'd far rather deal with a man like him where you at least knew where you stood, than one of the weasley buggers who'd come on all sweetness and reason then double back on you the minute you took your eyes off them. There were others, like Syd Hogg, the manager of Western Bridge, and George Randall of BC Marine, whose word could be relied on.

I tried to be the same way. I figured in a situation where you were dealing with the same people year after year your credibility was the most important asset you could have. No matter even with the bastards, I never broke my word to them once. If I said I'd do a thing, I'd do it. That's very important, with the employers and the men on the job too—if you can win their trust it makes your work a lot easier. Generally in later years our union had good relations with the majority of the employers, and this came from negotiations being conducted in good faith on both sides. That goes a long way towards peaceful industrial relations.

I personally negotiated the first forty-hour week clause our union had, the first union hall hiring agreement—(that was a toughie now, I'll tell you, we had to drop it several times before we finally made it stick), paid holidays, and paid medical. (That was the CU & C.)

We were the first union to come in under CU & C, which was an early medical plan set up under the Credit Union League. The CU & C wasn't offering group coverage til I went over to see the fella in charge, Tom Wiltshire, and put it up to him. We worked out the details between us, then I put it on our list of demands during negotiations. We wanted the employers to pay part of the premium you see, and by God, I got them to go for it. A lot of the Party guys couldn't see the value of the medical so I didn't get any support, but afterwards they realized what a good thing it was. I was talking to Wiltshire years later, and he said the CU & C was just getting its start on the West Coast at that time, and getting our whole union in one shot really put it on its feet.

I negotiated the first guaranteed annual income clause in this part of the country, down at Canadian Liquid Carbonic. They had very irregular hours, sometimes the fellas worked night and day and other times they were laid off for weeks at a time and it made it a hard job to follow. The company had trouble too, keeping the right kind of men around, so I came up with the idea of having a core of permanent employees who'd be guaranteed two thousand hours per year whether they worked it or not, and it panned out good for both sides. Another deal something like that was the hard hat divers—often they'd be called out on a job that would only take twenty minutes of actual work, but they had to sit around all day to get it, so I organized them and got them a contract for a hundred dollars a day flat rate. No matter if it was a dip or dive, they got their hundred bucks. Later I got the same deal for the skin divers.

We had a lot of guys come in to the office, guys from shops where there was no union or AF of L unions that didn't do anything for them, they'd just come in on their own and try to get our help. If it was possible we'd put them to work and give them all the help they needed to get their company organized into our union or some other, it didn't matter. I spent a great part of my time organizing. I moved the union out into the shops after the postwar shrinkage—I saw to the organizing of Western Bridge and the wooden yards as well. Sam Jenkins and George Brown took credit for those last two afterwards, but they were only a small part of it.

In organizing, the first important thing is your contacts. You get contacts inside the plant and you do all your work through them. We organized Morrison Steel and Wire and never set foot in the place until after the certification vote. The inside men did it all. The boss there was president of the Canadian Manufacturers Association too, old Hammett, who led the move to eradicate the scourge of industrial unionism from the face of the nation, and here his own shop fell to the foe right under his nose. He just about had a hemorrhage when he saw the application for certification.

We worked very quietly, starting with two or three men. And I said, only approach guys you're sure of at first. Leave the doubtful ones to last. That way you can build towards your majority, then you can go to the ones that say, "Ah, I don't know," and say, "Look. We got plenty for certification already. This union is coming in and all that's up to you is whether you're going to be on the inside or the outside." That way, if they figured the majority of their workmates were in, they'd come along too.

We'd have the favorable ones up to my office after work to

talk it over—"What about so-and-so," they'd say. "Oh, he's pretty stubborn . . ."

"Okay, we'll leave him. What about this other guy?" "He'd be a good one, he got gypped on that overtime and he's peeved about it . . ." We'd get a list of all the good bets and that'd be the key. You'd work from that list. All you needed was fifty-one percent of the workers in a bargaining unit, then you could apply to the LRB to take a certification vote. Once the union was certified as bargaining agent, then the company was bound under the Labour Act to recognize you as the worker's agent.

The ones you couldn't do anything for were the little family businesses, where a guy'd got all his relatives in working for him. There was one over on the North Shore like that called Canadian Mixermobile, a little shop that was some kind of a subsidiary of Dominion Bridge and just so goddamned anti-union. A few of our guys got on there, not many, and three or four of them come in to see me after work. They were getting fifty cents below union scale. "We wish to hell you could do something for us," they said.

I knew you might just as well try to organize the Vancouver Club as go in there, but we talked anyway, and one of the things they told me was the boss gave them a turkey every Christmas.

"Well," I said, "I'm going to get you guys a raise in pay."

"How?" they said. "They'd never join the union."

"You watch," I said.

I put out a leaflet. Oh Jesus, a real hot one, too. The title of it was "The Thousand-Dollar Turkey." I pointed out that they were four bits under the shipyard scale, and since the work year consisted of two thousand hours, they were missing out on a thousand dollars a year by taking the boss's Christmas turkey and staying away from the union. "The boss said that turkey was free, but he's making a thousand dollars on every one," I said. I went and stood by the gate at quitting time to pass these leaflets out, and do you know, some of those guys would bolt past me at a dead run! They'd look, see the leaflet, and turn their heads away, as if just seeing it was committing a sin. Others would look around, grab a leaflet quick and shove it under their coat to look at it later like a French postcard.

Well by gosh, a day or so later these guys come in, they were laughing to beat hell. The boss called them in and gave them a raise. Not the full four bits, but a raise. For three years those guys'd come in, laugh, say "Hey Bill, we need another raise. Is your printing press still working?" The union never did get in there, but it was able to get the men their wage hikes just the same.

You used to hear it then the same as you do now, all this talk about guys who were overpaid. But the queer thing about it, even though you heard about it all the time, you never run into a case of it. Any Joe you talk to, he's always earning what he gets, it's always the other guy who ain't. What really turns your gut is when the guy doing the bitching is some son-of-a-bitch who's pulling down a quarter million as head of MacMillan Bloedel or CPR, but invariably that's who it is.

People like this find something obscene about a mere worker making as good money as a professional, and it makes no difference which one of them works harder, faces greater danger, has the shorter working life or is more essential to the economy. Their feeling is based on class snobbishness alone. To them it's downright immoral for the worker to encroach on the economic territory of his "betters" just like in India it's unthinkable for untouchables to cut in on any of the higher castes. There was a doctor running in one provincial election here whose pitch was that logging truck drivers were getting as much as he was and it was time things were "put back in perspective." Well to me this is completely haywire, you see.

It never bothered me one bit to be in the forefront of wage demands, because I'm really not concerned about preserving the old class distinctions. I always figured the producer deserved just as big a share of the pie as anybody else, and he's a long way from getting that, even today.

6

Beyond the Union Hall

I

Y ou get an organization as good as that—especially during '44 and
'45 there when we had the biggest union local in Canada—well
it has a hell of a lot of influence. I was getting attacked left, right
and centre in the press. They loved me. Any time things were slow in
the newsroom they'd send a reporter down to get my reaction to some
damn thing and I'd always try not to disappoint them. They called me
"labour chief." Labour Chief Bill White says such-and-such. When
Gerry McGeer died there in 1947 they had a parade, some twenty
thousand people come out, so some fella asked me what I thought of
that—McGeer was the guy who read the Riot Act to the unemployed
during the Post Office riot and used police to break up the longshore
strike in '35, you see. "What do you think of that wonderful tribute
the people paid to old Gerry?" he said.

"That wasn't any tribute," I said. "Them people come out to make
sure the bastard was dead!"

Jack Webster the hotliner was a cub reporter from the *Vancouver
Sun* just fresh off the boat from Scotland then, he used to come down
calling on me all the time. Doug Collins, the columnist, too. I used
to have pretty good relations with them, but I used to have godawful

Vancouver mayor Gerry McGeer, pictured here in 1947, was a flamboyant populist who dominated city politics from the '30s through the '50s. CITY OF VANCOUVER ARCHIVES, PORT P965

wrangles with some of the publishers. The editorial page cartoonist on one of the dailies for a time was a fella named Fraser Wilson, who was quite a left-winger. Fraser was rep for the Newspaper Guild at the Vancouver Labour Council and once when he was called upon to say some hard things about his employer, he was fired. Well I hired him to decorate our hall and in the downstairs lobby he did a cartoon of a big overfed SOB labelled "Daily Press" standing on a prone woman in a white dress labelled "The Truth," stabbing her with a stick pen, and somehow it come out that the stabber looked a lot like his old boss. The boss heard about this and come down to have a look. Before long I got a letter from his lawyer wanting this slanderous depiction removed. I checked with our lawyer who took a look and said, "Migawd, get rid of that thing. Anybody would recognize that." Well, that rankled me because this paper was attacking me every other day and I never could get it to take anything back, so I told the lawyer to tell him we had no intention of removing this cartoon. "You just say, I am very surprised to hear your client claiming a resemblance to this drawing because I have queried the artist on this matter and found out that he had no intention of making a likeness of him and in fact he was only trying to depict a moronic-looking individual." That was all we heard on that one.

I used to get so goddamn mad, though. Everything we did the papers would somehow twist so we looked greedy or unfair or violent or worse. What made me maddest was knowing that they were misinforming people and people were getting hooked by it. I didn't care about their editorials or their opinions, it was the news reporting, where they'd go and cover some trial and quote only the witnesses who were hostile to us, or where they'd pick and choose the facts so it made things look opposite to what they were. That kind of slant is hard to catch for anyone who's not in the story, and it's hard to nail them on it. They might quote someone on our side to make it look fair, but they'd reproduce his bad grammar where the company rep would be talking like an Oxford scholar. They're so goddamned sneaky, you don't stand a chance against them. If you go after them, they really do a job on you.

And the *Sun* was by far the worst. The *Sun* was noted for yellow journalism. The Yellow Rag, they called it. I told the owner once that he owed his success to unions, and it was true. The *Sun* was just a minor paper, hardly any bigger than the *News Herald,* and the *Province* was the leading paper with all the name writers and all the big ads. What changed it was a strike. The *Province* went on strike in the summer of 1946 and stayed on strike for several years, although it was only off the streets a couple of weeks. I was down there at the old *Province* building at Cambie and Hastings. We had some fun there on the picket lines.

They run an issue off with scab labour and tried to bring trucks out through the picket line, but we were ready for them. We had four-by-four chunks with spikes drove through from all sides and threw those under the tires. That stopped them, and as soon as they stopped we got a bunch of guys rocking the trucks til they flipped over. Then we dove inside and pulled all the papers out onto the street. Then a streetcar come along and drove over the papers and set them all on fire and they had to get in the fire department. Bloody old Cornett, the mayor, ordered the police in to help deliver the papers, if you can imagine that. Cops delivering papers.

But during this time the *Sun* took over all the *Province's* readers and advertisers and by the time the strike was settled it was too late. The *Province* never got top spot back. So I told this guy he owed everything he had to unionism, but it didn't make him any more friendly. Once we took out a full page ad to reply to some damn attack they'd made on us, and they refused to print it. A paid ad for a thousand bucks. That's what they call the free press.

The only time I ever got a paper to make a retraction was in 1945, and that was the old *Vancouver News Herald*. The *News Herald* was a morning paper run by Slim Delbridge. This time I caught them completely off base—they'd misquoted me on something and we had the clear goods. I phoned up Delbridge and said I wanted an apology of this here.

"You'll get no apology!" Okay, fine, I says. We had twenty thousand members at the time, most of who came across to work on the old North Van ferries in the morning—Christ, there was traffic jams all over Vancouver when the shipyards changed shift—and they all bought the *News Herald* to read coming across the inlet. There'd be huge piles of papers there at the ferry slip and they'd disappear in a few minutes.

What I done was I called the stewards in and put the *Herald* on the hot list. Boys'd stay by the piles and keep the guys from buying and anybody seen reading a *Herald* would get shit. If somebody had a subscription to it a steward would say, "Hey, you're gonna cancel that, aren't ya?" "Oh, well, I guess so." "Good, do it right now." And they'd yard him over to the nearest phone. "Tell them why, too." Some of the things those guys said into the phone made even me cringe. Pretty soon the *Herald* stopped answering. It took four days. Delbridge called me at my office.

"White?" he says. "Call your dogs off. You'll get your goddamned apology." Slam. The next day everybody's reading Delbridge eating his words, hooting, pounding their fists. It gave them a feeling of power. This taste of power is one of the things that makes a union strong.

It can go too far of course. Some of the beefs that come up were ridiculous. One fella accidently set a fire welding, then refused to throw water on it. "I'm a welder, not a fireman," he said. I told him, "If that's all the brains you got then you deserve to be canned."

It was nothing for my phone to ring in the middle of the goddamn night for some stupid little thing. There was a little cafe, The Sugarbowl, down on Marine in North Vancouver and a lot of the guys on the midnight shift used to eat there. This one time it was closed for painting or something and when a bunch of them went to eat and found it closed, they phoned me up. "The Sugarbowl is closed and we can't get anything to eat. What's the union going to do about it?" This was about 2:30 a.m. I said, "I haven't got seven loaves and two fishes on me so I'm not going to do bugger all," and hung up. Stupid bastards. I used to tease old Malcolm MacLeod, who was secretary of the union by this time, I'd phone him up and talk broken English and tell him I was Joe Palookski and chew the hell out of him about the price of shoelaces or the weather—he was so apologetic, he'd say, "Just a minute, we're doin' everything we can . . ." Finally I'd get laughing so much I couldn't hold the accent, and he'd say, "Bill, you son-of-a-bitch!"

We used to take up a lot of issues. The Cambie Street grounds was one of them, next to where the Queen Elizabeth Theatre is now. It was the only park in downtown Vancouver but I guess the big shots didn't like it because it was popular for labour rallies and protests, so City Council decided to turn it over to BC Electric for a bus depot. We put up quite a fuss about this. I took a parade up to City Hall at one point. Cornett was mayor then. They boarded the hall up but allowed me to come in alone. There was just me, Cornett and two senators—Gerry McGeer and old Senator Farris. They had no official connection with council, either of them at that time, but they were running the city behind the scenes, you see, they called the shots for the establishment. They sat there not saying a word while outside was these couple of thousand men shouting and waving banners. Cornett stood up and read a prepared statement and his hands were shaking so bad he kept losing his place. We were turned down flat and I was given no chance to reply. Well, we had a sound truck, and as soon as I got out we wheeled her up to the hall door and oh Jesus, did I ever give them a blasting, now. It didn't save the park but the next day we found out they heard us alright. The council passed an ordinance prohibiting the use of sound trucks within city limits.

I got another shot at that one by accident. It was a City Council election you see, and the Non-Partisan Association—that was the establishment organization—they were holding a big fundraising banquet. Some secretary must have been given the job of sending out the invites and I was president of the Vancouver Labour Council that year and I guess that sounded like a bigshot to her, so I got one. Well, I went down there amongst all these tuxedos and diamonds just to have a look around. Cornett stood up and strung out his line of bull, got a big thunderous ovation, and they called for questions. So I stood up and put him on the spot over the Cambie Grounds. Oh gee, you should have seen the dirty looks. Every face in the hall just a mask of hate. Cornett stood up and waffled around for a minute and the chairman come out and brushed his hands off and says if there's no other questions, we'll adjourn—but before he could finish I rose again and said, "Just a minute—he didn't answer my question." And I repeated what I'd said. There was just a silence then. Cornett walked slowly up to the mike and stood there for a minute with his hands on his hips. He just bit off his words: "If I'd known you were going to be here tonight, I'd have been ready for you." Oh gee, they cheered and whistled and whooped. That was all the answer I got. They would have cheered just the same if he'd stood up and said, "Rotten fish!" They pushed the bus depot through over the objections of every union and community group in the city because they said it would only be there for two years, til they could get some other site ready. Thirty years later it was still there.

I started a radio broadcast on CJOR called "Labour News and Views"—the union bought fifteen minutes prime time and I'd interview other labour leaders if they were having strikes—the very first one was supposed to be an interview with Harold Pritchett of the IWA but he didn't show and I had to ad lib the whole program—or else we'd just take up issues where the people's interest was involved. One time I remember the lumber ration was on and nobody could get a board to build a birdhouse, this fella who owned Finning Tractor built a huge barn for his horses. Well I did a broadcast on that and the corruption in the rationing system. The program worked damn good, but after a while the station management started demanding to read my scripts before I went on the air, and they started taking a very free hand in running the blue pencil through anything they didn't like the look of. It got to where I couldn't say anything but God Save the King, so we had to drop it. It wasn't worth the money we had to pay for the airtime.

Our hall was a famous place in those days. Everybody knew the Boilermakers Hall at 339 West Pender—the Pender Auditorium as it was sometimes called. There was everything in there, from wrestling matches to ballet to revival meetings. It was the regular meeting place of just about all the Congress Unions and the Vancouver Labour Council and the BC Federation of Labour. You really had the feeling you were close to the heart of the city down there. There was no telling who you'd see in the lobby, from some junkie to the mayor. We used to get all the street people. I remember this little fella come into my office, he just sat down going sniff, sniff. I said, "Well, what can I do for you?" and he said, "Oh nothing, I just stopped in to shoot up in your john!"

Mostly it was union people, but you get a big active organization of twenty thousand people, you find you're involved in every goddamn thing that happens. The women used to flock into my office with their damn personal problems, they'd watch til you were alone then slip in and close the door. They'd want to cry and have me talk to their husbands, but hell, I'd have to show them out. A guy could've got in the bight of the line awful fast. We ran a lot of social programmes, too—classes for the wives and athletic programs for the men. We had a lot of top-flight professional boxers in the union. One was Eddie Weinstob from Viking, Alberta, who was a top heavyweight—he'd fought Schmeling and others. He was British Empire champ for many years but he didn't quite have the stuff to be world champion. And there was Tiger Jack Fox, Sammy Mandel, Len Girvais, who was our boxing coach—a real crew of them. We booked pro fights into the hall. I started an annual fishing derby, and we had an annual picnic and sports day. Often that would be at Bowen Island, we'd charter a steamer from the Union Steamships and take them up there for the day, wives, kids and all. I used to be able to run pretty good in the hundred-yard dash, and one time I almost won it. I tried to get them to cut it down to sixty yards for the old-timers but no, they said it had to be a hundred. I run anyway and led the field up to about eighty yards where I run out of gas. Some skinny bugger come up on me and

I tried to hang on but he got past. I strained myself so bad I just went down on my knees at the finish and puked.

We put on a series of public forums in the hall, too. We'd get the head of the Canadian Manufacturers Association in to debate with the head of the BC Federation of Labour, or if some top scientist or economist was in town we'd get him in for a lecture. I'd act as moderator and we'd have questions from the floor submitted on paper. We'd get real big crowds there, and I'd have to really watch so these speakers didn't get mauled too bad. Some of the questions the fellas wrote in were completely out of line—I'd just crumple them up. Different guys told me later, guys from the Department of Labour or the CMA, that their knees were just knocking when they went in there to speak but they were very impressed by the fair treatment they got. I insisted on doing it that way because I knew how easy it would be for them to go away and say we were a bunch of wild-eyed savages who couldn't be reasoned with.

We had to be so damn careful how we treated people, but they could be completely haywire in the way they treated us and still get away with it. I got invited to debate one time there on "Town Meeting of the Air." I don't suppose many people remember "Town Meeting of the Air," it used to start off "Hear ye, Hear ye, Hear ye!" The moderator was Arthur Helps, and this time I was debating the principle of the closed shop with a prominent lawyer who was very anti-union. The format was, each guy'd go on for ten minutes then they'd each get three minutes to rebut. It was before a live audience and after that they'd get questions from the audience. Well the buggers phonied up on me. They put me on first, I gave a straight talk and he did too in his main talk. In my rebuttal I stuck to the subject and answered the points he'd raised, but when he come up for his last lick, he just blasted me with both barrels. Said the labour movement was riddled with chiselers and racketeers and communists and all this—a real diatribe. I wanted to answer the bugger but they wouldn't give me the mike. "No, no, you've had your turn." We went into questions but there was nobody down on the floor to give me the bloody opening. When it was all over we were called to the mike to shake hands and say what a fine fight it was you see, so I come up all smiles. Helps was suspicious, but he had to let me at the mike and I just give him a good hip-check right out there.

"I very much appreciate this opportunity to come before you and explain labour's position on this rather contentious issue," I said. "But I very much regret that my honourable opponent here felt the need to break the rules and make charges that are outside the scope of this debate." Helps was just grab, grab, grab, you know, but I kept sweeping him away. "It is quite true that there's racketeers and chiselers in the labour movement," I said. "There's not many, and labour is at least making an effort to get rid of them. But I'll leave it to the listening audience to decide if there's more racketeers and chiselers in the labour movement than there is in the legal profession." Well sir, it just brought the house down. Guys come up to me the next day, "I want to shake your hand, Bill. You sure fixed 'em that time."

As well as the forums we held many and many's the concert. Paul Robeson, he was at the height of his fame then and in demand all over the world, he'd often come up and put on a concert for us. He didn't charge, either, he just took what we wanted to give. He said he'd a hundred times sooner sing free for a bunch of longshoremen on a dock than do it for big shots in hundred-dollar seats at the Metropolitan Opera. Later when the Canadian immigration put him on the shit list because of his working-class sympathies he used to come up and give outdoor concerts in Peace Arch Park, standing on the American side singing to us on the Canadian side. One time they hooked speakers up to the phone and he sung a concert over the phone. Thinking of Robeson—one of the finest singers ever, one of the great actors, a star on Broadway and in the movies, a distinguished scholar, even an all-American football player, and a man who'd rather abandon all his success than sell out his principles—there is no question he was one of the greatest men America produced. But they wasted him. He had to take refuge in Europe. We should think of that when they're showing us pictures of the president receiving Russian dissidents with flags waving and arms open. Robeson died shut up in an apartment in New York, a broken man.

I remember driving him around town in my '37 Ford—him and Ivy and me in the front seat, it sure didn't leave much cargo space.

||

I went on many and many's the junket to Victoria or back East, representing the union or the labour council. Hopping city to city over the mountains and across the prairies in old Lockheed Lodestars. During the war you had one hell of a time getting on a plane and often you ended up spending a week somewhere you didn't figure on. Ottawa was worst, both because it was the place you got stuck most and it was the worst place to be stuck. This one time I was there to badger the Deputy Minister of Labour over some change in the Code we wanted and he asked me how I was getting home. I told him I was on the waiting list for a flight but didn't have much hope of getting away before the week's end.

"I'll get you on a flight tonight," he said. And he did too, lickety-split. Ottawa is like an iceberg, the part you see is only ten percent. All the rest is behind the scenes. I felt quite good about being on the inside track til I got home and realized I'd forgotten about half the things I was going to say to the bastard. He'd done a good job of getting me out of his hair.

I was on a trip once to Trail where I was going to give a talk. Harvey Murphy of Mine-Mill was having quite a struggle holding off a raid by Steel and he asked me to come up because a lot of ex-shipyard guys had gone up there after the shrinkage and he figured they might listen to me. We were waiting for our flight in a cafe at Castlegar and this other passenger says to us in a low voice, "We've got quite a notorious character with us today."

"Who's that?" I said.

"Bill White, the Communist."

"Is that so," I said. "Do you know which one he is?"

"I think I saw him coming in, but I'm not sure," she said.

"Well, I tell you something," I said, "you seen him alright, and not only that, you're talking to him right now!" Jesus, I had to laugh. She lit up like a neon sign.

We'd go to conventions mostly by train, and the train trip was often the best part of the convention. All the factions would be there, the left-wing Party guys, the right-wing CCF bunch, and they'd all be plotting and spying against each other, and trying to figure out how to foul each other up most effectively.

Harvey Murphy, head of the Canadian Mine, Mill and Smelter Workers Union, was always a standout on those trips. He was very good company, a great gossip and an easy guy to buy a drink for. He was the heavyweight of the Party bunch and the right-wingers' favourite target when it came to making an attack. They knew his position in the Party as well as we did but the Party was in camouflage those days and all they

Harvey Murphy, once head of BC's Mine and Smelter Workers.

could do when they wanted to call a guy red was claim that he espoused the Party line. That's where the term "fellow traveller" came into use. If he's not an out-and-out red, they'd say then he's at the very least a "fellow traveller." I remember one time going to a convention when the plotting was quite tense. Murph and I were walking down the aisle and we come to the car where all the right-wingers, Mahoney, Baskin and them, were getting their heads together. We knew they were there, but they were keeping to themselves, so Murphy bust open the door, poked his head in and hollered, "Greetings, fellow travellers!"

Murphy had a very striking head with big bushy brows—a lot like Harvey MacMillan, the timber magnate, as a matter of fact—and I think the sight of it poking in there just about wiped the whole right-wing out with a mass heart attack. If they had guns, I'm sure they'd have all been drawn right then. Murphy laughed like hell.

Murphy wasn't his name, you know. How he come by Murphy, he was down in Pittsburgh many years ago, probably organizing for the CIO, I don't know, but he got in on a ruckus and got hauled up in court. The judge was a real Irishman who hated only one thing as much as he hated labour agitators and that was Bohunks, as they called them. A lot of the guys Murphy was in with were Ukes and Poles and he could see this judge just giving them the heavy hammer one after the other. When Murphy's turn come this judge was just starting to lick his lips and enjoy himself.

"What's your name," he said. I don't remember what Murph's right name was now but I think he had a "ski" or a "chuck" there.

"My name is ah . . . Murphy, Your Honour," he said and crossed himself.

"Murphy!" this judge says. "What are you doing mixed up with this bunch of hooligans?"

"I was misled, Your Honour," Murph says, crossing himself again.

"You certainly were, my son. How long since you've been to church?"

"Too long, Your Honour," Murph said, crossing himself again.

"Well, I think you've learned your lesson," the judge said. "Case dismissed."

I noticed though, in later years he didn't like it too much if anyone said anything about his old name.

He had a tremendous history in the labour movement, Murphy. He'd been organizing since he was a kid and he'd been in damn near every big battle you could name. It was well on in his career when he came to the coast and built up Mine-Mill.

The conventions moved around, but most of them seemed to be in Toronto or Montreal. Whenever I was in Montreal I'd go around to the shipyard unions there and renew contacts. I kept in touch with the Quebec unions at all times and they were always very interested in our union because they couldn't get near the conditions and wages we had. I used to send them lots of advice and the odd donation so I always got a good reception when I went out there. I was there for the big Vickers Strike and seen them run in the scabs. And I mean run, now.

The strikers tried to block the gates by forming a crowd but they set up a double line of riot cops and the scabs bust out of the trucks and run down the line for all they were bloody worth, with the strikers on the outside straining their French to let them know what they thought about it. The air was pretty thick with rivets and nuts too, and a lot of scabs went down. It was a sickening sight.

That was under Premier Duplessis. Duplessis had spies at the convention, sitting in the galleries. The union guys told me about them and I pointed them out when I was on the floor speaking. I said, "Let's give these distinguished guests the welcome they deserve." They sure got it.

There was an awful lot of partying and drinking at those conventions. The establishment made sure of that. The breweries used to rent the floor above the convention hall and send girls in to serve free booze to all comers. Guys would go up in the morning and stay there all day. We had to lay the law down to a few of our guys.

We had delegations til hell wouldn't have it. Once we were in Ottawa and everybody was in town with us—the CCF, the craft unions, the AF of L, even a preacher. The Reverend A.A. Cook—he was quite a guy. There was about twelve of us went down and there was some big function on at the Chateau Laurier. We couldn't get rooms there so we had to go over to the Standish Arms in Hull. I had a room with John Turner who was secretary of the Labour Council and four doors down was Tom Parkin and Roly Gervin, who was secretary of the Trades Council. Roly Gervin was a city alderman and very well known in Vancouver as a friend of the establishment. In the provincial election of 1949 he campaigned for the Liberals and tried to pull labour away from the CCF by talking up the red scare, and later he became a representative for the employers. Between sessions we'd go up to Tom and Roly's room to hoist a few and Roly kept saying he had to have a bath, he had to have a bath. When he was out I said to Tom, "Go hide all the bloody towels, and when he gets done his bath this is what you do." So I told him. Tom hid the towels and Roly went in for a great long soak and he winds up hollering for Tom to go borrow one of our towels.

"To hell with you, go get it yourself."

"Come on, you bastard."

"Hell with you. The walk'll do you good."

So Roly gets out of the tub you know, looks up and down the hall—it was a bit chancey because we were four doors away around a corner and right at the head of the stair—but he comes dashing over and bangs on our door.

"Who is it?"

"Roly. Quick, let me in."

"What the hell do you want?"

"I want a towel."

"We need our towels. Use your own damn towels."

"Come on, for Chrissakes. I got nothin on."

"The hell with you. We don't want you in here like that."

So he scuttled back to his room, but Tom had locked the door.

We kept him out in the hall for about fifteen minutes. Cursing us through the keyhole—I thought he'd go right nuts. Jesus! I seen him not too long ago and said, "Bout time we took another trip back to the Standish Arms, Roly."

"You bastard, I'll piss on your grave for that," he said.

I guess if I made twenty trips to Ottawa, ten of them would be over the merchant marine. Apart from Compensation and the Kuzych Case that was the biggest campaign we ever put on, the campaign to set up a Canadian Merchant Marine. You see, the wartime shipbuilding programme, in spite of everything that was haywire about it, turned out a great success. Today I don't think there is an average of one ship a year launched on the West Coast, and when one is, they get royalty out to christen it. But during the war West Coast yards put out three hundred and forty-nine ships inside of four years. It's almost impossible to imagine the scale of the work that was undertaken. We started with green workers—ninety-nine percent had never seen the inside of a shipyard. They had to start from scratch and the ones who knew the trades had to teach the ones who didn't. By the peak there they were popping ten thousand-ton ships out in sixty days. They were good ships too. We were damn proud of what we done. We wanted to keep the thing going, and the way to keep it going was to maintain the fleet

Launch of the *Westend Park* at Burrard Drydock in 1944, the 300th Canadian-built cargo ship and Burrard Drydock's 85th. NORTH VANCOUVER MUSEUM AND ARCHIVES, 9792

as a peacetime merchant marine, hauling commercial cargoes. This was no damned pipedream either. Canada had every need of a merchant fleet and we did all kinds of research to show how it could be worked.

We held a mass rally in Athletic Park at the war's end and just about everybody in Vancouver came except the mayor, who'd been invited to speak and sent word he was going to the beach to relax. We got a letter from the Minister of Veteran's Affairs, Ian A. Mackenzie, which said, "Vancouver's shipbuilding record is unsurpassed. This is due to the skill, zeal and energy of you, the workers. Canada extends her thanks and the assurance that your skill and ability will be required for the tasks that lie ahead.

"We are not going to repeat past mistakes. It is the determined policy of the present Government that Canada is in the shipbuilding business for good. The Merchant Marine that you made is going to be maintained and expanded."

When that letter was written in 1945 Canada was fourth among the ship-owning nations of the world with over five hundred ships employing at least twenty thousand men. In 1948 she was down to a hundred and forty-five vessels employing six thousand men. By 1955 she was down to fifteen dry cargo vessels. By 1963 she was down to one ship, a ten-thousand-tonner with the laughable name SS *Federal Pioneer*.

This decline had been brought about as a direct result of federal government policy. The public-owned Park Steamship Company which operated most of the wartime fleet had been broken up and given away to foreign interests. We lobbied for legislation to have Canadian goods carried in Canadian bottoms and stop foreign bottoms from trading coastwise, which is common fare in other countries, but never a thing was done. We fought for government assistance to build the service up—there's hardly a shipping country in the world that doesn't subsidize its merchant fleet in some way—but here it was out of the question. There have been no end of official studies, all finding that Canada is losing out by not having her own merchant service, but still no action is ever considered. Meanwhile employment in the shipbuiding industry in BC has fallen from 31,200 at the peak to less than a thousand today. The skill and ability they assured us would never be wasted is not only lost, it's forgotten we ever had it. Canada has fallen further behind the times in shipbuilding than she was at the beginning of the WW II. If you take that great effort the Canadian people made to build them ships then you put beside it the dismal damn effort the government made to save those same ships, it's just about enough to make you sign up with the Red Brigades.

Part Two

THE COMPENSATION BOARD

7

Case By Case

There was no doubt about it, by the war's end the Boilermakers Union was one of the most powerful organizations in Vancouver. When we spoke, people listened. Our record in fighting for social causes was tops and we pioneered many new labour practices. When I look back I realize that what I was seeing during that time was the formation of the modern labour movement. At the beginning of the war unions weren't recognized by industry or government and were not considered a real part of society. Companies were not required to recognize a union even if all its employees belonged to it. Union activists could be discriminated against with impunity. It was the strong Party-dominated labour movement in BC that forced the first big change with the Provincial Industrial Conciliation and Arbitration Act of 1943, and this showed the way for federal action. That came on February 17,1944, when parliament brought down Bill PC 1003, which might be called Canadian labour's Bill of Rights. When wartime wage controls were finally abolished in 1946 and the wartime gains were consolidated in permanent legislation, Canada took its place with the US in the forefront of modern labour development.

As I look back on my term as president of the Marine Workers and Boilermakers Union and think of my personal involvement in the labour developments of that period, two things stand out in my mind. These are the Kuzych Case and the Royal Commission on the Workmen's Compensation Board of 1949-51.

Before starting on the Compensation Board I want to read a quote from the *Encyclopedia Brittanica* regarding the history of workmen's compensation legislation because most people think it was set up to protect the worker and it's hard to make them see the other side of it.

"The old common law liability of employers to employees has been largely replaced by workman's compensation laws. Under these, industry, on an insurance basis, bears the cost of injury arising out of, and in the course of, employment. All questions as to the fault or negligence of the employer are eliminated." Under common law you were responsible for any injury that happened to me as a result of doing your work, which is only fair. But under modern law the worker has had this fundamental right taken away and replaced by Compensation Laws which are manipulated to cheat the worker wherever possible.

The problems injured workers have had trying to collect that which was rightfully due to them from the Compensation Board are well known amongst the working people of BC. Strictly speaking it wasn't my business as union president but guys used to come to me complaining about the various raw deals they were getting and I took an interest in it early on. What was happening was these fellas, ordinary working stiffs with no experience in dealing with government bureaucracy, they'd come in before the Board expecting all they had to do was state their case and they'd get fair treatment, and the bastards would just chew them up and spit them out in a lump. So I'd help them. I'd go down and present their case for them and see if I couldn't get them a better shake and I got to where I knew my way around the Compensation Board pretty good.

Some fellas didn't even know they'd been screwed and I'd put them up to making a squawk. One fella I remember, Pete Bidin, come into my office just before Christmas wanting to know if I could get him a job. "I'd like to get a few bucks in for Christmas. I'm broke," he said. I could see he'd had an accident to his hand and only had a thumb and one finger left and I asked him, "Did you get a pension for that?" Well, he hadn't because the Compensation Board ruled there wasn't serious enough disablement. I said I'd do what I could to find him a job in the yards and phoned up a super I knew at Pacific Drydock, Hank Hayes, who wasn't too bad a guy. "Look here, Hank," I said, "ol' Pete was in today flat on his ass—what's the chances of putting him on somewhere he can make a few bucks for Christmas?"

"Well," he says, "Chrissake Bill, I'd like to but, you know, he's a hazard. With that hand of his, he hasn't got grip on the tools and if he gets up on staging or anything he's liable to brain somebody. It's too damn bad, but he's just not up to the work any more."

"Would you give me a letter to that effect?" I said.

"I sure as hell will." So he give me this letter and I went right to the Board with it. This was proof, you see, that his ability to earn a living was impaired.

I got Pete a pension, he got seven hundred dollars in back payments, and they put him through for a course in watchmaking.

Oh Jesus, he was really pleased.

Bobby Jackson was a guy who come to me from the IWA. He was running a forklift and he backed over a bunch of ties and wrecked his back. Well, the Compensation Board just laughed at any guy who said he had a bad back. "Another CPR back!" they'd say. In their books anybody with a back complaint was just a goof-off, you see.

Well, Bobby Jackson couldn't work. He was off for a year or more and this thing had him just ruined. His own union had give up on it, his doctor couldn't get anywhere and finally he ended up in to see me.

I checked with his doctor, because without medical evidence you're beat before you start, and he said yeah, he'd back us up, so I filed to reopen. What it come down to at the hearing was the Board's Chief Medical Officer Giles Murphy said Jackson had a previous history of back trouble and they were hanging their hat on this. Okay, I says, how do you know this? Giles said they had a letter. He didn't want to produce it, but I demanded it and the commissioners made him show me this letter. It was from the personnel manager of the sawmill

Jackson had been injured at; all it said was he had a long history of back trouble—it didn't offer any proof or anything.

Giles couldn't offer any proof either, so I asked for an adjournment so we could bring this personnel manager in to testify. He came and I questioned him. I said did you write this letter? Yes, he did. Well what was his authority, I said. He said, well, he *understood*. That's not good enough, I said, you must explain to us where you got this information. He couldn't answer.

I let him have it good. I said, "I accuse you of fabricating this information and making this here story up out of whole cloth!" He couldn't deny it. So I turned to the commissioners and said, "This information was plainly false and must be disregarded." They had no way around that, and since this'd been what they based the case on it had to be allowed and Jackson got his award.

This just shows how the Board would work together with the companies to block a worker's claim to compensation. There were hundreds of things like this come up, and thousands more that never come to me. In Jackson's case we had a strong union and we were able to force them, but an ordinary worker can't do that so they walk all over him.

The Compensation Board was made up like all the labour-management boards with a representative from labour, a representative from management, and a neutral chairman appointed by government, and it functioned like the other boards too—two to one against labour. When I first got involved the labour man was Chris Pritchard who wasn't too bad, and the management rep wasn't that strong, but the "neutral" chairman was a fella named Adam Bell. He'd been Deputy Minister of Labour during the big strike at Bralorne and Pioneer Mines. He'd been sent up to settle it and the guys at Bralorne told him to go to hell. So then he went to Pioneer, called a big meeting there and announced that Bralorne had just settled and gone back to work. But these fellas weren't absolutely stupid—a couple of guys from Bralorne had followed him over. They got up and branded him a liar right on the spot and the company had to escort him out of town to keep him from being lynched.

This was his qualification for the job of neutral chairman of the

Compensation Board. I used to fight with him something unbeliev-able. We had a fella, Mac Kuthar, fell into the hold—twenty feet, head first—and landed on the steel deck. He had a fractured skull, eleven fractures in one hand, nine in the other, his teeth were smashed, his jaws were smashed—but he recovered. With considerable impairment. So we tried to get a pension for him. The Chief Medical Officer at that time was an old doctor, oh he was an obnoxious bastard. Being Chief MO for the Compensation Board was a political plum you see, a very high paid position, for someone in with the establishment who's proven he's a good dog, but once in there he's got to do his job, and his job was to flim-flam the claimants. There was one MO—not this old doctor, but a guy who was just as bad—used to tell the story of how when he was company doctor at Princeton he went down with a bunch of goons and threw Slim Evans, the famous union organizer, in the Similkameen River and damn near drowned him. I never got on with any of the Chief MOs, and this bastard was one of the worst. And he rejected Mac for a pension.

So I demanded a re-examination with me present. Well, you don't tell these bastards that, you see. But I insisted and they gave Mac a reappointment and I come with him. It was just a bare room with a table and there was no heat on. It was freezing bloody cold. A WCB doctor come in and told Mac to undress and get up on this table and took kind of a quick look then went out. We must have sat there three-quarters of an hour with Mac bollock-naked in this cold room, waiting for him to come back. Finally the doctor's assistant came in and said, "What are you doing here? Get on your clothes—'way you go, 'way you go."

"I want to have a talk with the doctor," I said.

"The doctor's busy," this fella snapped.

I knew where his office was so I just bust in there. And oh Jesus, he just hit the bloody roof. "Outside you, outside you," he screeched at me.

"I want to talk about Mac here," I said.

"I'm not talking to you," he said. "Get out!"

So I just took a big step forward and jammed my finger in his face. "Look you old son-of-a-bitch, I got some advice for you," I said. "You need a bloody psychiatrist. You're nuts, you old bastard. You're crazy as a shithouse rat."

I walked out then and down the hall to Adam Bell's office. There was two offices, a front one with a little son-of-a-bitch of a male secretary, then Adam Bell's. They knew I was coming so of course the secretary said, "He's not in." I walked around his desk and he stood up in my way so I put my hand in his face and shoved him down in his chair again and walked in on Bell.

He was really fussed up. Bell was sure as hell biased, but he wasn't that strong.

"What do you want, Bill?" he said nervously.

"You bring that old son-of-a-bitch of a doctor up here," I said. I want to talk to you about him but I want him here to hear it."

"Wh-what's the trouble Bill?" he stammered. I told him about Kuthar and the treatment this doctor had give him, but I didn't want to say what I really had to say about that goddamn freak unless he was sitting right there to listen. I was just going to peel him alive, you know.

"Now look Bill," Adam said, "I-I think I know what you mean and I think you'd best leave that to me. I-I want you to know, Bill, I'm not a bit happy about this Kuthar case. You leave it to me. I think he deserves it. A pension, I mean."

Well that's what I went in there for. Mac got a forty-buck pension which in them days was good. But you see the kind of justice that's dealt out by these goddamn government agencies. They put it up to you, it's all so cut and dried, the policy is this or that and the policy is beyond the influence of ordinary mortals. But when it comes down to it, the whim of the official is everything and the rules are nothing. The thing with the Compensation Board was they were dealing with guys' lives. Guys with families to raise and a long life ahead where they might get by with a little help, but otherwise they were sunk, it made no difference. Cut them off. Keep the expense to industry down.

I got the first award for industrial cancer that was made to that time— the first time it'd been recognized by a compensation board anywhere in the world as far as I know. A welder had a piece of hot slag go down inside his glove and burn his hand and it developed into a cancer. The Board turned it down but I happened to catch an English cancer specialist who was in town lecturing and he wrote up a diagnosis for us. Well how could a bunch of goddamn backwoods shitheels like was on the Board there tell an internationally renowned specialist he was talking through his hat? They had to allow the claim.

Another one was heart attacks. Work-induced heart failure. We had a guy working down in a double bottom in all them fumes take a heart attack and die. I contacted some heart specialists and told them I had this theory I was going to argue that if a guy's ticker wasn't too good to begin with, the strain of working in there without enough oxygen in the air could put him over the edge. These doctors told me I could push that just as far as I wanted.

I did this, and of course they just hooted me down at the Board, so I brought in the attending physician from the coroner's inquest and he backed me right down the line. He even went so far as to say he had only admiration for the men who work in these conditions. The pathologist went even further. He said my argument was sound and in his opinion was exactly what had happened in this case. But for having gone into this confined space, he said, this man could probably have lived a long and useful life and even played golf.

That was all you needed to show—that working conditions contributed. The case developed quite a twist after that—the widow's brother-in-law asked me not to pursue it further because he was the comptroller of some big bridge-building company with connections to the Board through Masons and what-not, and he said he could probably get a better settlement by taking the paternalistic approach. So I let the case drop but the widow come to me several weeks later and said she'd been turned down. It turned out this company the brother-in-law was working for also had an industrial heart failure case they were fighting and he was actually trying to obstruct settlement so as to avoid having a precedent set. I phoned up the labour delegate to the Board, Chris Pritchard, to ask him why this thing had been turned down and he insisted it hadn't been processed yet because he'd never seen it. So I took him this letter of refusal and I said to him "There's something goddamn rotten going on around here,

Chris." He was furious, you see, because he had been gone around and this was absolutely illegal.

"You tell this woman to disregard this letter," he said. Three days later she got another letter—her claim was allowed. But you see how bold the bastards were. Some guy down in the heap somewhere just took it on himself to do his lodge brother a favour and cut this widow off. You'd be damn well amazed if you knew how much this kind of thing goes on.

I can't begin to remember all the battles I had with those guys, and I sure as hell didn't win them all. Lots of times you'd have some perfectly solid case but you couldn't get a doctor to testify, or the goddamn doctor would file evidence against you. That was very common and there was nothing you could do. I generally wouldn't push a thing like that because I knew it was a waste of time. I met old Adam Bell one time after I was out of the union and he told me, he said, "You know Bill, when we heard you were bringing some case in we knew it was going to be something serious. You never brought in any of this doggone silly stuff."

"Does that go for the guy that lost his pecker, too?" I says. He had to laugh at that. This fella come to me all the way from Kitimat. He'd been working in the mill up there grinding some tool on an electric grinder. The stone was full of frost and flew apart and took the head off his pecker. There was no argument about him getting compensation for being laid up, but he wanted a pension. Disability pension. Just for the hell of it and to see what the old farts would do, I took it up. Asked for a regular meeting and presented the case in complete seriousness before the commissioners. They shifted around in their seats, stole glances at each other, you know, trying to figure out what the hell I was up to now. There was a silence after I finished, some mumbling and nodding, and very carefully Adam said, "Now Bill, I'm sure you're aware the Act requires an injury must impair a man's capacity for work before he can be considered for pension. The Act is very clear on this point. The Board extends it sincerest sympathy to this young man— but how can this, ah, injury, affect his pursuit of a livelihood?"

"Well," I says, "there is more to this here than meets the eye at first glance. This fella, his real trade where he's got his reputation established is as a chauffeur for wealthy ladies out in Shaughnessy Heights and ever since word got out about this accident he hasn't been able to find any positions at all."

Pritchard and Bell chuckled a little but the industry rep didn't crack a smile. I think he lived in Shaughnessy.

8

I Get a Royal Commission—1949

I

What made you mad was you knew, okay you'd work like hell on some case to get it past the Compensation Board, but you could see it didn't change a goddamn thing. They didn't change their thinking. They were actually defiant—you could see them thinking—alright you bastard, you got this claim through but there's more of us than there is of you. The next case come in they'd put the screws to him a bit worse to make up. I could see the only way to make real headway would be to go above the Board itself, and that's why I started agitating for a Royal Commission. Every time I caught them off base I'd try to get it publicized and I put other unions up to the same thing. I editorialized on them in our paper, *The Main Deck,* on radio, at the Labour Council, and everywhere I got the chance. Meanwhile I started files on their bad decisions and followed up on the cases and kept track of what these fellas went through after they were rejected. I worked at this for five years and finally when I figured I had enough of a case I went to the Attorney-General in Victoria, old Gordon Wismer, and laid a charge of gross malfeasance against the Board. He wanted proof, so I turned over my files and it hung fire for quite a while.

I guess old Gordon went down in history as kind of a blackguard, but really he wasn't such a bad old shit, you know. He was every bit as crooked as they say, but he was one guy in the government you could talk sense to, too. He was the guy that made that goddamn coalition government work. Boss Johnson, who was premier, didn't have the nose for politics that Wismer had. The two main parties in BC at that time were the Conservatives and the Liberals, they'd been trading power back and forth since WW I, but had joined forces to make a united front during WW II. After the war there was no real excuse to keep on with a formal coalition where the two parties shared cabinet appointments and all, but the CCF was really coming on by this time and that gave them a different reason to band together. Old Gordon told me one time when I was up in his office there, he said, "You know, Boss and I don't always see eye to eye." They had just had an election in June of '49 and the Liberals picked up enough seats to go

on their own, but Johnson figured he owed it to the Conservatives to keep on with the coalition. Wismer, who was a strong Liberal, wanted to make the split and restore the Party's independence, but he couldn't fight Johnson. He said to me, "Now Bill, I'm going to make a prediction. I predict that the Liberal Party is through in BC for a decade at least, and maybe for all time." It didn't seem very damn likely then, they'd been in power as long as most people could remember, but by Jesus he sure called the shot on that one. A few years later the coalition lost to a new Party, not the CCF, but the Social Credit, and the old Liberals were wiped off the map.

Incidentally, I was over there in Victoria just around the time W.A.C. Bennett bolted from the government benches and set up his own version of

Gordon Wismer, Liberal Attorney General in Johnson coalition government and noted "political" lawyer famous for his back room deals.

the Social Credit Party. He was working on putting the new Party together and one day when I was sitting in the legislative cafeteria he come up, introduced himself and right off the bat invites me to join up with the Social Credit and run in the election.

"We're going to form the next government and we want to have some of you labour fellas in with us," he said. I don't know if I laughed out loud or not. Can you imagine? Him to the right of the Conservatives and me to the left of the Communists. We'd make a fine team. Ivy always says that's where I missed my big chance.

Wismer damn near became premier, you know. He run against Johnson for the Party leadership and he only lost by eight votes. He was well and away the better politician and I think people knew that, but what hurt him was his reputation. He was quite a boozer and he had a kink used to come out when he got drinking. He liked to take his clothes off. They used to say Wismer had to become Attorney-General just for his own protection and there was more than a grain of truth in it. Harvey Murphy of Mine-Mill pulled a good one on him there one time, they'd been after the government over some goddamn thing and not getting anywhere, and the Liberal Party was having a convention. The Party big shots were holed up in the top three floors of the Georgia Hotel having a real wing-ding. Wismer put on his usual strip show and Murphy heard about this, I don't know what all it was. Next Monday Murph shows up at Wismer's office to bring up this issue they were trying to settle, and he says to old Gordon, "I come up to see you about this in the Georgia Saturday night, but I guess you wouldn't re-member that, would you, Gordon?"

"Oh Jesus, were you there?" Gordon said. "Jesus Murph, whatever you do, don't say anything about that. I'll see this here gets taken care of for you. Just don't let on about Saturday, to anybody." Wismer kept his end of the deal better than Murphy did.

One time I went over to Victoria to see Wismer about the Compensation charge and he was just coming off a ten-day drunk. The bugger, his face was just a blue-grey colour, you know. He'd have given anything to get rid of me. I put the screws to him and finally he says to me, "Are you going to be in the House tomorrow?"

I'd been planning to go back to Vancouver that night but I said, "Yeah, I'll be there."

"Alright. I'll make a statement on this."

The next day I was sitting there in the visitors' gallery. Wismer rose at his desk, looked up to where I was and said, "The government has decided, after considering numerous questions which have been raised, to launch a Royal Commission of Inquiry into the Workmen's Compensation Act. I will announce further details next week."

I'm not sure I ever did understand his reasons for doing it, because he had lots of things of a more politically pressing nature to attend to, but there it was.

I went home and went to work. I had a couple of months before they started hearings and I had a pretty good idea of the things I wanted to go after, but I knew the key to it all was the doctors. It was the doctors who were most involved with the Compensation Board and they were the only people who could tell the story—but getting them to say anything was like getting an angleworm to stand on its tail.

What keeps a guy going doing this kind of work, though, is there are a few people around who aren't part of the herd, who are individuals, outstanding individuals. And every so often you come across one of these and it kind of restores your hope. In this case it was a neurosurgeon on staff at St. Paul's Hospital named Frank Emmons. I'd had some dealings with him and I knew he had no use for the Board. He'd been on a case, a logger come in who'd been struck by a falling limb and it drove a piece of his skull down into his brain about an inch-and-a-half. Emmons' approach was first of all to minimize trauma and save the guy's life, then build him up strong enough for an operation. The Board come to him then and asked him what his plan was for plugging this hole in the guy's head. Emmons wanted to retrieve the bone and reconstruct it back in its place, which was the best way to go, but it was going to take a lot of work and time. Well, the Board couldn't see going to this kind of trouble for a logger and instructed Emmons just to install a metal plate. He said he wouldn't do it, so they took the case away from him and give it to a guy who as he said, "needed the experience." The logger come out of it a gibbering idiot. There'd been other cases, too.

"I tell you what's going to happen," Emmons says to me. "You're going to go in there and they're going to hammer you from pillar to post. You won't get anywhere unless you really know what you're talking about." So he and another doctor, Norman Kemp, who was an ex-staff doctor on the Board, started coming over to my house evenings to give me a crash course in medicine. We'd discuss different problems, different techniques, and study cases, mostly on backs because we planned to really press for the recognition of back problems. I even learned all the doggone Latin names. For instance, slipped disc, that's a *herniated nucleus pulposus*. And where you strain that big back muscle, you tear it and it scars—that's hypertrophy of the *ligamentum flavum*. I had them all down. Emmons even took me into the hospital disguised as a doctor to study myelogram x-rays. He told me, "You stay right at my elbow. I'll be lecturing to a group of doctors but pay no attention—it's you I'm talking to."

I was a bit nervous—you had to go into this dark room to adjust your eyes, then you put on these dark glasses and one thing and another, gown and mask, but it come out okay. In fact I very much enjoyed it.

But that's the kind of a guy Emmons was. Real bold, real outspoken. The medical establishment hated his guts because he wouldn't cover for them. "Yeah, I knew what happened," he'd say, "you got your goddamn clumsy paws in there and made a mess of it, I know." He just went after them to beat hell. According to them he was unethical.

One time there, he told me, he was just leaving the hospital after an operation. He had an intern with him and just as they were getting to the door this air commodore come up to them.

"Are you a doctor?" this fella says.

"Yes," Emmons says.

"Well, come with me," this guy says. So Emmons follows him to this ward where this air commodore's brother is, and what's got him upset is there's another patient there just coming out of the ether and he was puking up a little.

"Just look at that," this fella says. "I never seen such a disgrace! I want you to do something about it."

Well, it wasn't even Emmons' patient. He takes a look around the ward and says, "They all look like men in here to me. I wouldn't worry about it."

So this air commodore rears back and says, "Well! You're a cold-blooded son-of-a-bitch, aren't you."

"Just a minute now," Emmons says. "You can't talk to me like that in front of my assistant. I want you to apologise for that remark."

"Well you'll have to put up with it, because I don't apolo-". And Emmons let him have it right there. They fought out the door and down the hallway and the air commodore ended up taking an unscheduled flight through a glass door. Emmons told me, "I figured I was through. This was unheard of—a doctor fighting in a hospital! Next morning, sure enough, I got a call to go up before the old Mother Superior." He figured this was goodbye Frank Emmons. So he went in. His mind was made up he wouldn't apologize.

"Doctor Emmons," the Mother Superior said, "on behalf of St. Paul's Hospital I feel I must thank you for your actions in upholding the integrity of this institution!" She was proud of him, she said. Emmons socked some other doctor in there, too.

What saved Emmons was his ability. He'd spent several years with the Mayo Clinic at their invitation and his reputation as a specialist was tops. He put me on to a doctor, Jack Hazard, in Kimberly, who'd been Chief MO for the Compensation Board and I spent a couple days up talking to him. I found out all kinds of goddamn haywire things about the Commission, and he told this story about a patient he'd sent down to Emmons.

This fella, some kind of supervisor in the mine, had been in an accident and got a head injury. Ever since, the least jar would give him a headache. Hazard was a great shooter and he told me one day he was out in a duck-blind with this fella and a big flock come over. He fired one shot. "You know it's bad when a duck hunter will let ducks fly over him and he's afraid to shoot," he said. This fella'd been all over—Mayo, New York, Europe—everywhere. So Hazard told him, he said, "Go down and have a talk with Frank Emmons. I got great faith in that guy." He went down, Emmons listened to his story, and he prescribed a treatment for him. And what this treatment was, was epsom salts. Told him to take them just as dry as he could stand, by the spoonful. Don't drink any water. He kept it up for a week and Hazard told me, last fall, when this fella come back, he won the trapshooting contest here. His head never bothered him again. These various brain specialists from different parts of the world had been telling him he was beyond the help of medical science and Emmons fixed him with a twenty-nine cent bottle of epsom salts. How it worked—epsom salts isn't a laxative when you take it like that—they dehydrate your system. The trouble with these head injuries, the brain swells just like anything else, but there's nowhere for it to go. It's tight in the brain box. So it has to compress. And as long as it's compressed, it sets up its own inflammation, you see. Then it stays swelled. And eventually it can start to deteriorate. But if you can take the swelling off, let the inflammation go down, well, it has a chance to cure itself. So he was really good, Emmons. Anybody else would have gone through a bunch of mumbojumbo and worked it into a tremendous fee, but he just said, go home and take some epsom salts.

Norman Kemp, the other doctor who was helping me, wasn't a stupe by a long-shot either, now.

Kemp told me one time there while he was still on staff at the Compensation Board they broke a fella's leg right on the examining table. They had him lying there on his gut and this bloody medical examiner wanted him to turn over so he just grabs his foot and twists it, instead of asking him to turn over. And this prick twists so hard he breaks the guy's leg. This is what it was like. This was the attitude that the whole organization was infested with from top to bottom. Kemp, he was feuding from the day he got in there over stuff like this and eventually they fired him.

Another one was Allan Inglis. A real fighter of a guy and a fine doctor. He come from Gibson's Landing and he got to be the Medical Chief of Staff at the Vancouver General Hospital. He told me once, a guy, quite a wealthy guy, come into the hospital and he was old as hell—there was only one thing for him and that was to die. They knew if they touched him, that'd be it, he'd just blink out. And Inglis seen these two doctors in there late at night scrubbing. "What's up fellas," he says. "Got an emergency?"

Yeah, they say, they're going to operate on this old guy.

"Well, he's dying," Inglis says.

"We're going to operate at any rate."

The rush was, they knew the guy would die on the table but before he did they were going to stick their hands into him and lay hold of some of his dough.

Inglis sent them home.

Another thing Inglis told me was they had a practice in that hospital, when they got a fracture of the femur—that's this big bone in your thigh here—their procedure was to open the thigh up to the bone and set it, then place it in a cast. But when he went over to study in Edinburgh he noticed they were just setting the bone from the outside, and he asked them, wasn't it better to cut it open."

"Christ no," they says, "that's been obsolete for donkey's years."

"But that's how I was taught to do it in BC," Inglis tells them.

"Well you know why, don't you?" So they open the fee book up and show him—if you have to open a guy and go in it's just about double the price. Emmons told me the same thing. He showed me the fee book and he said, "This is the real medical bible."

He told me more than once, you think you know all about scabs and deadbeats and swindlers from being in labour. He says, "You don't know a damn thing, compared to the medical profession." And you know, Emmons never charged a cent for the time he put in on that Commission. If he'd charged regular consultation fees we could never have paid.

Once other doctors heard I had the support of guys the calibre of Emmons and Kemp and Doc Hazard, well then they started to peek their heads out of the brush, too. They all had a few hot stories to tell about the Compensation Board, and one doctor would send you down the street to another one. All the ones I figured were solid, I'd line them up to come give evidence.

II

The hearings started in Victoria. I was there at the opening. The guy they got as commissioner was Gordon Sloan, who was Chief Justice of the BC Supreme Court. They sat I forget how long in Victoria and then came to Vancouver and that's where the bulk of the hearings were held.

For the first while the only ones there besides myself were the delegations from the various companies and employers' councils, who hired all the big shot lawyers and put up extensive briefs. The rest of labour weren't participating at all—there were all kinds of ordinary guys coming up with beefs of their own, you see. Not represented by any union or anything. I'd jump in there, maybe catch them in the lobby and interview them. Try and advise them and coach them and act more or less as a counsel. I could cross-examine them, you see, and bring out whatever it was they had.

And bloody old Giles Murphy, the Chief MO, was there to carry the ball for the Board. Well, one of the first things that happened was one of these loners come up to testify, and he had a buggered back. Soon as he was done old Giles was on him like a wolf on a spring lamb, just like he done over at the Board, writing this guy off as if he was nothing, saying backs was a congenital problem and this sort of thing. Once Murphy was finished I had the right to cross-examine, so I started to question him. I says, "Now Doctor Murphy, I'd like you to explain how you were able to prove this here problem is congenital," you see, starting to work him out into the open a little. Well, oh, Murphy just hated the sight of me, and he couldn't stand this. That I, an ignorant layman, would have the temerity to question his

Chief Justice Gordon Sloan, former provincial Attorney General and chairman of the 1950 Royal Commission on the Workman's Compensation Board. He was one of labour's few friends in court during the '50s.

medical knowledge. So he got mad. And he started right off heavy into the Latin, all sarcastic, going to bury me in my own ignorance, you see. So I started heaving Latin right back at him. And it rapidly become apparent to me and everyone listening that I knew more about backs than he did. He'd graduated in 1906 and he'd never taken a post-graduate course since, and there were tests and so on that he didn't even know existed. I got him tied up until he couldn't answer. He just sat there red and steaming. Sloan stepped in then and said, "I'm going to stop this cross-examination. I don't mind admitting it's way over my head. Evidently Mr. White is very familiar with his subject."

Old Giles never went on the stand again. When the hearing moved over to Vancouver the Compensation Board had their lawyer, C.K. Guild, do all the talking.

I didn't start my own presentation until we got back on the Vancouver side. I called eighteen doctors in all, and eight specialists including the Chief MO of Oregon State, all dealing with different types of cases. There were forty or fifty cases that I went into detailed discussion on.

I forget just how long I gave my direct evidence, but I know Guild cross-examined me for three days. And you know, I don't think I ever enjoyed anything so damn much in my life. I had held back so much you see. I knew—I'd studied so damn much—that the more he cross-examined me, the more I was able to bring out in my own support. Guild really wasn't a very aggressive lawyer, and these other company lawyers were getting quite a kick out of the way the more he kept after me the deeper he got in the grease.

Old Emmons was just smiling. "There wasn't once he got a touché in the whole three days," he said. And oh, Jesus, when Emmons got in there, he got a backbone you know, a skeleton, he worked it and showed them—Sloan was *really* impressed. Kemp put on a good show too—he wrote a pamphlet *What is Wrong with the Compensation Board?* and just laid into them. He had the real dope on them from the time he spent on the Board's medical staff, and it really caused a stir. Because here was one of their own doctors you see, exposing them from the inside. It got headlines all over and they brought old Adam Bell, the Board Chairman in to say Kemp was just a crank whose nose was out of joint because he'd been fired.

Jerry Heffernan was Commission counsel and at first, three days was all he was going to allow us—when I said we might need as much as two weeks he said, "Preposterous!" Altogether I think we took twenty-one days.

The Party fellas generally tended to pooh-pooh the whole affair— "There he is on that Compensation Board business again," sort of thing. But one day when we were right in the thick of it there, making hay with these big-name doctors and getting publicity on it, Harvey Murphy come down to watch, and after we adjourned for lunch he came to me and said, "Jesus Christ, I had no idea this was what you were up to. This is big league stuff. By God, we're going to get in on this." He sent Ken Smith over from Mine-Mill, I think he was secretary, and we worked together all through that commission. He was goddamn good, too.

You see, what we were doing was setting out to show that the Compensation Board was absolutely rotten. Case after case we showed where guys had suffered disability and had claims disallowed. So our basic demand was for an appeal board where a fella could go to some outside authority and have his case re-examined if the Board rooked him. We figured this would be the only way you could ever make them really come honest. It's like in court—any time a judge thinks he might start abusing his power and give some guy shit, well he's got to consider that it can go to appeal and his actions will be put under scrutiny by superior judges. Half the time the Board wouldn't even tell you the reason they were turning you down. They'd claim to have some evidence, but they wouldn't produce it, and you didn't know if they had it or not. Their word was God, and of course that's the way they wanted to keep it. They hated the thought of anyone coming in to watch over them.

When Chris Pritchard came on to testify I asked him the procedure. I knew the procedure but I wanted it on the record. I asked him, if a fella come up and his case was turned down, what was his procedure. He said, well, he appeals to the Board. Well I said, in effect, he's asking the Board to admit they were wrong in the first place. It could have that effect, he says. Okay if it's against him again, what's his procedure. Presuming this man is entitled to compensation—and we have seen case after case where legitimate entitlement was ignored by the Board in the past—what would he do, where would he go after being turned down twice? He said, "I don't know." So I stopped right there. That was the answer I wanted.

We made our point. When Sloan done up his report, one of his main recommendations was that an appeal board be established. But it wasn't done. The Commission went on for two years and by the time the report come out the Liberal-Conservative coalition had been defeated and replaced by Bennett and his Social Credits, who didn't implement a third of what Sloan recommended. Instead of an appeal board they put in some kind of a damn ombudsman who was just about as much use as a pocket in your underwear.

There were other things though. We wanted a reduction in the seven-day waiting period, increased compensation payments, increased pensions, increased widow's allowances, allowances for travel and therapy increased—I can't remember them all but it was well thought-out. Many of these demands were also recommended by Sloan in his report, and quite a few of them did get put into practice. In fact the first year after Sloan's report come out the monies paid out to injured workers of BC by the Compensation Board increased by approximately three million dollars.

Part Three

THE KUZYCH CASE

9

Tools of Power

I

n the old days when a union guy started to shape up as a threat to the establishment they'd kill him. Early union leaders in the US were shot and hung by the dozens. And here in BC when the dockworkers went on strike in 1903 the CPR hired armed strikebreakers, shot organizer Frank Rogers and smashed the strike. In 1918 Ginger Goodwin, who was vice-president of the BC Federation of Labour, was shot and killed by another hired union-fighter after he'd helped organize the CPR-owned smelters in Trail.

The trouble with this method was it could backfire—Ginger Goodwin's murder brought on what was I guess the first general strike in Canadian history, and his name is a powerful rallying cry for labour still today. So what they do instead is go for harassment through the courts.

The courts have been one of the establishment's most effective tools in fighting unionism down through the years and this is still the case.

It is still possible for an employer who's being picketed over some dispute to phone up some friendly judge and get an *ex-parte* injunction to stop the picketing just on his own word, with no argument from the union until later. A lot of judges are all too happy to put the crimp on a union, too. There used to be a story about old Judge Manson, the Hanging Judge. Someone phoned him up in the middle of the night and said, "Sorry to disturb you Your Honour, but we need an injunction." "Injunction granted!" Manson said, "What union is it against?" I don't doubt for a minute but it's true either. That goddamn Manson, all the lawyers agreed—he was a menace to the legal profession. There was more successful appeals to Manson's judgements than all the rest of the judges together. He would take a disliking to a guy and it didn't matter what the evidence was, he'd get him.

Charlie Caron was telling me one time he come up before Manson for something and while he was waiting this other fella was going through divorce proceedings. His name was Duncan McAlpine or Angus McDougal or something like that and he wasn't even contesting this case—his wife was initiating the action and he was going along with her. So old Manson, who was Scotch and a big wheel in the Presbyterian Church, he was listening to the evidence against this guy and he said he couldn't understand it. He simply couldn't believe a man with a good Scotch name like this and no doubt a Presbyterian too could have done such things as he was being accused of, but there was nothing he could do if the fella wouldn't even contest it. When Caron heard him say this he laughed out loud, the old guy was making such a blatant thing of his prejudice. Jesus Christ! Manson stood up and made Caron stand up in the audience and gave him the damndest dressing down and said, "Any more outbursts from you and I'll see you in my chambers!"

He was a bugger. He'd chew tobacco and spit into a spittoon on the floor all the way through a trial. He had the face for the job too— he was a real mean-looking bastard. Imagine the feeling you'd have walking into court accused of some capital offence and seeing that bastard crouched behind the bench scowling at you. I guess he hung more guys than any other judge in modern times.

I was up before him once with seven other guys on a conspiracy to intimidate charge. It was all union guys but it wasn't union business. There was a guy there who was going after one of our men's young daughter and a bunch of us went down and paid him a visit. He laid charges and it come up before Manson and to try and save spending the rest of our lives behind bars we elected for jury trial. He still sat on the case, but the final verdict went to a jury. What we done was, we knew that they'd empanel a bunch of prospective jurors and we'd work through them til we got twelve we agreed on, but if we didn't get the full twelve the judge would instruct the sheriff to walk out on the street, lay hold of whoever he run into first and that'd be our jury. This was the procedure. We each of us had twelve challenges, making ninety-six total, so we used them and made sure we had lots of guys from the union walking around outside the court.

Well, Manson convicted us but the jury acquitted us.

There was another dandy, a dried-up little shit always wore a string bow tie. He was a police court magistrate and the cops on night patrol used to pick him up passed out in the gutter, but any of the guys came up before him on a drunk charge, Jesus, would he ever come down hard on them. Another judge was a strong Catholic and anybody the least bit left-wing had a hard time with him. Dealing with prejudice like this all the time it's easy to see how unions got to forming up in flying squads and dishing out their own brand of justice. Often it was closer to the mark than what was being served up in the courts.

The seamen and the dockworkers were the ones for scab nabbers. Geordie Gee told me a story one time, he and this other guy'd been sent out to fix a longshore scab and they were following him down the street waiting for the right opportunity. The scab had to stop at a light so they were window-shopping about half a block back, and out of the corner of their eye they saw this car pull up at the light and stall right beside the scab. The driver got out with a crank and walked around the front as if to start the car, brought the crank down over the scab's head, got back in and drove away. They never did find out who it was, but it was very reassuring to them. I always wanted to set up a flying squad in our union but the others wouldn't go for it.

II

For years there, I practically lived in court. I couldn't look sideways but I was nailed for some damn phoney thing or the other. It damn near come to the point Ivy'd have to look in the papers to see if I was going to have dinner at home or at the pokey.

One time there I got charged with assault for saving a guy's bacon. This was over at the Celtic, the BC Packers boatyard on the North Arm. We were in a real pickle there, and the worst thing about it, we brought it on ourselves. What happened was, we'd just won a new contract in the steel yards and got a good boost in the wages. The contract with the wooden yards didn't come up for another six months and it was bugging us that the guys in the wooden yards were going to have to go all that time working at the old wage.

Bill Stewart was back on the executive by this time and he proposed we break the contract. Which was typical for him. He was great at setting up battles from behind the scenes, as long as it would be somebody else going out to fight them. I wouldn't fall for that, but I agreed to try and get the contract opened some other way, because I felt pretty sure we could get the guys a raise. It was stupid, you see, because we didn't have to do it. We were just doing it because we thought we could.

We started by asking the companies to open their contracts voluntarily, and they refused, which was natural. I didn't want to get into a confrontation over it, so I ruled out any illegal stuff like sitdowns or walkouts. Our position wasn't strong enough for that. We needed something that would be legal but would cause just enough nuisance, too.

I went over the contract looking for an idea, and what I noticed was there was nowhere in it the men had committed themselves to working more than eight hours a day. There was nowhere it said they had to work overtime; overtime was voluntary. Well, the wooden yards had to work with the tides a lot and they really depended on the guys working overtime, so I thought, we'll call a halt on overtime. I checked with the lawyers to make sure, and they said no, we were in the clear as far as the law went, so I called a meeting and the guys agreed to put a freeze on all overtime.

There was instant bloody uproar. The companies charged us with going on strike, and illegal strike, because we were too greedy to wait for our contract to come up. The papers gave us shit. I said we weren't on strike, we were just working "to the letter of the contract." The term "work-to-rule" wasn't known in those days. In any case, it wasn't an accepted practice like it is now, and the companies right away took it to the Labour Relations Board.

The LRB was another one of these three-men boards with one labour rep, one employer rep, and a neutral chairman who was neutral as hell on the side of the boss. The chairman at this time was a fella name of Johnson, but it was actually run by Fred Smelts, who was for the employer. We couldn't get anything from them. Smelts, there was no getting to him at all. He was just rabid. And smart, boy he had a bloody brain. He was the toughest guy I ever sat across a table from, bar none. When him and I got together the other guys' ears would be ringing for a week after.

One of these hearings there was quite a crowd, a whole bunch of lawyers and fifteen or twenty people around this long table all waiting for me—I was a few minutes late. When I come in old Fred said some goddamn sarcastic thing, he always had some scorcher right on the tip of his tongue, you know. And rough talking? Christ, he'd a made a bullpuncher blush. Fock this and fock that, right in formal hearings. Great big guy, just like a frontline football player. And he was quite a noted horseman, he got up every day at five a.m. and rode his horse around Point Grey for an hour or two before he come to work. So I said to him, "Bygosh, Fred, you learned to ride in Alberta?" I knew he come from Alberta.

"Yeah, that's right, I did," he said. "Why?"

"Oh, I run into a guy the other day that knew you. Told me that's where you'd learned to ride."

"Oh, is that so? Did he say his name?"

"No, he didn't," I said. "He said you run a big cattle spread there raising purebred cattle. He said you shipped purebred bulls all over Canada."

"Are you sure?" he said. He was really puzzled, who could've said this.

"Oh yeah, it was you," I said. "In fact he said you had the reputation of being the biggest bullshipper in all of Canada."

None of them was expecting it, you know, it was so serious in there, and they all broke up to beat hell. Fred was so disgusted he just about turned purple. "Fock you," he growled. You didn't catch him off guard very often.

We expected nothing when we went up before the LRB, but this time we couldn't see how they could find against us, because it was so clear that all we'd done was follow our contract to the letter. That didn't bother them though.

"In the opinion of the board it is more than a coincidence that the decision of all employees to refuse and to continue to refuse overtime followed hard upon the decision of the employers not to re-open the wage clause of the unexpired contract," the decision read. You won't get away with it, even if it is legal, is more or less what it meant. But the bombshell was, the Marine Workers were declared "decertified" in all the wooden yards. It turned out they'd lined up the AF of L to come in and take over from us and they figured they'd just wipe us out with a stroke of a pen and deliver the men over to the Carpenters Local 506. Smelts announced in the papers the Marine Workers Union was no longer recognized as the bargaining agent in any of the city's wooden boat yards and invited "any other union" to come in and sign them up.

This was so heavy-handed the Congress was even roused to take an interest. It was haywire as hell you see, because what if the men refused to jump? The new Labour Act provided that any union that had a majority of the workers in a plant was legally entitled to certification and the company was legally bound to bargain with it. So what happened when you took the certification away but the union still continued to hold the majority? Could the union go on strike and force the company to bargain outside of Labour Act provisions? They said oh no, you can't go on strike because to call a legal strike under the Act the union has to be certified. It was a Catch-22 situation.

I figured as long as we held the men we had the bosses over a barrel just as bad as they had us, so we sat tight and held onto the men. Then they locked us out and got the AF of L to bring in scabs.

We found out when the scabs were coming and made a pact they wouldn't get through. Stewart was to take a gang of pickets to Macdonald's shipyard, Lawson to Benson's, and I went out to Celtic, which was the biggest. It did all the work for the BC Packers fishboat fleet. We had to stop the scabs or we were down the tube.

Out at Celtic there was a little bridge about twelve-fourteen feet wide going into the yard and we just set up on that. They had several carloads of scabs and they would come up and start to push on us with their bumpers but we wouldn't move, just hammer on the hood you see, so they'd back off.

There was an old guy there about sixty, name of Bob Newlands. Nice old fella, too. He didn't want to be at the front so he was back behind us a little. And there was a car come along driven by a strikebreaker named Roy Loop. He had three other guys in with him and they all had these ironbark clubs about two feet long and an inch-and-a-half square. We wouldn't let them through, so the bastard, he backed up and took a run at us. The guys, some of them jumped up the hood of the car, rolled off the sides, he just rumbled through and nailed this old guy, who'd been running away with his back to us. Hit him from behind so he went backwards over the hood and carried him for two hundred and forty-seven feet—the cops measured it after. Then he fell off and they run over him with the front wheel and up on top of him with the back wheel and stopped right like that so he was pinned under the back wheel of this car full of strikebreakers.

I was the first there and I thought old Bob was dead. Just as white as this paper and lying under the back wheel.

I yelled at this scab to back off so we could get him out but instead of backing off, he locked all his doors and windows and set his emergency brakes.

Well, there's no time to fool around then, you know. I hauled off and hit the car window on the driver's side. It was this damn shatter-proof glass and I cut hell out of my hand but she caved, so I pushed it in and unlocked the door. I had only one thought, which was to get the car off the old man.

This scab grabbed his club and swung himself around with his feet on the ground ready to come out, but he had to kind of duck his head through the doorway and right as he was ducking I unloaded on him. Jesus, I lifted him too. I don't think I ever hit a man so hard in my life. Split his jaw and he just dropped, and I flung him into the ditch, released the brakes and a bunch of us pulled the old fella out. I was sure he was dead, you know.

This was right directly in front of the shipyard office and every window had a head in it looking out. I just run over and butt in there, never asked them anything, and phoned for an ambulance.

No time at all, out come the ambulance. We loaded our guy in and the attendants seen this other guy, still laying in the ditch out cold. This was about twenty minutes after.

"What about that man?" he said.

"That ain't a man, that's a scab," I said.

Away they went. Left him lying. The office staff was still all plastered to the windows, and when they seen we didn't grab their scab, they phoned for an ambulance, too. That ambulance come, and they had to drag this guy out of the ditch. He still wasn't moving.

Then we hear the music coming and here's two carloads of harness bulls.

"What happened here?"

I told them. They got out their tape measure, took pictures, and one guy come up behind me—"Good for you," he says, "I'd have done the same thing."

I thought, Jesus, this is pretty damn good. Couple minutes later out come another couple of guys in a car. I stopped them.

"Who're you?" I said.

"Who're you?"

"I'm Bill White."

"You're under arrest!" They were plainclothes detectives.

The buggers wouldn't even let me take my car back downtown. They loaded me in the wagon and down to the slammer I go. The guys sent word up to the union and they come down to bail me out, but the cops said, "We don't know any Bill White. He isn't here."

All this time I was feeling pretty good because after all, we stopped the scabs. We'd done what we had to do and as long as it went okay at the other yards we had the situation pretty well saved. Then I got out and they told me we hadn't held the other yards. Apparently the scabs just walked in and neither Stewart nor Lawson lifted a finger to resist. So we lost the wooden shipyards to the AF of L. It was a major setback to the union. And it was my fault. It was up to me to tell the men to wait til their contract was up and that's what I should have done. I accepted full blame.

But you see how the establishment works. The law, the government, the press are all just tools of power. There was no investigation at all, except the harness bulls who figured I done the right thing. But BC Packers has all the connections and somebody made a call to somebody else and bam! I'm in jail. I'm brought before a labour-hating judge and convicted of assault. There's testimony from a dozen guys that I was acting in defence of human life, which is backed up by the attending officer's report and medical evidence, but the judge rejects this for the testimony of the company and its scabs and writes in his decision that I beat this strikebreaker senseless while union thugs pinned his arms. That was Judge O'Halloran. I just about fell over when I heard it. Where he got it from I'll never know. It wasn't in the evidence. But the papers carry this story and not one person in a thousand questions it, because it's the words of a judge. For trying to better the welfare of my men I'm made into a bloody villain and for crushing their workers' legitimate union the company comes out smelling like a rose. Beside this, Ginger Goodwin-style assassination is crude. There's no general strikes this way.

10

The Courts Get On Our Case

I

One of the most effective weapons when it comes to legal harassment is the paid agitator or *agent provocateur*. Working through an agent the union-busters can get the job done without having to show their hand. Instead of an establishment gang-up on a legitimate workers' organization it seems as if the union is just having embarrassing internal problems. Sometimes an agent will be picked out, trained and sent in like a mercenary to carry out a programme of disruption and other times the same thing can be accomplished simply by finding a way to encourage dissent which already exists within the union. The latter method is the slicker one because it's almost impossible to trace back the source.

I have to make it quite clear at the outset I have no proof that Myron Kuzych was a professional agitator. We were never sure even in our own minds whether he was picked out by the Canadian Manufacturer's Association and sent in to make trouble for us or whether he was on his own. The CMA was certainly aware of labour's advance during the war and organized to fight it. At a secret meeting in May 1941 a CMA delegation tried to get the federal cabinet to outlaw the new wave industrial unions such as ours and return Canadian industry "to the good old days when there was little trouble with labour." The CMA proposals were so vicious, according to the minutes of this secret meeting, that even Munitions and Supply Minister C.D. Howe, who was sure as hell no friend of labour, accused the CMA of "the most flagrant disregard of labour laws so far encountered."

The West Coast was the real breeding ground of labour militancy and our union was a standout in this regard. If the CMA went out shopping for an agent to send in against us, Kuzych might have been a logical person for them to approach since he'd recently been expelled from the Hod Carriers Union for alleged anti-union activity there.

On the other hand Kuzych himself always claimed that he was acting entirely on his own and following the dictates of his own conscience. According to him he was fighting for the freedom of the individual Canadian worker to work without being forced to join a union and to speak out against the union practices he disagreed with. The newspapers called him "Vancouver's battling welder" and played it as a David and Goliath story, the solitary man of conscience standing up against the big red union. When our lawyers asked him where he got the money to carry on his side of a legal campaign so costly it nearly broke our union, the only answer we got was the money came from his "friends."

It's possible for a guy in Kuzych's position to be used without his realizing it. Ernie Dalskog of the IWA was telling me one time about a guy he met when he was up the coast organizing logging camps. This was in the days when he'd have to hide in the bush and sneak into the bunkhouses at night, and he was signing a bunch of guys up after a talk when this guy come up to him. "I was listening to what you said about scabs and finks and I've got a question," he says. "When I hired on in town they told me I'd get seventy-five bucks a month if I wrote a letter back to head office telling them what the men say in the bunkhouses, so every month I bin sending them a letter and they bin sending me seventy-five bucks. Is there anything the matter with this?"

"Yes," Ernie said. "You're scabbing on the real informers. They get a hundred bucks." So maybe Kuzych wasn't pro, but he couldn't have served the bosses better if he was. It didn't matter what he was, really. He was just a springboard to get the union into the courts, and

Myron Kuzych, instigator of the Marine Workers' long court battle on the right-to-work issue.

once we were before the courts the lawyers and judges took over. They made a test case out of it and in test cases the guy they use to start it doesn't matter. It helps if he's a bit of an actor, but he can be anybody.

Kuzych first come to the notice of the union in 1942 when we were trying to organize the West Coast Shipbuilders which had just been started up in False Creek by old W.D. McLaren. It come up to a conciliation hearing and Kuzych appeared at this hearing to give evidence for the company. Against the union. He was opposed to the closed shop and everything we represented, although he claimed he supported some kind of true, pure unionism that was very hard to find in Canada.

As a result of his action, Kuzych was charged with working against the interest of the union and expelled. He promptly sued the union for reinstatement and damages. This was back while Stewart was still president and he put a Party lawyer named John Stanton on the case. Stanton advised the union to back down and Kuzych was given fifteen hundred dollars and reinstated. They figured give him what he wanted and he'd shut up you see, but they were dreaming. It just added fuel to the fire. It gave him credibility, he was successful then, and he got more support, among the public and no doubt among his "friends" too. Then the election came in 1944 and he helped Henderson defeat Stewart for president of the union. He held meetings to organize opposition and he bought airtime on radio to denounce the union and its leadership. He compared the closed shop to the slavery that existed in the US at the time of Abraham Lincoln and said Canada should follow Arkansas' example and outlaw it. He said the union was "spurious and a fake" and that there wasn't a trade union in Canada whose principles he agreed with.

There was some feeling that we should go on appeasing him and not be baited into more litigation, but I figured what the hell, we were in the right and there was no reason we should have to put up with this kind of bullshit. If the CMA wanted to take labour on in the courts, we couldn't run away forever. Better we meet them head on and get it settled. So when Henderson resigned and I went in as president I pulled Stanton off the case and got a new lawyer, Jack Burton. And I said, alright, we're going to give this fella what he's asking for but we're going to do it by the letter of the law. So we set up a press and investigating committee, it held a trial, it produced a report, the report came before a general meeting and the membership voted to expel Kuzych. The vote was four hundred and fifty-four to twelve.

When Kuzych brought action this time we were waiting for him. The Oath of Obligation which he had signed to become a member said: "I promise that I will not become part of any suit at law or in equity against this union or the Federation, until I have exhausted all remedies allowed to me by the said Constitution and Bylaws." The Bylaws read: "If any member feels that the decision (of the Press and Investigating Committee) is unfair . . . he may, within sixty days appeal in writing to the Executive of the Shipyard General Workers Federation."

We argued that the Oath of Obligation was a legal contract and by going to the courts directly Kuzych broke it. We lost the case and appealed. At this point our defence made quite a serious blunder by changing strategy and adopting a kind of gambler's defence, where we said the law didn't apply because we were outside the law. You see, a union doesn't have any kind of formal existence at law. It's not incorporated like a society or a company. It may have a charter granted by some parent organization like the CLC or AFL, but that is only a sign of affiliation, that isn't a legal document. So the question arises, what is a union in law? For the purposes of this argument the claim was that a union is an illegal association because one of its objects is to obtain the closed shop, which is in restraint of trade. And in capitalist law one of the worst sins is to be in restraint of trade, better you should commit murder. So the effect is to render all union contracts, including the membership contract, void in law and remove any claim founded therein from the jurisdiction of the court.

It was a stupid argument really. It's the kind of thing lawyers get you into if you don't look out. It had worked in other cases but here it took away from our best argument, which depended on the sanctity of the membership contract. I think it might have been in the back of our lawyers' minds too, that the Constitution and Bylaws of our union hadn't been professionally drawn up. When we dissolved the Boilermakers and Steel Shipyard Workers to form the Marine Workers in 1949 we drew up all new constitution and bylaws ourselves, or rather it was done by one of our men, Gene King. If it hadn't been for Gene King, we might've got a lawyer, but he was so damn keen on this, we let him go ahead. He worked on it for months.

He was a queer duck, Gene King. He was a loner. Very secretive. Nobody knew where he stayed and his only address was a post office box. He wasn't in the Party but he was a very sound trade unionist.

If we'd realized how much we'd end up counting on those bylaws we would have hired all the most expensive legal brains in the country, but we figured we were saving money, you see. In any case this new argument got away from leaning on the bylaws too hard and the Appeal Court ordered a new trial to consider it.

In the new trial the judge more or less brushed the illegality defence aside and gave weight to Kuzych's argument—that our expulsion proceedings weren't right. They got two witnesses, Mole and McPhaetor—one a fire warden in the yards and the other a security guard—and these guys testified that there'd been intimidation and irregularities during the expulsion process. We had dozens of different witnesses to contradict this and all sorts of documents, Christ, we had done it with a lawyer mapping our every move, but the judge ignored us and took their word as gospel. They claimed we'd denounced Kuzych before the vote was taken and that names of the dissenting voters were written down, and that I'd shown pre-judgement and bias by telling McPhaetor to lay off or he'd get the same treatment Kuzych was going to get. This was five years after the fact, you see, so our lawyer asked this McPhaetor how it was he could remember all these details with such clarity and be so sure of himself. Well, he said, as a matter of fact he'd always had a very outstanding memory. He had total recall. Well, I'd like to just test you a bit on that, the lawyer says. He was going to trap him into going too far you see. He says, now for instance can you remember what the weather was like yesterday? Yes? Okay, a week ago? Yes? How about a year ago, four years ago . . . What was the weather doing, say, at ten o'clock in the morning, April 10th, 1945? McPhaetor looked thoughtful. "I remember that morning. It was cloudy that morning. It wasn't raining, it was a dull, dull morning." The lawyer'd give him another date and McPhaetor would give him the weather in detail. The lawyer figured he'd totally discredited him as a witness, and so he should have. The judge should have said, alright, take this witness away, his testimony is simply not credible. But Whittaker took his word against an army of completely sound witnesses from our side.

The truth of it was Kuzych was such an outcast in the union nobody had to denounce him or warn people off him. I mean here he'd been—expelled twice and once from another union before that, he was denouncing the union on the radio and in the papers almost every day, claiming the leadership was crooked and dictatorial and inferring the members were a bunch of dupes—Christ, it would have been a waste of time for anyone to try and make him any more unpopular in the union than he'd made himself.

But the way they pictured it in court Kuzych was a respected member of the union that we were trying to destroy by underhand means because he was a threat to us with his high principles. They made a big thing out of the fact he run against Stewart for president, as if he'd been a real contender and not just a nuisance candidate. I think he got a total of fifteen votes, and this was before the so-called denunciation.

The judgement read, "It is almost inconceivable that so determined an effort should have been made to influence the members against (Kuzych) while the charges were pending . . . In light of the facts above, I am of the opinion that the purported expulsion of the plaintiff was contrary to natural justice." He ordered a reinstatement and awarded five thousand dollars damages. Now the goddamn trouble of this is that even in an appeal the senior judges are bound to follow the trial judge as to evidence. They can disagree with his reasons but they can't disagree as to which witness to believe.

This was just before Christmas, about the 22nd of December. I can remember quite well because I was working on the Royal Commission on Compensation. We were in session in the courthouse in Vancouver and I was examining a witness. It was about a quarter to twelve, and Doc Emmons sent up a note that the sheriff was waiting to arrest me as soon as I come out. Well I hung onto this witness then, I was asking him questions and trying to think about the other thing at the same time, but finally Sloan, who was head of this commission and also Chief Justice of the Supreme Court, he cut in and adjourned for lunch. I wasn't finished so he said, "I trust we will have the pleasure of hearing from you after lunch Mr. White?" He was always very polite, Sloan. I said yeah, okay.

Soon as we adjourned the sheriff come up and grabbed me. Arrested me. They wanted to take me to Oakalla right there.

"Well I think you better see Sloan first," I says. "I think he wants me back here to finish off my witness." The mere mention of Sloan put the wind up them. The Chief Justice, you see. They went and seen him and he said yes, he wanted me back. After lunch I went back there and I really had nothing left to ask this witness so I just played around with him for a few minutes and let him go.

"Well, my Lord," I says, "I'm afraid I'll have to ask for an adjournment. I find I have a pressing engagement I must keep."

He kind of smiled, "Adjournment granted," he said. "I trust your engagement will not detain you too long, Mr. White?" he said.

I rather liked Sloan. You wouldn't think it, but he was a very self-conscious man. He often didn't seem to know what to do with his hands. It was strange because he'd been in public life for many years. He'd been Attorney-General in the Pattullo government until one day he was suddenly kicked upstairs into the Supreme Court. It was a surprise move that was never satisfactorily explained and it remained a question mark in the public mind for many years.

What had happened was some big shot in the Liberal Party had caught Sloan in the wrong bed and threatened to blow the government apart, so Pattullo had to pull him off the firing line.

But I had no complaints with the guy, he did all right by us. He was probably a lot better judge than a politician. He had the most fantastic memory of any man I ever run across. You could get into an argument with some counsel about what some witness said maybe three weeks before, you'd say that witness said so-and-so and the other guy'd say no, it was such-and-such. Sloan would think for a minute and say no, I think this is what the witness said, and you'd swear he was reading it out of the transcript, he'd reel it off so perfect. The recorder would check and there wouldn't be a word out of place.

I come to know Sloan very well and many's the time we sat in his chambers and just talked about how things could be done different. He asked me once what I thought about a labour court where reasoned discourse would replace confrontation tactics as a way of settling industrial disputes. I told him as far as I was concerned that was the only civilized solution, but I said it would be a long time in the future before it would ever work.

"Why do you say that, Bill?" he said.

"Well," I said, "you know just as well as I do that the composition of all these boards, conciliation boards, arbitration boards, the Labour Relations Board, the Compensation Board—every time, without exception, they're always stacked two-to-one against labour, and in our experience the Supreme Court is usually two-to-one against labour also."

I said, "Labour would be worse than stupid if they ever gave up the strike weapon to have it replaced by any kind of setup where they had to depend on the objectivity of government appointments. They'd just be committing hari-kari."

He said yeah, he knew what I meant. He admitted it.

Another time Sloan asked me if I ever considered going to university to get a law degree. There were a few old guys did that—A.G. Crux's father was one—and he give me to understand he'd set things up if I ever took a mind to do it. I sure would have loved to've been a lawyer too. I would've been one of the busiest lawyers in Vancouver just defending myself.

So bingo, out to the damn pokey I go. They took Stewart with me, they had it pegged he was in on this refusal to effect Whittaker's order to reinstate Kuzych. I think that was the only time Stewart ever seen the inside of a clinker, though you wouldn't know it to hear him talk in later years.

You see, what they were doing was working a squeeze play. Kuzych's lawyers had entered a contempt-of-court motion to have me

This faded newspaper clipping shows Bill Stewart (centre left) and Bill White (centre right) Oakalla-bound on a contempt of court charge, cited for refusing to re-admit Myron Kuzych to the Boilermakers Union.

committed for failing to reinstate Kuzych to membership in the union. They come before the same judge who ordered the reinstatement in the first place and naturally he allowed the motion. Oh, he hated my guts. They knew goddamn well we'd appeal the motion and that would stay action on it, but the appeal court was adjourned for the holidays and here they were going to pop us quick into Oakalla and leave us stuck there til the court opened in the New Year, you see. That's how vindictive the goddamn judges were. They had the papers all alerted ahead of time, Christ, there was bulbs flashing on every side of us. They must of took a hundred pictures. Ivy never knew til the evening paper come with me on the front—WHITE GOES TO OAKALLA. I seen Kuzych sitting there smirking and boy, you know, it was all I could to stop myself sliding over there and nailing that guy. I'm not sure but it would have been worth it, too.

They took us out along with a bunch of other criminals, they kind of save up til they've got a full wagonload, and it was past suppertime when we got there. They strip you bollock-naked and walk you through a disinfectant shower to get all your goddamn lice off, get your mug shot and prints, give you your number and they shove you around and bark at you, you see, and by the time you're through that, well, you feel like you're a convict alright. You've left your old life behind you, you've left your name and your rights and any respect people may have for you, you've been stripped of that and come out of it something else, a number, an animal in a cage, you're not sure what. It's something you can't really get the feeling of until you've gone through it. It's your rights you miss. You've suddenly got no rights, less than a school kid, less than an idiot.

They sent us something to eat and I'll never forget that. It was some kind of mutton stew but dinner was well past and all the goddamn tallow was set up hard around the plate. You could no more eat it than you could eat puke from a dog. I'd brought out a tin of tobacco and they let me keep it—they took the tin away and put it in a paper bag, but I had the makings anyway and that made me real popular. Everybody was crowding around wanting to know what our rap was.

"Contempt," I says.

"What's that? What's that?"

"Well, we just didn't obey a court order."

"When do you get out?"

"Well, when we obey it," I says. They couldn't see that.

"You're not gonna stay here are ya?"

The lawyers got busy and got hold of Sloan and a couple of other judges and sprung us the next afternoon. Sloan just raised shit. "This man shouldn't be out there at all!" he said.

But you know, I've never had a minute's regret about going to Oakalla that time. It's a bloody experience everybody should have. Especially the goddamn judges. Every time they appoint a judge he should have to go do a stretch himself before he could send any other man in there.

There's guys in there should never have gone in in the first place and there's guys they should never let out. You could look down into murderer's row and see some of Judge Manson's victims sitting there. They were stringing them up then quite regular.

II

Another thing come up which give you some idea of how the courts operate was this assault case. This was not too long after Kuzych was expelled. He'd often come around trying to get into our meetings but of course he couldn't because he was no longer a member. We had several incidents where he was ordered out or escorted out.

This time, it would be about February of '45—we were having a morning meeting and for some reason I wasn't in the chair. I don't know who was—one of the Nuttalls maybe. I can't remember why I wasn't in the chair—maybe I had an appointment or something but I was there when the meeting started.

Before the meeting come to order there was a photographer and reporter from the *Vancouver Sun* come up into the hall. I knew them both so I went over and said, "What the hell you guys doing here?"

"Oh, just thought we'd drop in," they said.

"Why?" I said.

"Oh, in case something happens."

"Well if it does you're not going to see it because this is a closed meeting," I said and showed them out. Now the way our hall was, you come in off the street, turned to your left, went up a flight of stairs about ten feet or so, there was kind of a big landing and then the stairs turned at right angles and went up to the main auditorium. I guess it was about fifteen feet from the one up to the next one.

They went down and they stood in this here elbow in the stairs, you see.

Well Kuzych came up, with his usual big bundle of books and stuff under his arm, and somehow he pushed his way past the guard and got into the hall. Guys seen him though, and when the meeting was called to order, somebody stood up and pointed out Kuzych was in the hall. The chair asked him to leave and he refused. What the chair should have done then was to quote the constitution which says only members can attend union meetings and have him hauled out then and there, but instead he put it to the meeting. There was over five hundred guys there and I think the vote was about five hundred to seventeen to kick him out.

Kuzych still refused to leave so the guard went over and Kuzych got up and quite willingly accompanied the guard the full length of the building and across—until he got to the head of the stairs, where he was in view of these newspaper guys. There he took a swing at the guard.

It was the wrong guy to swing at because this guard was an ex-pug. He pulled back about that far and smack, hit Kuzych on the eye and opened his eye up.

You should have seen that bugger put on a show then. He leaned over holding his head making a sound for all the world like a cow bawling: unnh, rooo-unnnhh, oh, the awfullest roars, you know.

There was two guys coming up there, coming in late—one was Bill Gee and I don't know who the other was—they didn't know one another and weren't together, but they had to walk past Kuzych at the top step and they both got the same idea at the same time. It was a beautiful thing to watch. Just like one body they stepped up, hauled off and booted him square in the arse. Both of their boots landed at the same time, and it just picked Kuzych up and sent him head first down the stairs. That did it. He picked himself up and hustled out of the building. The photographer of course was trying to get his picture but there was another guy coming up the stairs with a bloody *News Herald* in his hand, and he just put his paper up in front of the camera, turned the photographer around and walked him out onto the street.

That night, big write-up in the paper. "Kuzych Struck, Kicked at Union Meeting." And who assaulted him? Me. They had me hitting him on the head from behind and then putting the boots to him. Well I thought, what a bloody joke, you know. There was five hundred guys there seen what happened and I hadn't been within fifty feet of the man.

Nevertheless I was charged and it came up in court. We had about fifteen witnesses there that gave rock-solid testimony as to what happened. Kuzych had a witness who said he was driving down the street looking for a parking space, in the rain and with his windows rolled up, and he said he just happened to be passing the door of the hall when he seen Kuzych come flying out, and I slugged him as he came through and said, "Get out and stay out." We had the girls from the downstairs office who both worked right there facing the door, and they insisted Kuzych come down and left on his own with nobody near him. The guy that really did hit him, Cornado, he got up in court and said, "I don't know why White's charged! Kuzych was only hit by one guy and I'm the guy!"

The judge found me guilty.

You've got no idea what something like that does to you until it actually happens. Hearing about somebody else having it happen's not the same. It's actually a painful thing, to finally be stripped of all faith in justice. It's depressing. But when something as plain as that happens you can't kid yourself. You have to conclude the courts here in this country are just goddamn tools of the establishment and nothing more. I didn't even bother to appeal it, I just paid the fine.

11

Trade Unionism in Trouble

I

You know, I just can't recall all the twists and turns we went through in the course of that entire Kuzych court battle. I've seen it written up in different books, none of which describe it exactly the same way and none of which catch all of the ins and outs. Let's just say it started in 1943, the first case, and it went on until 1953 and it went up and down through the court system several times. We'd work our way up to the Supreme Court of Canada, then it would be sent back down to the lower courts and we'd have to start working our way up again. We lost in every court in Canada.

And the more it went on, the worse it got for us. Not only was it a drain on the finances of the union, every time a new judgement come in it was a worse setback for labour. We'd figured at first it was just a campaign to break our union because of its size and power and the fact it was under radical leadership, and there's no doubt in my mind that was a big part of it, but we began to realize they had another aim as well—they were going to try and cut back on the growing power of labour by making certain practices such as the closed shop illegal.

In the BC Appeal Court, Justice O'Halloran went from saying we give Kuzych a bum trial to saying "the question the Union Trial

Committee sought to decide here was beyond the competence of *any* union to decide . . . civil liberties . . . cannot be decided by a . . . committee set up by a labour union. That is the prerogative of the constituted courts of the country."

Now you can imagine if this decision was followed, every time some matter of internal union discipline come up you'd have to go before some labour-hating bastard like Manson. It would be like sending chickens for the hatchet.

What they were getting around to, you see, was right-to-work and in another part of the judgement O'Halloran spelled it out: "A man has a right to work at his trade. If membership in a union is a condition attached to working at his trade, then he has an indefensible right to belong to that union." You could have a union, in other words, but you had to let everyone in and you couldn't throw anyone out. If you went on strike the company could bring in an army of scabs, and not only would you have to let them take your jobs, you'd have to welcome them into your union!

I practically lived in court through those years. I went to every hearing. It was a real drain on my time and there's no doubt it hurt me in my job and hurt the union. The money was an even bigger worry. In fees alone the case ate up $60,000 from our treasury and another $40,000 from other unions, which is like a million today. That put us right on the rocks. We didn't have that kind of dough to spare. There was a lot of uneasiness about the whole thing, especially since it seemed there was no chance of us ever getting justice anyway, and there was a lot of pressure on me to drop the whole thing. The big worry was the settlement. If we caved we'd be liable for all costs and damages, which started at $5,000 and was balling up bigger and bigger every step like a man pushing a big ball of snow up a steep hill. If you know you'll never make it over the top, you might as well let it come back on you before it gets any bigger, you see.

All this time Kuzych was getting lots of publicity. Every time he beat us they'd play it up to beat hell in the papers, he got to be a kind of a folk hero. Christ, he even got written up in *Time* magazine. Lone Ukrainian-Canadian welder takes on big bad union and brings it to its knees—single-handedly. It was the kind of story people find irresistible. He was supposedly standing up for freedom, the law seemed to be on his side, so he was a real hero, you see. And to complete the picture they had me for a villain. They had the story of me jumping him from behind and kicking him, and they tried to put out the story his life was in danger. He was supposed to live in a little shack down on Fraser Street and they claimed we tried to bomb him out of there. He supposedly heard a noise on his porch early one morning and here was this bottle of gas with a glove stuck in the neck, on fire. The newspapers had pictures of him pointing where he'd found it and holding this glove up. I don't remember if they went as far as to say it was the same type of glove used in the shipyards by members of the red-led Boilermakers Union, but being a glove and not just an ordinary rag helped people to get the connection. As if anybody would be stupid enough to leave one of his own gloves on a firebomb for evidence, and set the damn thing on the porch instead of busting it through a window.

But you can see how it was going for us. Between the papers and the courts they were just frying us in our own juice. We kept trying to bring up the point about where he got his money—because that was just so damn obvious, if you could get people thinking on it. For years there Kuzych had no visible means of support. He wasn't working in the yards and according to his lawyer he couldn't get work, he was prevented from earning a livelihood by our action in excluding him from our union—this was one of the claims his lawyer was making in the damage suit. But during this whole time he was out of work he went on living, he went on supporting his family, renting his house, and not only that, he bought prime airtime for his regular radio broadcasts against the union, and he held up his side of one of the most expensive court battles in the history of Canadian labour to that time.

There was tens of thousands of dollars coming from somewhere, but we could never find out where.

It was all sitting pretty heavy on my shoulders but I'll say one thing—one guy I never had to fight was myself. I've been accused at times that I tend to be a little blind to viewpoints other than my own and whether or not that's completely true, there's times it has its advantages. I never doubted but that we should fight this one out til one of us got to the end of the line. To me it was a key battle in labour's long war against the combined forces of industry and government and it was worthy of any sacrifice I or the union could make.

II

I had a new idea I put to the union, and that was to appeal the thing to the Privy Council in England. What give me the idea I think was right around that time there'd been a shift in Canada's status from a British Dominion to a fully independent nation, partly as a result of the role we played in the war, and they were bringing an end to the practice of having the Privy Council as overseer and last court of appeal over the Canadian court system. It was already too late to take any new law cases to the Privy Council but they had a rule that any that'd started before such-and-such a date was still eligible. The union executive accepted my recommendation and we became one of the very last Canadian cases, if not the last one altogether, to be heard by the Privy Council.

In order to raise money and also to try and get some public support on our side of the thing I decided to go on a speaking tour around the country. I spoke all around BC—Kimberley, Trail, Copper Mountain, Victoria—then I went back East and spoke all around down there. I sometimes talked to three locals a night. It was a grind, now. You had it set up, you see. You'd get permission from the office beforehand. You're asking quite a favour, to be able to come into their meeting and ask for money. You'd bust in there and they'd suspend their regular order of business to hear you, then away you'd go to the next one. You'd hit the last one maybe just as the meeting was breaking up. Generally I was pretty well received. The Canadian Congress of Labour took a sympathetic position and helped out a lot with their affiliates, even though they were CCF and we were Party and they were trying to rub us out.

I went down and seen Pat Conroy who was secretary of the CCL and he was all for it—we always got along good together, Pat Conroy and I—but he said, one thing, before you go into any of Steel's locals you should probably go see Charlie Millard. Millard was the international rep for Steel then. Their top man in Canada. Well, I figured then and I still figure today, that Steel is as phoney as a three-dollar bill. It was them headed up the big drive to purge the Party out of BC unions that was going on around then, and I'd personally gone out to speak against them in Trail that time I mentioned earlier when they were trying to raid Mine-Mill.

"You got a lot of nerve coming here for favours," Millard told me when I seen him. "I personally will see that you don't raise one red cent out of a Steel local."

"This case has nothing to do with Trail," I said. "If they win this case we've got right-to-work in this country right now."

"How much you need?" he said.

"Twenty thousand bucks," I said.

"Go back to Trail and speak for Steel and you'll get your twenty thousand," he said. I told him to piss up a rope and went into a bunch of Steel locals anyway. And I did good in them too.

Their biggest local was Hamilton and there was some Party guys in there. They had meetings with three thousand guys and the night I was going to talk a couple of these Party guys come to me and said, "Christ, you better watch yer Ps and Qs because they're really layin for you here. You're in for a real rough ride." Millard had heard what I was doing and he had I think five CCF members of the Provincial Parliament who belonged to the Steelworkers all primed to strip me down at this meeting.

There was nothing for it but to plunge ahead so I got up and give them my best, hit them for a donation, and sat down. There was about a ten-second silence after I sat down and then way down at the back of the hall some Joe got up. Who this guy was, I don't know. I'd never seen him before and I've never seen him since. He couldn't speak worth a shit.

"After settin' here listening to Brother White th-there can't be no doubt what th-this l-local will do," he stammered. "The only question is h-how much. And I m-move we give him a thousand bucks."

Somebody seconded and it went through just like that. The MPP's didn't get a chance to stand up.

So often I've seen that, you know, where it just hangs in the balance and it could go either way. And all it takes is a nudge. The timing of it is all that matters. Another five seconds and I'd have been rabbit stew.

I had the feeling more and more during those days that the whole Canadian labour picture was like that meeting, hanging in balance and the Kuzych case was one of the things that could tilt it. Igor Gouzenko, the Russian defector who exposed a red spy ring, had come along and offered the Canadian establishment a cause to bring Canada in on the anti-leftist hysteria of the Cold War, and after fumbling around a bit the government had took him up. Canadian business was lobbying for a big crackdown on unionism and the States was showing the way with their Taft-Hartley Act which set American labour back to where it was in the pre-Roosevelt days. We'd followed the US lead in the past and Canada as a whole had followed BC's lead into the modern era of labour relations. If the Canadian Manufacturer's Association won against the closed shop out West, then BC might well lead the country back out of the modern era.

C.S. Jackson was head of the CIO Electrical Workers.

The big Party union back East was UE—United Electrical Workers—led by Clarence Jackson and George Harris. Jackson was one of the real Party warhorses on the Congress for years and years and I hitched a ride down to Niagara with him to speak at one of their locals there. "I don't know how the hell you can raise money out of these bastards," he said to me. "We can never get anything out of them down at headquarters." These were his own locals. I went to a lot of UE locals and they were pretty good, but I told them, now don't bother giving me a lot of small cheques, just send it in to your head office and they can wire it through to Vancouver in one lump. So they did that, and you know, we never got a cent of that money.

They just hung onto it in the head office. So we did real good off Steel and real poor off our friends.

I think I raised altogether $12,000 which was a good hunk of dough in those days. Stewart was really knocked out by it when I got back. Christ, I figured maybe a few hundred, but twelve grand's real dough, he said. For all his wonderful oratory Stewart never raised a tenth of that in his life. The money was really the least part of it though—the real important thing was it acquainted the trade union movement as to what was going on. I tried to get that working-class resentment going—guys would stand up and say "D'you mean to say these bastards are trying to tell us we can't kick some son-of-a-bitch we don't like out of the union? Who the hell do they think they are?" And this is what you want, you see.

You'd learn from one meeting to another what got a rise and what didn't. "The closed shop wasn't invented by labour," I'd tell them. "If you want to find out what a closed shop is you try and set yourself up as a doctor or a lawyer. They got the toughest closed shop there is. What I want to know is how come it's so good for them to have it when it's so bad for the working man. This is class discrimination of the rankest kind." And I'd say, "They talk about the 'right to work.' Isn't it nice of all these big shots who've been robbing the Canadian worker for years, how they're suddenly so concerned about his 'right to work'? Whenever anybody talks to me about 'right to work,' I say 'You're damn right, I'm all for that. Every worker has the right to work at a decent job for decent pay and if there's no job for him it's the duty of society to create one for him.' But that's not what they mean. They're talking about one worker's right to take his brother's job by offering to do it for less pay, so the boss can make more profit." I felt after we got back we had real strong backing amongst the working class all across Canada, let *Time* magazine say what it wanted about Kuzych waging a one-man battle for freedom.

12

The Law Lords

I

I think it was April of '51 we were over in London to take our case
before the Privy Council. You could still see the results of the Blitz.
You could see where a bomber had gone through and dropped a
stick of bombs—everything smashed down in a straight swath like a
tornado'd gone across town. The first thing I done was I checked to see
if my case of whisky came. Liquor was on ration in England then, they
had a rule all you could have was one mickey after you'd been there a
month. I knew this before I went over, but the thing was, you could
order liquor here in Canada and have it delivered in London from the
warehouse in London. So I ordered a case of Seagram's and when I got
there to the hotel it was waiting for me. Well Jesus, that was like a drop
of water in the desert, and before long the whole goddamn case was
gone. I wondered what the hell to do so I got in a taxi—you could ride
all over London for a shilling—and I went down to the Seagram's office there, and I told them I wanted a case of liquor. Oh, they couldn't
do that. Didn't I know liquor was rationed in this country? Well you
already sent me up one case, I said, what's so hard about sending up
another one? They had to go into conference on that. Finally an old
fella come and he says very soberly, we decided there is nothing to

prevent you having another case Mr. White, with one provision, and that is you not pay for it until you're back in Canada. Alright, I said, you drive a hard bargain, but you've got my word I won't make you take a cent as long as I'm here. And was that whisky good, too. Export grade. Way, way ahead of what you get here. Way cheaper, too.

I got quite a write-up while I was over there, in one of the newspapers. A guy run into me on the street and said, "I beg yaw pawdon, but may I awsk what pawt of the colonies aw you frohm?"

"How do you know I'm from the colonies at all?" I said.

"By yaw necktiiie."

He was a reporter and he wanted to know what I was doing there so I told him and he done quite a spread on the thing. It was a lot better coverage than we'd ever got back home, I'll say that much. They gave us good coverage all through the trial. I gave a speech to the British Labour Council while I was there too. They had moose heads up all around the bloody hall. Didn't cause much excitement—just some bloke over from the colonies, you see. About fifty came to hear it.

We'd had John Burton doing most of our law work in BC and he was good, but when the Privy Council come up I figured we better go whole hog and get as high-powered a lawyer as we could, so we got old Senator Farris, who was certainly the most prestigious lawyer in BC, if not the whole country, at that time. He'd been before the Privy Council numerous times and they liked him over there, so we figured we were lucky to have him. Nathan Nemetz came along as his assistant. Nemetz became a Supreme Court Justice later, but he was just wet behind the ears then.

Nemetz was very eager to do all the correct things while we were there and every night damn near he'd be wanting to go see some damn high-falutin' thing—Royal Opera, and this here Sadler-Wells you know, see this here Margaret Fonteen. We went over to Paris, too, seen the Folies Bergère and so on. I had to go along with him, but Christ, it was way over my head.

We were at the International Theatre one night. They had on a bunch of gruesome goddamn things—I couldn't see anything to it—but did they ever have that joint fixed up nice now. You sat in upholstered chairs, you know, each guy in his own fancy chair. One play was where they threw some guy in the pokey with some great big giant who was about eight foot tall and blind. And this giant got into his head that if he could take one of the eyes out of this other guy's head he'd be able to see. So he was after him you see, and he got him down between his knees, jammed his head back and he got like a screwdriver, jabbed it into his eye, you see, and Christ, the blood just squirted all over—and he roared and yelled . . .

That was one of them. Another one was this dame was in bed some-place, some gruesome damn deal, hell of a storm on and some guy was going to murder her—the lightning would flash and you could see this face outside the window looking all blue, you know—hell of a look-ing thing—Nemetz was sitting there all stiff, taking this in so I leaned back and just drew my finger across the back of his neck—skkkch! Talk about jump! Thought his head was cut right off.

I stayed in the Park Lane which wasn't a bad old hotel, and Farris and Nemetz were in a real ritzy place called the Dorchester. We were in the lobby of the Dorchester one day and at about 3:30 they'd bring around tea and biscuits. Free, you see—anyone sitting in the lobby they'd come and pour you a cup of tea. Nemetz and I were sitting there and there was a Eurasian woman at the next table over. Jesus, she was a stunner, boy! We got talking—she was that close you see—and boy oh boy, was she ever a radical! You bet your sweet ass she was. She was from Bali. She was over in London studying economics. I said to Nemetz, Christ, invite her up to the room, I'd like to talk to this dame. So we set it up.

She said sure, she'd come the next day. She brought a bunch of stuff that she'd made—not sarongs, but something like that. Native dress of Bali. Jesus Christ, she was a smart dame now, I'll tell you. She give us a rundown of the history of Bali, see, it was a Dutch possession like Indonesia at one time.

"We fought the Dotch for many years," she said, "and finally we drove out the Dotch. Then we got the Yank, and the Yank is worse than the Dotch."

They were still under Yank control but they were going to take over their own government, and she said she wanted to be prepared when they took over, to govern. So she was in London studying economics.

Nemetz had to go someplace so her and I stayed there, and this was when I really got acquainted with her.

That dame was smuggling diamonds. In from Bali. And she wanted to enlist me for a contact in Vancouver. She had the damndest bunch of diamonds with her, too. Like kernels of corn, and peas. She'd worn a lot of them into England in made-up jewellery, and this was what she was paying her way with. She gave me a lecture there on all the grades and different types of diamonds—boy, she knew it, too. And she told me before she come over she'd had a couple of fifty-ton freight boats trading in around the Malay Peninsula there. She'd got in with the Australian High Commissioner and rigged up some damn way to slip goods in under tariff you see, oh she was quite a gal. Sri was her first name, I forget the rest.

We were over there six weeks. I don't think the trial went more than two or three days altogether but there was a lot of sitting around between sessions.

II

That was the most informal affair you could imagine, the Privy Council. It was in some goddamn dingy little place like a third-rate police court and the law lords'd sit around a table there having tea and biscuits while they heard the arguments, ask a question here and there, just as nonchalant as you please, Lord Porter, Lord Morton of Henryton, Lord Asquith of Bishopstone and Viscount Simon. Their word was the very last word in British law.

The first time we went in there we just had an hour or two before closing time and it was a goddamn good thing, too. Farris was terrible. This was the first time he'd argued on the case and I could see right off he didn't have a goddamn clue about it. He just floundered like a gaffed fish in there. Kuzych had his regular lawyer and they had the thing completely in hand. I just felt sick.

As soon as he come off I got ahold of him and asked him what the hell went wrong, because I could see we'd never win it that way. The old fella was quite shook up. He said, "I know, I know, I'm afraid I've slipped up here, I just haven't had the time to prepare this like I should

The British Privy Council hearing its last Canadian case. Foreground (left to right) Nathan Nemetz and J.W. de Beque Farris for the Marine Workers Union; A.W. Johnson for Myron Kuzych.

have." He had another case he was presenting and he just hadn't got around to ours.

Well, it was a fine time to be finding that out. Here we had one of the most drawn-out pieces of labour litigation in Canadian law. The goddamn transcript was about six inches thick. Lawyers had argued on it for years without getting to know it completely. And here we were with just hours before we had to go in and make our final stand. I was pretty mad.

"Look here," I says to them. "There's only one way we're going to do this and that's if I help. I don't know the law but I've lived with this case for seven years and I know that transcript better than anyone alive. So let's just sit down and work this out together."

Well you don't have much hope, arguing law that way, not at the Privy Council. But the old Senator, you know, he was quite a man. He said okay, you know where to find the stuff we need, you make some notes and give them to me tomorrow morning. I'd sit up half the bloody night making notes, give him the page and paragraph and line and everything. Time and again he'd say, "And now my Lords, if you will turn to page so-and-so, paragraph so-and-so, line such-and-such, you will see the defendant said the following—" and he would be reading it for the first bloody time himself! Jeez, you could have crossed him up good if you'd wanted to you know. But the old guy, he took that case on the fly, and you know, he done a wonderful job on it. Once he got them notes you'd have thought he'd been on that case half his life.

You see, what you was paying for when you hired Old Senator, as much as anything, was his manner. He had a way he could take something that if you or I said it, no one would pay it any mind but he'd make it sound like it come from a parting in the clouds.

He had a big thick mane of hair that was absolutely snow-white. He could intimidate a witness, not the rough way guys like Owens tried to do it, but just by his manner. He had a habit when he was cross-examining a witness, he'd get his chin down on his chest and be kind of wrinkled there—he had sort of a bulldog face—and you'd just see this great white head of hair. Stand there a long time, you see. The witness would start to fidget then—"Wonder what the old bastard's up to?" And just how much he used this—one time when I was on that Royal Commission I called the Chief Medical Officer for the State of Oregon, and he was stone blind. Farris was acting for the bosses in this case and you know when he come to cross-examine this blind fella he tried everything but he couldn't make any impression whatsoever. The doctor couldn't see how impressive the old fart was. Farris was just another voice to him.

The bugger sure worked it good on those law lords though. In his windup he went into a farewell and told them how he'd been there so many times to represent the young Dominion and how he'd watched her grow even as he himself had gone from youth to age and he could see the passing of the years in the faces of the Lords as well each time they met, and now Canada was ready to strike her own path in the world and this was the last time and so on and so on—he just about had the Lords in tears by the time he was done. It didn't hurt our case one bit.

Nemetz and him flew back. I come back on the boat. It took six to eight months before we got the decision. I was over in Victoria on the Royal Commission and Nemetz phoned me at my hotel, early in the morning. Got me out of bed. "Well I knew you'd want to know right away," he said. Ken Smith, the fella who was helping on the Commission from Mine-Mill, a hell of a swell guy too, he was over there but in a different hotel. I had a bottle of whisky and I got into Ken's room there and woke him up.

"Here, have a drink," I said.

"Christ, it's a bit early, ain't it," he said. I guess it was six-thirty.

"We won that Kuzych case," I said.

Ken sat up and said, "By God, I'll drink to that!" He was really thrilled. And so was I, too. You bet. After all those years. Unanimous for the union and Kuzych had to pay us, I think it was $18,000 and costs.

The papers didn't know quite what to do with the story, after the way they'd been so partisan to Kuzych all along. The *Sun* said, "The widespread importance of the decision given in London on the controversial Myron Kuzych-Boilermakers Union legal fight has prompted the *Vancouver Sun* to print the judgement in full." It filled a whole page. Kuzych himself put it out that he'd lost on a technicality and the decision was of no consequence, and that became the accepted line but it was a long ways from true.

Basically what the Lords done was accept the argument we'd made at the very first trial before Judge Macfarlane in 1945—that Kuzych was bound by the membership contract to exhaust his grievance remedies within the union organization before going to court. But on the way to that decision they had to rule on all arguments raised along the way, which included the legality of unions as a social institution, the competence of unions to discipline their members and the legality of closed shop. Much of the argument was around the union constitution and the legality of the processes laid out in the union bylaws. Gene King's "amateur" job of drawing up our by-laws had been subjected to the intensest of legal and philosophical scrutiny, by every court in Canada and now by the highest of all courts—and had come through it all a winner. I always wanted to tell him how proud I was of that, but he left the shipyards and nobody knew where to find him.

The case became a legal landmark throughout the British Commonwealth and it still has that position, but Canadian courts have allowed its precedence value to be chipped away.

I think, looking back, that it was necessary to create a bulwark against the erosion of union rights at that time. It was and still is possible for labour to lose the closed shop and other fundamental gains, as you can see by looking at states like Arizona and Tennessee where right to scab legislation has been passed. The same thing could have happened here at any time, and I'm convinced it still will happen the moment you have an establishment government in office that sees a way of getting away with it.

Kuzych vs. White et al., it's referred to as. So I've got my mark in the books there someplace anyways. It kind of looks like that'll be the only place, too. I don't give a damn though. I'd just as soon have my name on an important labour case as an opera, and my name's got as much right on that one as anybody's.

What that session in the privy Council really showed was how rotten the judicial system in this country was. Senator Farris said as much in the Vancouver Club there just after the decision come down, these big shots were sitting around running the country and one of them asks how this here Privy Council could get away with overturning the rulings of the Canadian courts like they done. Farris told them, well, the Canadian courts held that Kuzych couldn't get a fair hearing in the union but the Privy Council found that the union couldn't get a fair hearing in the Canadian courts. And that about said it. The judicial system in this country isn't set up to dispense justice, it's set up to protect the established order.

A couple of years later we got a Supreme Court writ that looked to be starting the Kuzych case all over again from scratch. They'd gone through the motions of seeking appeal within the union—which was just a joke because the bylaws said it had to be done within sixty days, not six years, and the Boilermakers Union had merged with the other unions to form the Marine Workers by this time and ceased to exist as an independent entity. But the court went ahead and entertained the action and there we were.

The union had shrunk quite a bit by this time and there was no way we could afford to go through the wringer all over again. What would be the point, anyway? We no longer had the Privy Council to look to and we'd proven that there was no justice for us in Canada. I put it to the union we could go two ways. One was we could fight it all through the courts and I would represent the union. I could have argued it as good as any of the bloody lawyers by that time and without the expense of legal fees we could maybe get by. The other option was to get us a political lawyer. Old Gordon Wismer was back in private practice by this time and I'd an idea he could fix it properly for the right price. The union elected to go the latter route so I delivered Gordon five thousand dollars and told him to go to it.

We'd entered a motion to stay proceedings on this new suit for the reason that Kuzych hadn't paid us the eighteen thousand he owed us through previous litigation and was coming to court with unclean hands. If I'm not mistaken we lost that in the Supreme Court, but in any case it went to appeal.

I remember when I walked into the courtroom that last day, who should be sitting in the audience but old Allan McDonnell, the head of the Canadian Manufacturers Association. "Well, Allan," I says, "come here to see if you're getting your money's worth today?"

"Oh no," he says. "No, no. I'm a friend of Gordon's. I just wanted to listen to Gordon argue."

"Yeah, bullshit. Look," I said, "I'm going to give you a tip. You better give up on this bloody Kuzych case. This case stinks all over Canada."

"I, ah, I got nothing to do with that . . ." he said, all red.

"Bullshit," I said. "Don't give me that."

Now you have to understand that all through our whole struggle in the Canadian courts there were judges that were for us and judges that were against us. Always the same judges. Whittaker, O'Halloran and Smith were against us and Sloan, Bird and Robertson were for us. But always we'd get one of the good ones with two of the bad ones so we'd lose out.

When I come in this time there was Sloan sitting and Smith and O'Halloran with him, and I thought, of all the goddamn rotten luck. They were finishing up another trial, and when they were done Sloan called an adjournment before we started. So they all went out and a few minutes later Sloan come back in, only Smith and O'Halloran weren't with him. He had Bird and Robertson instead. So we got a unanimous decision and that finished it because a unanimous decision is very difficult to appeal.

How Wismer set that up I don't know and I made a point never to ask. But there it was. That was the last we ever heard of the Kuzych case. To the best of my knowledge he never paid the union the money.

Part Four

THE PARTY

13

The Militant Tradition

'm a trade unionist. That's my politics and my religion both. It's like a religion. It has its goddamn rituals, it has its martyrs like Joe Hill and Ginger Goodwin, it has its unbreakable codes that go back to past centuries. If you talk about sin, it's every bit the sin for a trade unionist to cross a picket like as it is for an Orthodox Jew to eat pork or a traditional Sikh to shave. In strong trade union towns crossing a picket line can create a black mark that takes generations to wipe out. In Nanaimo they'll still point out the descendants of guys who scabbed the Great Coal Strike of 1913 and in Vananda there's guys who've never lived down the time they scabbed the Blubber Bay Strike of 1937. And to me, that's the way it should be. I love to see it. It makes you think people learn something after all. There is talk today on the left and the right both that unions have outlived their usefulness but I doubt the day will ever come when this will be true.

The right-wingers say unions may have been needed once to fight for a living wage but now that they've got it they're just in the way. They think wage disputes should be solved by a computer. I suppose wage disputes could be solved by a computer but you'd still have strikes over who would get to programme the computer.

Most people who believe in labour courts are complete know-nothings. When I hear somebody talking up labour courts I get the impression they believe in the tooth fairy too. We had a sample of what labour courts would be like with Trudeau's Wage and Price Control Board in the late 1970s. Even Pepin, who headed it, admitted they weren't near as tough on companies raising prices as they were on unions raising wages. The only reason it didn't create more violence than it did was the unions figured they could gain back the ground they'd lost when it was lifted.

People who believe in book solutions to labour disputes forget that one of the aims of the labour movement is to create more equal distribution of the country's wealth and stamp out injustice between the different classes. The labour movement has had some success at this but it's had to fight all-out every inch of the way. If history proves one thing it proves that no class will give up its power over the classes below it unless it's forced to. The force the working class has used up til now in capitalist countries has been the strike. If we give that up, how long would we continue to gain in our share of the wealth? How long would we even hold our own? The Wage and Price Control Board has given us the answer: the minute we sign away the right to free collective bargaining that's the minute we'd start to lose.

Trade Unionism gives power to the class that never had it under the capitalist system before. It puts it toe-to-toe with the exploiting classes. What's so bad about that? It's the adversary system, the same system that our courts are based on. The same system we have in government. A balance of powers.

This might be as good a system as there is. It keeps both sides honest.

On the left they're against unions because they figure they've become a "capitalist appendage." They figure the true struggle should be aimed at the overthrow of the capitalist system. They figure it should be replaced with communism, or anarchism. Or Maoism. Or Trotskyism. Or anarcho-syndicalism. There is quite a choice of revolutionary persuasions, each one fiercely dedicated to stamping out the others.

But workers' organizations by one name or another would be needed no matter what the system of government. There's just no system devised where the worker wasn't at the bottom of the heap holding it up and the struggle to make his job easier and more beneficial to himself will never be over. It's true, workers fare better under some systems than others, but there will always be leaks in the factory roof to be fixed or dangerous machines that need shielding or haywire foremen who should be canned, and there will always be a need for some means through which the ordinary worker can make his wishes felt by those in charge. No matter how well-thought-out a system of government is, there will always be sharp edges to be ground down and fitting to be done, and this is the work of unions.

To me the rise of trade unionism is one of the few things in the last two hundred years of our history that makes sense. Trade unionism has nothing to do with the guilds of the Dark Ages. A lot of people think there's a connection, but the only thing we've got to thank the guilds for is the bloody Masonic Lodge. Modern trade unionism is also a separate thing from socialism, though both movements come out of the industrial revolution together. They have the same aims, but where the socialist movement was mostly full of middle-class intellectuals trying to save the working class from itself, the labour movement was made up more of uneducated workers trying to raise themselves by their own bootstraps. There's been damn few eggheads leading labour, and even today it's one of the few places a working man can work himself up into an influential position in society and still stay a working man.

Some of the first unions were the best. They took as their aim improving the workers' lot in the broad sense, and there was one group, the Syndicalists, who went so far as to say governments should be done away with and replaced with unions. The Syndicalist movement had a million members in Spain alone and raised their own army to fight Franco in the Civil War. One of the first labour organizations in North America was the Noble Order of the Knights of Labour, founded in 1869 in Philadelphia by Uriah Smith Stevens. It *was* noble, too. They believed in industrial unions, with everybody in the particular industry from architect to ditchdigger as members. The only ones barred from the Knights was doctors, lawyers, politicians and bootleggers.

The phonies showed up early on too.

The Knights of Labour believed in a brotherhood of all workers united in the struggle to better their class—it was the type of union-ism that I believe in and that I think is the true type of union. But the Knights were pretty well on the skids by the turn of the century and it was the other kind of union that was responsible. This was what they called the "business union" or "craft union." The difference is that craft unions were horizontally organized—just with workers across one level, such as carpenters—instead of embracing all workers top to bottom. This appealed to guys who had a trade under their belt who figured they were a cut above the guys that didn't. They figured they could do better on their own, bargaining on their valuable skills and not carrying the ones with no skills. So it appealed to selfish motives and played on jealousies between workmen in different types of work. It went against the idea of a brotherhood of all workers and divided the labour movement into thousands of tiny factions whose aims went no further than their own personal wages and job security. It was a step backward, a sellout of the true unionism and just plain damn phoney but it naturally got lots of establishment backup and took over centre stage of the labour movement til John L. Lewis started the CIO fifty years later.

The great father of phoney unionism was Samuel Gompers, who was a cigar-maker and apparently quite proud of it. He set the AF of L up in opposition to the Knights in 1886 and broke them by scabbing the big railroad strike in 1894. He rejected strike action in favour of boycotts and generally did what he could to disarm labour from the inside. Oh Jesus, they honoured him and toasted him and he addressed the Canadian House of Commons and they sent him as an overseas ambassador—but in Europe huge crowds of workers come out and rioted. They understood what he'd done.

When Gompers died a reporter asked John L. Lewis if he was go-ing to the funeral. "No, I'm not," Lewis said, "but I heartily endorse the occasion."

There was still a lot of opposition to business unionism and vari-ous attempts were made to set up opposition to Gompers. Eugene Debs, the American socialist leader, and Big Bill Haywood started up the IWW or Wobblies, which was based on the old Syndicalist idea of union control of everything. They organized hop workers, loggers, miners and others the craft unions spurned, and forced better conditions through direct job action. The Wobblies are usually seen as a bunch of wild-talking vandals who flew apart of their own accord, but it was actually an effective organization that ran very down-to-earth campaigns for things like the eight-hour day and clean bedding in logging camps. They operated on very tough ground and proved themselves equal to the job. They were masters of industrial sabotage and one of their favourites was to drive big spikes into the logs so the mills would break their saws. Just to make sure the boss got the message they'd paint a grinning black cat on the office door, which was their symbol. They introduced slowdowns too, and the symbol for that was a clock face with the hands weighted down by a pair of wooden shoes. They got the name Wobbly from being the first union to let in Chinese—when a Chinese worker tried to say IWW it came out "eye-wobbly-wobbly." The Wobs were tough and smart and gave hope to a lot of workers in a time when there wasn't much of it around.

What really happened to them was they were smashed. After they pulled a big loggers' strike for wages and conditions in 1917 the US government ordered mass raids on Wobbly halls and filled Leavenworth Penitentiary with Wobbly leaders. Police opened fire on a boatload of union demonstrators in Everett and killed and wounded nearly a hundred men, and in Centralia, Washington, goons shot a Wobbly officer named Wesley Everest and hung his bullet-riddled body from the bridge. Big Bill Haywood got twenty years for sedition and had to take refuge in Russia, where he died.

The Wobs were tough but when they got the establishment up in arms they were crushed like ants. The survivors took to fighting amongst themselves almost the same way the Communists did later when they were under the gun. I suppose the IWW still exists on paper, but it long ago ceased to count for anything.

The IWW was never big in BC and part of the reason was that here on the West Coast the labour movement was already quite progressive. The counterpart of the AF of L in Canada was the Trades and Labour Congress or TLC which had been set up at the same time in 1886. Each district had a council and one time the Vancouver Trades and Labour Council refused to forward its dues to the TLC. The AF of L sent Gompers himself out to try and calm things down but all that happened according to Gompers was, "They denounced me in the vilest language I ever heard."

Finally the western delegates to the TLC Convention in 1918 set up a new industrial union called the One Big Union. The OBU was special in that it was completely a Canadian undertaking from start to finish. Later movements like the Workers Unity League and the CIO were carried out by Canadians but always under the name of some American or Russian parent body—and often use of the name was all the help they got. The OBU had quite an ambitious programme—to take over the entire labour movement in Western Canada and rebuild it on vertical or industrial lines, but they had good experienced leadership, strong support and by 1920 they had fifty thousand members. It was a militant active organization, and their Lumber Workers section alone pulled off thirteen successful strikes between 1918 and 1920. It was too successful. The government got together with the companies and the big US international unions and smashed it, too.

The TLC had labour all to itself through the twenties, but they still refused to help anyone but skilled tradesmen and left the common working stiff to go hang. The twenties weren't very damn roaring for the Canadian labourer.

There's no doubt when the Bolshevists got in in Russia it gave new life to left-wingers over here. In 1921 the Russian Communist Party called leftists together from all over the world to form a united front which came to be known as the Communist International or Comintern. The key strategy of the Comintern was what they called "boring from within," meaning they would first of all convert people in various countries by a process of class education, then move these people into key positions of power and eventually take over control without a shot being fired. Unions were the most important target and a special apparatus known as the Red International of Labour Unions, or RILU, was set up to oversee operations on the labour front. From that time on the history of the labour militants in North America, the old line of dedicated working-class progressives coming down from the Syndicalists in Europe through the original Knights of Labour, Wobblies and

OBUers, was a process of being absorbed and unified under the banner of the Communist Party. After years of frustration and fruitless struggle in the name of causes that popped like bubbles at the first pinch of the iron fist, here now was a cause with an iron fist of its own. The real thing at last. This is how it looked to me and to anybody who was seriously committed to changing the system at that time.

Through the twenties the Party got nowhere. Then the Depression came and it took off. Partly it was the economic trouble, which seemed to prove what the reds had been saying about the collapse of the capitalist system, and partly it was the viciousness which the establishment unleased on the public. The sort of thing I was talking about before, the store owners who raped their serving girls, the banks that grabbed family homesteads for default of a twenty-dollar payment, the yard bosses who made men fight like gamecocks for job tags, the big companies that cut loose and just gobbled up independent operators, the rampant police brutality, the complete heartlessness of the government, all this.

As far as I am concerned it was the Depression that set the Communist Party up in this country. They give great credit to their efforts at "education," but there was nothing they ever did that come close to the education the capitalists themselves dished out through the course of the Depression. The Depression left the Party with experienced leaders and ready followers both, and this was the key to their success.

Through the Depression it was impossible to "bore within" the labour movement because it was so bound up in craft unionism it didn't exist in most areas of industry. The Party as a result had to go organizing on its own hook and to do this Moscow ordered the creation of a new national organization called the "Workers Unity League." The WUL was a good aggressive radical organization and it was a great success. It set up a network of industrial unions across the country that for the first time in years brought the strength of the Canadian national unions up even with the American Internationals, right across the country. If it had kept on, the history of unionism in Canada might have been a good deal more Canadian and less American than it has been. The trouble was the WUL wasn't really under Canadian control, and what happened next proved it. One day it received orders from Moscow to disband and turn its members over to the TLC. Just like that, like a command from the heavens. No one really understood why and no explanation was offered that made much sense. The byword in Moscow that year was "a united front against fascism, " and quite possibly some high Russian Party muckymuck who didn't know beans all about Canadian labour or care a whit for Canadian nationalism just gave a wave of his hand and ordered this merger. It was questioned plenty within the WUL and the Canadian Party but it became an issue of Party discipline, so it was done.

It is possible this had something to do with the CIO. In this same year, 1935, John L. Lewis of the United Mine Workers led a rebel group within the AF of L to form a new American labour organization called the Committee for Industrial Organization, which was to re-establish true unionism—industrial unionism—to the North American labour scene for the first time since Gompers rose to power. The new organization scored huge victories in the rubber, steel and auto industries and soon all those whose wages were low and conditions were bad in Canada and the US began to pray for John L. Lewis and his CIO to come and save them. The Communist Party no doubt saw that this opened a great new opportunity for the kind of work they were good at, and it may be they decided they would be better off pushing this new breakthrough and gaining control of it than following a separate course in the WUL. In one respect they were right. The red labour organizers with their experience did a tremendous job for the CIO and laid the groundwork for all the big industrial unions of today— the United Auto Workers, Steel, Mineworkers, Fur and Leather, IWA, Electrical Workers, there's not one of them doesn't owe their existence in a large part to the organizational work done by Party personnel in the early days of the CIO.

One group that wasn't impressed with the CIO was the old executive of the AF of L, who stuck fiercely to their phoney craft union convictions and expelled the CIO, creating a nationwide split in the American labour movement. The AF of L then turned around and demanded its Canadian arm, the TLC, expel the new CIO unions too. A good deal of the reasons for the split were personal hatred between

Lewis and old line AF of Lers in the US, and the TLC didn't feel near the same hostility to the new industrial unions which had come into being in Canada, but the AF of L forced the Canadians to go ahead with the expulsions. This left seven big Canadian CIO unions with over twenty thousand members without a roof over them, and after some shuffling around they joined forces with Aaron Mosher's old All-Canadian Congress of Labour to form the Canadian Congress of Labour. Mosher was made head, and so Canada had a split labour movement too, with the CCL industrial unions under Mosher on one side and the TLC craft unions under Percy Bengough on the other side.

I know it's hard to talk about this kind of union history without sounding like you're reciting the Begats but I'll try to finish up here in one thrust. The situation during the time I was active in labour was that the movement had these two branches, the conservative old-line craft unions on the one side and the more progressive new-look industrial unions on the other. The craft unions were mostly under Gompers' old AF of L and its Canadian branch, the Trades and Labour Congress, or TLC. The industrial unions were mostly under John L. Lewis's CIO and its Canadian branch, the Canadian Congress of Labour or CCL.

Both of these Congresses in turn had smaller regional groupings in each city called councils. The craft union councils of the TLC were called *"Trades and Labour Councils"* and the industrial union councils of the CCL were called just *"Labour Councils."* So in Vancouver you had the Vancouver Trades and Labour Council and the Vancouver Labour Council blasting away at each other. The Boilermakers and Marine Workers Union, being an industrial union, was in the VLC whereas the Teamsters, being a reactionary bunch of phonies, were in the TLC. The BC Federation of Labour was a CCL organization that brought together the industrial unions on a province-wide basis.

Is that completely clear? I hope so because now I'm going to turn it back to mud again. There were some industrial unions like the United Fishermen which were in the TLC and there were some craft unions like the Electrical Workers in the CCL. On top of that, you had completely right-wing phonies like Aaron Mosher at the head of the CCL and you had left-wingers like Pat Sullivan in the top executive of the

TLC, so to some extent the war between left and right cut across the war between trade unionism and industrial unionism.

The Party in the meantime had bored holes in the ground and disappeared from view.

14

Canadian McCarthyism

I

n this book the Marine Workers put out in 1977, *A History of Shipbuilding in BC,* Jeff Powers, who was union president at the time, said, "Our union has been under fierce attack, especially during its formative years which coincided with the Cold War, as 'Communist-led. ' This was not true then and it's not true now." During the Cold War, which flared during my term as president, it was very common to hear spokesmen for the establishment charging that the labour movement was under communist control and to hear the labour movement deny this as "red-baiting" and "scare-tactics. " The public for the most part I don't think ever did decide who was telling the truth.

You can take it from me, the establishment was right, at least as far as the West Coast goes. The Party had a special branch called the TUC or Trade Union Commission where the top Party men from various unions could get together and plan things out. When I sat on the TUC I could look around the room and see top leadership of all the big industrial unions in the province: Ernie Dalskog or Harold Pritchett of the IWA, Harvey Murphy of Mine-Mill, Homer Stevens of the United Fishermen, Ed Leary of Dock and Ship and the Vancouver Labour

Council, George Gee of the IBEW and many people out of many of the lesser unions too. We had all the major industries in the province covered and the vast majority of the unionized workers.

Very few amongst the public would be aware of the existence of the TUC let alone know when its meetings were but if they did, cabinet ministers and captains of industry alike might well have been sitting outside its doors fingering their hats and knocking at the knees, because what we were talking about was the kind of year both of them were about to have. The implications of our decisions for the economic and social life of the province were quite considerable.

To say the Party didn't have anything to do with labour is just bloody poppycock. Furthermore, I don't see a damn thing wrong with the Party being involved with labour. Other political parties have tried just as hard to get into bed with labour and their intentions haven't been half as honourable. In my own case I was led to the Communist Party through the desire to better the lot of the working stiff of which I was one, and most anybody who counted for much in the Party come the same route. The ones who had my respect did anyway.

And they did one hell of a job. Many established unions like the IWA and the Steelworkers owe their existence to men like Dalskog and John McCuish and Slim Evans who camped out in the bush and crept into camps to organize in the dark of night, and guys like Dick Steele and Harvey Murphy who once slipped into a barricaded company town dressed as a rabbi to pull some all-or-nothing strike out of the fire. Harold Pritchett, Don Barber, Bill Rigby, Homer Stevens, Tom Parkin, Jimmy Thompson and Digger Smith were all in the same category. These guys were bloody heroes in my book and I sure don't see anything to be ashamed of in what they did. The labour movement owes the Communist Party an enormous debt on their account and if the Party won't stand up and take credit for them it's time somebody else did.

One thing the establishment give out that wasn't true was that red unionists were foreign agents and subversives. For the most part they were patriotic Canadians whose disloyalty to the establishment was more than made up for by their loyalty to the working class. The discussions that took place in the TUC were union business strictly. We were working together as a block of radical unions to better conditions for our members and of course to better our own position against the right-wing unions and against the government. This was the day-to-day business. Any influence Moscow might've had on this was very general and remote. There was no pipeline to the Kremlin. Some of the more dedicated ones like Bill Stewart would take the odd trip over to Russia but I always got the impression they come back disappointed with the level of interest in Canadian labour they found there. There was certainly many attempts to influence union policy by the Canadian Communist Party acting on its own or in concert with the American Party, but to the best of my knowledge very little of this originated from Moscow. I think the Party brains got most of their Moscow news out of the newspapers.

Just as an example, when the Second World War broke out Hitler and Stalin signed a non-aggression pact to keep Russia out of the hostilities. The Party guys in Canada took the line from this that Canada should stay out of it too and every chance they could they denounced it as a phoney war, an imperialist war and all this. Some of the strong Party unions like the UE pulled a lot of little strikes and things. In June 1941 Hitler invaded Russia. The next day the same Party guys were raving about all-out effort to stop the fascists and denouncing the government for not fighting hard enough and advocating all Party unions sign a no-strike pact.

A lot of people took this as a sign the Party was in close contact with the Rooskies but Christ, they didn't know no more about it than anyone else. In most cases they were just trying to guess what Moscow would like them to do and hoping they'd be noticed sometime and get a pat on the head. But even at that, very few of these unions were able to do much. There were strikes and demands for better conditions before and after Russia come into the war. The idea a Party-dominated union leadership had total control over its membership was malarkey. Propaganda went out that we could just snap our fingers and close down strategic industries, and this was the threat we posed to the national security, but the minute we tried anything like that the membership would throw us out on our ass.

This foreign agent scare was an old tactic they used on the leaders of the Winnipeg Strike. Old J.S. Woodsworth quoted a piece of the Bible there, something about "Men shall not plant vineyards to have them eaten by another man and each man shall enjoy the work of his own hand." The Mounties took this as proof he was in with the Bolsheviks and slammed him in jail. Dick Steele was another example. He was one of the original organizers in Steel and during the war the government had him in a concentration camp as an "enemy of the war effort." He was such an enemy of the war effort the first thing he did when he got free was enlist and get killed in action after winning a bunch of medals.

The government knew bloody well we weren't foreign agents—Christ, they had enough of their own agents in the Party to know it better than us—but they did know the communists were giving Canadian labour real good leadership and that was what they really wanted to stop.

II

The CCF was always very anxious to have labour in its camp but they didn't do like the Communist Party and go out organizing the unorganized and building strong unions where there weren't any before. The Party was in there organizing when nobody else even thought of it and the labour movement wouldn't be what it is today if they hadn't. The CCF wasn't near as effective at organizing and wasn't too interested in it—their approach was to move in on already established unions and take them over at the top. The Party had no use for the CCF programme of watered-down class-collaborationist socialism so it was just natural they would get tangling.

And tangle they did. On every issue that came up. No matter what side one took the other would take the other. We used to have some godawful fights down there in the VLC. The Party and CCF fought each other a damn sight harder than they ever fought the boss. The Party even went so far in the 1943 federal election as to back Mackenzie King over the CCF—they said the Liberals represent the capitalists who understood labour. They tore that one up after King won though.

In the Congress too, hoboy. It was just one long pitched battle between the right and the left, that's what they called it instead of the CCF and the Communists—the right-wing vs the left-wing. Charlie Millard was the big push for the CCF—he was a CCF member in the Ontario Legislature and a close ally of David Lewis, the CCF national secretary. Millard was phoney from the word go. I don't think he worked a day in his life. I don't think he did any organizing to speak of either. He was one of these guys who walked into labour at the top, a bureaucrat more than a worker. He got started with the UAW in the Oshawa Strike but they soon got rid of him and Steel picked him up. He was big in the CIO too but it wasn't on account of his talent.

Then of course there was old Aaron Mosher. Jesus that guy was phoney, I'll tell you. Right-wing reactionary red-baiting son-of-a-bitch. Call a man like that a leader of labour, now. The only good thing he did for labour was when he died. He was president of the Congress, Millard was vice-president and Pat Conroy was secretary. Conroy was the only trade unionist between them, a red-haired Irishman from the Alberta coal mines and a real fighter. He built the goddamn Congress and made it work in spite of Mosher and Millard. He was very, very strong. I guess he did as much to shape the Canadian labour scene the way it is today as any single guy. It was him cut the CIO off at the border and insisted on Canadians running their own show, and whatever small autonomy Canadian labour had in the following years, Conroy is largely to thank for it. He was sure no friend of the Party but he didn't like the CCF either. Him and Millard hated each other's guts. They had a scrap at the 1951 Congress convention in Vancouver, which Millard won, and Conroy just up and resigned. It stopped the whole convention. No one had a clue beforehand, and one of the great unending arguments is just why he done it. I'm not sure he knew himself. I was talking to him not half an hour before, I run into him on the floor while the votes were being counted in this election they were squabbling about, and he says, "Bill I've been looking for you, there's something I want to talk to you about." I was supposed to meet him up in his hotel room after the vote count but then he walked out and

I never did find out what he had on his mind. I don't think when he talked to me he was figuring it was his last few minutes in the labour movement. He later became labour ambassador to Washington I believe, and Donald MacDonald took over in his place as secretary of the Canadian Congress of Labour.

The big charge against the reds always was that they caused trouble, everywhere they turned up it would be all squabbling and wrangles and wasted time. They tell a story about old Birt Showler who was with the Teamsters and just as phoney as a three-dollar bill. They had some strike some place and they had a twelve-man strike committee and it just so happened that all the other members were communists but old Birt didn't know it. Well this committee worked out pretty good and they won the strike and everything went just fine. So Birt congratulates them and says, "This is why we've gotta keep the reds out of this union. If there'd been one Party guy on this committee he'd've torn it wide open." They didn't put him any wiser at the time but the Party got a lot of mileage out of the story later.

But this is just real BS you see, to say that somebody's no good because they cause dissension when in fact they're arguing for something that has merit. If they're just agitators that's one thing, but the Party never was that. They had a very clear purpose, and that was to make the labour movement more militant and aggressive in fighting for the Canadian worker.

For instance that Ford strike where Rand made his famous formula. This was the first big strike after the war. What was at stake the way the Party saw it was all the gains labour made since 1939. You see, during the war the government had been forced to seek labour's goodwill and co-operation with favourable legislation, and with cost-plus a lot of companies had found it cheaper to give workers what they wanted and charge government extra than to put up a fight and lose production. So there had been big gains in conditions and in wages, and especially in labour legislation, but the concessions which had been made were made under the War Measures Act and there was a good chance it would all just evaporate when the War Measures Act was mothballed. The Party had it figured that there would be a coordinated move by the establishment to get things back the way they'd been before the war and Ford was going to show the way. They had an old-style regime there that was noted for rough treatment of labour and the workers had gone two years without a contract. They were at odds on just about everything including closed shop and union recognition. There was lots of feeling and the Party figured that here was the place labour had to make a stand. The CCF'ers in the Congress come back with some phoney line that it was "too soon after the war" for a strike and did everything they could to put it off, so the Party just went ahead on its own and sent in its top people, Joe Salzberg, and Jackson and Harris of the UE and a bunch of others to organize, and the men went out on the 12th of September.

The strike went on for a hundred days and there was one key point there where the guys went in and shut down the plant's powerhouse. The company went to the Ontario government and claimed if it didn't get the plant back in business the whole factory would freeze up on them and cause millions of dollars of damage, so the government decided to send in a brigade of RCMP to smash the picket lines the next morning. The strike committee got wind, so real early before the cops got up, they had every person who owned a car drive it as near as they could get to the Ford Plant, stop it in the street and walk away with the key. When the cops got around to making their move they couldn't get within twenty blocks of the place. Every road, every alley was plugged solid with abandoned cars. It stopped them completely and turned the strike in the union's favour. But the CCF'ers in Congress, they thought this was terrible, it was unlawful and they denounced the communist radicals for misleading honest auto workers and CCF unions refused to contribute to the strike fund. Jackson called a meeting and charged the Congress with sabotaging the strike. The strikers managed to win in spite of that, though. Rand was appointed arbitrator and he give a good settlement which he's gotten a lot of credit for, but the credit really belongs with the strikers and the Party organizers. It was them who forced the situation to where Rand had no choice but to award a good settlement. His "formula" was actually quite an obvious type of a compromise and had the effect of putting off true union shop agreements for quite a few years. It allowed guys to come on the job without joining the union but they still had to pay dues. The reasoning was that all workers received the benefit of gains won by the union so all should contribute to the cost, which was true enough, but once they'd admitted that much there was really no reason for not going the rest of the way and granting full union shop.

There's no doubt about it though, the strike was a tremendous victory for labour and set the pattern that was to follow for the next ten years. The wartime gains were cemented and all the editorializing about the peacetime economy not being able to carry the burden of wartime working conditions come to a stop. But Mosher, Millard and the big CCF guns in the Congress refused to admit they were wrong. They never got done carping about the way the Party guys flouted Congress authority during the Ford strike. They couldn't deny the success of the strike but they quibbled that the Party's only interest in it was to advance their political campaign to enslave the Canadian worker under a totalitarian dictatorship. Millard tried to set up a purge of the reds in the Windsor UAW local and when that didn't work he laid charges against Jackson and Harris for treacherous attacks on high-ranking officers of the Congress, namely himself and Mosher. It went on and on and on. All the top reds, Jackson, Murphy, Pritchett of the IWA, were constantly being suspended and reinstated for things they were supposed to have said or written that Millard and Mosher didn't approve of.

Jackson introduced a motion to set up a national wage policy to go after thirty percent raises right across the country, and Mosher decried it as "too high" and "too soon" and denounced it as "just more left-wing agitation." But the executive council, which was made up of delegates from all member unions, went for the idea and it was another success. Mosher's response was to arbitrarily abolish the executive council, which was set up as the CCL's supreme authoritative body between conventions, and take all its powers onto a small executive committee which was controlled by himself, Millard and Conroy. This was totally against the constitution but anything was fair to fight the reds, you see.

They finally expelled the UE for non-payment of dues. Jackson was an accountant and very careful about his bookkeeping but what happened was, his dues for the Congress were first of all sent to the CIO across the border then sent back to the Congress headquarters in

Ottawa, and the CIO had just expelled the American division of the UE as part of the purge down there, so although Jackson thought he was sending his dues in, they were getting hung up at the UE's head office in the US.

There was a part in the constitution that said any Congress affiliate who got more than three months overdue in per-capita returns could be suspended, so when Mosher's bunch noticed what was happening they kept mum. He told later how he waited for the mail every morning with his heart in his mouth praying it wouldn't contain the UE's overdue cheque. On what he figured was the last day he slapped UE with a suspension and gave a phoney new union, the IUE, authority to take over the UE's jurisdiction. This was only supposed to be done by resolution of the executive committee but he couldn't wait to call them. He called them afterwards instead and had them pass the motion retroactively.

This was a bit much even for Mosher's cohorts to take, and they weren't a bit happy. Jackson came in with a cheque and showed them how as Mosher miscounted and dropped the axe fifteen days early.

All this came out at the Congress convention in 1950 and Mosher really didn't have a leg to stand on. But McCarthyism was right at its height and the Congress put out a paper calling communism the greatest tyranny the world has ever known and said it promised freedom and bread but delivered only dictatorship, poverty and the echo of firing squads gunning down innocent men and women. On that basis they convinced delegates to support their purge, which included most of the big Party unions—Mine-Mill, Fur and Leather, United Fishermen, all of them. The Marine Workers was left alone because they weren't big enough to be a threat on the national scene by this time.

But just think of that now, here you had the CCF screaming about the scare tactics the establishment was using against them—especially in the 1949 BC election where the newspapers printed pages of solid black ink warning about the red menace, the only time I ever saw pages in a daily newspaper solid black—and on the other hand, at the same time, you had the labour wing of the CCF using the same McCarthyist hysteria against their opponents in the Congress.

15

How the West Was Lost

On the West Coast the right-wing purge was a tougher job because the Party was so much more powerful. They had the big Congress unions and controlled the Vancouver Labour Council and the BC Federation of Labour. The CCF out here was non-existent as far as its union influence. The reputation of old-time union leaders like Pritchett and Dalskog and Murphy was unshakeable amongst rank and file union members in BC but there was no hope of making a dent in the Party's hold on things without knocking them out of the IWA and Mine-Mill because those two unions could almost control the labour scene between them.

Against the solid wall of Party strength the Congress sent out a young organizer from Steel named Bill Mahoney. His orders were to break the Party's back in BC and "clean up" the BC labour scene and he was given two years to do it.

The laughable goddamn thing is that he pulled it off and not only that, he did it in one year. He had a lot of help and a bit of luck but to give the guy credit he done a hell of a job. Basically he did just what the Party itself did for years and years, he got out on the road and organized his support. A lot of the right-wing locals stopped sending delegates to the labour council, so he went around and gave them shit and lined up delegates. Then there were the paper locals—unions that had gone under but still existed on paper. He looked them all up and got delegates to stand for them. The Party protested, but the Congress naturally ruled in Mahoney's favour whatever come up. Besides, they'd pulled the paper-locals ploy themselves often enough. Anyways, in the 1948 elections the Congress got control of the Vancouver Labour Council.

The Fed wasn't so easy for Mahoney because the control of the IWA and Mine-Mill was proportionately much greater over the province as a whole than it was in Vancouver city. It was all pretty phoney how he done it, when you look back. We were all over in Victoria putting on a demonstration against the coalition government and in the evening there was a banquet. Pritchett was MC and the main speaker was Murph, but Murph was quite a booze artist, you know, and there was never any shortage of booze at any Party dos. When Murph come to speak he was pretty well oiled—but not that bad. Not near as bad as he could get and not near as bad as they made out later. I think he'd just come from back East, anyway it was right around the time Mine-Mill was having a lot of trouble with its international president, Reid Robinson. He'd come up to Canada to escape the Taft-Hartley Act but the federal government arrested him for deportation and it came out the Congress was behind it. So Murphy was full of this, on top of the Mahoney business, and he took a pretty good strip out of the Congress. It was a pretty good speech actually, but the press wrote it up that it was vicious, vituperative and made lurid references to the personal lives of Congress officials. I never could figure out where they got that. The thing that seemed to have most of them upset was where Murph said when the establishment asked Mosher and Millard to kiss their arse the only condition they made was they asked them to pull their underwear down first. The papers said parts of the speech were so gross it couldn't be repeated, but when you asked anybody what parts, they'd say, "Oh that underwear business." So it went down in history as Murphy's Underwear Speech.

You hear people blame the downfall of the Communist Party on Murphy's Underwear Speech, but Christ, they were just waiting for any phoney goddamned excuse and that happened to be it, that's all. Mahoney laid charges in the Congress and had Murphy suspended. Well this meant they couldn't be seated at the BC Fed convention, you see, and as it turned out without the twenty-two Mine-Mill delegates Mahoney had a one-vote margin.

That was some rhubarb, that goddamn convention. That topped them all. Mahoney had his votes figured so close that when Bill Stewart beat Pen Baskin for vice-president by one vote, he knew which one of his delegates was going the other way on him and for the rest of the convention he got George Home to go sit beside this guy to help him mark his ballot. I remember it well. It was some fella from Retail-Wholesale, there was quite a fuss about it but it was just pandemonium down there. But with that straightened out, Home beat Pritchett out for secretary by one vote, and the right-wing got the rest of the executive. Except president, old Danny O'Brien held that, but he wasn't one side or the other, he didn't count for much.

That Danny O'Brien was a consummate actor. He was a natural mugger. Oh Jesus, could he put on a show, you know. I would put him beside Stewart at bringing a crowd around to his way of thinking—the only place he fell short, he had to get somebody else to do the thinking. He was on the executive of the Congress at first, he was their Regional Director in charge of BC, but Murphy got to him and swung him around to the Party's side. That's when he got in as head of the Fed. They put him up to scrapping with the Congress so he got on the outs with Millard and the CCF bunch, but Murphy promised him if he'd go to bat for the Party and got bounced by the Congress they'd fix him up with an organizing job in Mine-Mill. Danny did get bounced and Murphy come through with the job alright—for about three months. Then they dropped the old bugger and that was the last you heard of Danny O'Brien.

But I seen him up there, he'd imitate like a parrot, he'd do these here impersonations of Mackenzie King and different ones, Christ you couldn't mistake it. He'd have long pauses, talk asides to himself, pull faces, talk out the side of his mouth—when he come up to speak everybody'd just settle back in their seats and get ready to have a good laugh.

He was a queer bugger too. He was going quite grey there so he got a dye job, absolutely jet black. It just about knocked your eyes out, you know, it looked so damn phoney. You'd hear guys say to him, "Jesus, what happened to you Danny, you fall into some axle grease?" And he had very poor eyesight, Danny did but he'd never get glasses. To read something he'd have to bring it right up to the end of his nose. I remember one time at a meeting there, a Fed convention, I guess, some damn right-wing phoney from one of the hotel unions was trying to get recognized and Danny kept ignoring him and only giving the floor to Party guys. We knew this fella's background—he'd been a hotel dick. The Party saw to it that this was well-known. Finally after he'd stood up about ten times and Danny'd passed over him about ten times, this fella let out a roar. "You better get yourself some specs you old bat," he hollers, "you're so blind the only colour you can see is red." There was a bit of a chuckle over this and Danny waited til it was quiet.

"I'm the first to admit my eyesight isn't what it used to be," he said, "but I will say this—at least I never ruined it peeking through keyholes in hotel rooms." Well this really got a roar out of the place, and the guy shut up. Danny was quite quick.

Old Danny pulled a pretty good move at that convention that would have saved the Party's bacon if they'd been smart enough to take advantage of it. There were ten delegates there from the IWA local in New Westminster who were part of the "White block"—the anti-red faction—and a dispute come up as to whether they were legally elected. Danny said, alright, we'll have to put this to the floor and until it's settled the delegates in question will have to refrain from voting. Mahoney challenged this ruling, it went to vote and O'Brien won it by about twenty votes. This was the first vote of the convention and Pritch right away took it that the left had a twenty-vote edge. So he decided to be big you see, and he stood up and said he'd give these New Westminster fellas the benefit of the doubt and move they be seated. He figured the left would still have a ten-vote edge. But he didn't have things figured as close as Mahoney did. There was some right-wingers broke Party lines and supported O'Brien's ruling, because they thought it was right, and this had Pritch fooled. It was one hell of a blunder.

So Mahoney and the CCF got control of the two main labour councils in the province, but they still couldn't pretend to be in control in BC while the Party controlled the IWA, which was much the biggest union in the province and the real power.

This is where the Party made its worst blunder. It's doubtful Mahoney ever could have permanently captured the IWA if the leadership had kept its head, but it didn't. They were under terrific pressure from a lot of sides—they had their own white bloc after them, and the International—the parent body in the US— was fighting with them all the time in addition to the Congress, but they had just won big in the '46 strike and they still had the strong support of most of the membership. There was the usual baloney about crooked bookkeeping and Mahoney backed them into making an audit which was quite critical, but he was really still sucking air.

Then the leaders of the IWA themselves turned around and handed the union over to him. They decided to secede from the International and set the union up on their own under a new name, the Woodworkers Industrial Union of Canada. They figured this way they'd get away from all their troubles you see—they could just tell the International and the Congress both to go to hell. They figured they'd be better off financially since they were sending $120,000 across the line every year and getting bloody little of it back, and now they'd be able to keep it all. They had prepared carefully by transferring all the union bank funds to secret accounts and even hiding the furniture out of the office and hiding their organizing ship, *The Logger's Navy*, in a bay up the coast.

But here you get back to the question of what is a union, you see. It's not a legal entity as I said before. In a sense the charter that says it's a local of an international or an affiliate is just a piece of paper that can be ripped up. In this case you had the men who built and run the union figuring that they were the real union and they could take it with them wherever they chose to go.

Well they were wrong. The vast majority of the membership stuck to the IWA name and let the new union wither on the vine. The IWA went over to the complete control of the right-wingers and the old officers who led the break were blackballed for life. They couldn't even go back logging. Ernie Dalskog, who done as much to organize loggers in BC as any one man, was reduced to working as a first aid man in non-union camps.

It's always been one of the big mysteries when guys sit down and talk about the things that happened, how the Party with all its experience and after all the years they'd controlled the IWA, could have misjudged things so bad as they did over that pullout. Both Dalskog and Pritchett claim they were against it, and I believe them, but that leaves you wondering just who the hell was responsible. They say Ernie's writing a book about it and I hope he throws some light on that.

This was the end of the Party as the dominant force on the BC labour scene, and the end of any widespread militancy in BC labour. They figure they were victims of fanaticism and the rankest injustice, which is true. But that is always what any group trying to change society runs into to one degree or another, and the way I see it the Party was the author of its own destruction to a large extent.

16

Cannibalism

I

They say if you take a bunch of rats and subject them to enough harassment they will turn on each other—the mothers will eat the young, the followers will cannibalize the leaders and they will appear to lose all sense. If you take a political movement and smash it like they did the left in the Cold War, you can see the same thing happen. Everybody gets suspicious of everybody else, the leaders lose their sense of direction and cannibalism becomes commonplace.

You could see it as soon as things started to go sour on us, and one of the first victims they picked on was me.

You see, one thing I could never concede was that the Party brain trust there had all the goddamn know-how. They wanted all the goddamn say all the time and you were supposed to just take their word like it was the word of God. I could never concede that this was true. In fact I figured that guys who were down at ground level, out on the job, often had a better idea of what should be done than the ones stuck away in their offices at Party headquarters. So any time they handed down some decision I thought was wrong or against the union's interest, I'd do like I did for anybody else I figured was out of line, and tell them.

They didn't like that. They wanted guys who would jump when they snapped their fingers. So I guess I began to be seen as not the best Party material after all. I was too independent. Then there was a lot of guys in the Party I had no use for at all and I guess I didn't do a very good job of keeping it a secret. The way I figured, such success as the Party had in labour was the result of the efforts of old-timers, the guys who'd fought the cops and lived out of the bush and spent the better part of their lives down on the front lines organizing the men and leading strikes. Most of these guys had put in quite a stretch as working stiffs themselves during the bad old days and had a real feeling in the gut for what the workers' struggle was all about. I'd been through a lot of that too and this type of guy I always got along with first class. I'm thinking of guys like Murphy, Dalskog, Hjalmar Bergren, Ed Leary, Slim Evans, George Gee—the old warriors.

Joe Salzberg and Tim Buck, too. I knew them very well and they were both very fine men. Salzberg was the most powerful communist in the Party's trade union setup. I don't know if he was from a working-class background but he was a hell of a swell guy. He was the one that called the shots on the Party's trade union activity in Canada. And he was good, now. I had dealings with him often and I always found him very objective. When the IWA broke away there he sent a telegram ordering them to reverse the action at all costs, but it come too late. He was on the national executive of the Communist Party. He was an MPP in the Ontario legislature for many, many years and he was well thought of by everyone. From the Jewish section of Toronto, probably in the needle trades. I always liked him very much.

Tim Buck was an awfully nice fella, too. Very soft-spoken and gracious, a

Joe Salzberg, a labour brain-truster and back stage manager at conventions.

real gentleman. He had a big scar across his forehead where they tried to shoot him. They had him in jail for some damn thing, thinking the wrong thoughts I guess, up in the Kingston Pen, locked in a cell. They staged a phoney riot there one night with the lights out and came and poured a bunch of bullets into his cell. He laid down on the floor and a bullet ricocheted off the floor and cut a big skive across his forehead. I knew him very well. He gave me a picture of himself one time and signed it too. I still got it.

But even in the Party guys like this were in the minority. The rest of them were a pretty mixed lot, with opportunists, screwballs, parlour-pinks and phonies of various kinds in large numbers. Once I had a guy figured for a phoney I wouldn't waste my time on him, but a lot of these guys where they weren't effective at anything else they were quite effective spreading rumours and scheming to cross a guy up.

Another thing that was happening, there was a scramble for paying jobs what with the shipyards shrinking and the Party losing its big union, the IWA. A lot of guys could see their salary disappearing and this led to some pretty anxious pushing and shoving in the Party's back rooms.

The first open attack that was made on me was engineered by a fella who was secretary of the Shipyard General Workers Federation, Gary Culhane. The Federation was a Party front that was set up as a result of the union's battle with the Congress back in '44 and it was supported by a per-capita surcharge on all the shipyard unions of about ten cents a member. During the boom years this come to a considerable sum and the Federation was able to support quite a staff, though I never did get a clear picture of what they all did. Culhane had about fifteen girls there all on payroll, at least that's what it seemed like. But when the shrinkage come all this dried up and Culhane started campaigning for my job as president of the Boilermakers.

In this first episode I found I was charged with consorting with anti-Party elements or something, it was the most ridiculous goddamn thing. There was a fella in the yard by the name of Gordie McQuillan who belonged to the SLP—the Socialist Labour Party. The SLP never had more than a few dozen members but they were Trotskyites or something and the Party just hated them like the Reverend Henry Ward Beecher hated the devil. But I couldn't see losing sleep over them and this Gordie McQuillan was one hell of a fine trade unionist, which gave me more respect for him than a lot of guys on the Party side. I was leaving the yard one day when I run into Gordie so I stopped to pass the time of day with him. A fella by the name of Cinnets, he didn't get along with McQuillan, he didn't get along with anybody, he saw this and the first thing I know I'm called up to answer these charges of cavorting with Trotskyites or anti-Party elements or whatever the hell it was. They laid on a full-blown trial committee—Nigel Morgan was there, and Tom MacEwen—and Culhane. Culhane, the same guy that laid the charges was on the committee to try them, and boy did he ever lay into me too.

I knew what the drift was, so I went right for the bastard's throat. I pointed to Culhane and I said, "There's the most expensive monstrosity that ever hit the trade union movement. You don't need to take my word for it," I said. "You'll remember the big project he was supposed to be carrying out was a guide-book for shop stewards. We heard so much about that when he was putting the arm on us for the money, maybe some of you guys would like to know what become of it. Well, I'll tell you what become of it. It got exactly as far as buying great big fancy useless covers for it. There's a thousand bucks worth of covers sitting right in there in the next room all covered with dust and if you don't believe me go take a look.

"That's one thousand bucks of the workers' money he's squandered, but that's just an appetizer to the main course. What the Party should do instead of fretting about who I might happen to say hello to in the course of doing my job, is get an accountant to go over the books of that Federation to see where the hell all the money is going to."

Well this really shut them up, because I guess they knew where a lot of it was going. There was thousands and thousands poured into the Federation over the years and it just disappeared. This was a line of speculation they did not care to hear about, you see. They wound the trial up smartly. I was found not guilty but I was given a lecture on my attitude. I should be able to take constructive criticism, it was only meant to help me and all this bullshit.

I never expected any better from the likes of Culhane but to see Morgan and Tom MacEwan in on crap like this kind of threw me for a loop. I had great respect for these men, you see. To do the kind of job I was doing and have all this public hostility blasting down at you constantly you really had to have a strong faith the track you were on was the right one, and a lot of my faith at this time was tied up in the leadership of the Communist Party. That's what it all centred on. The best I could think was Morgan and MacEwan somehow weren't wise to this Culhane, but any way you looked at it, it was damn hard to credit them for giving such chickenshit goddamn crap a serious hearing, after all the goddamn work I'd done. It stung me, I tell you. It really stung.

II

After the president the most important guy in the union is the secretary and in the Communist scheme of things this was even more so because they always played the position of secretary up, I don't know why. But it makes the president's work go a hell of a lot better if he's got a secretary he can depend on a little and up to 1949 my secretary was Malcolm MacLeod who I always got along with first-class.

I don't know if I mentioned it before but MacLeod was the first Party guy to get a position in the Boilermakers Union and I was there when he got voted in. It was just a few months after I started work in 1941 and I was coming off shift with Joe Belanger. It was hot and what Joe wanted more than anything else was to go over to the pub for a few beers but I said, hell with it, let's go check on that union meeting. We'll have a soak later. So I dragged Joe in there and here we walked in in the middle of an election for business agent. MacLeod was one candidate and Lush Campbell was the other. I just knew enough to know MacLeod was the outsider so I told Joe to vote for him and when they counted, Malcolm got it by one vote. So that was the seed that started the Party off in the Boilermakers Union, and if I hadn't wrestled Joe Belanger away from the beer parlour that afternoon, it might never have got planted.

It's funny how the picture gets warped by time. I was reading a history book a guy give me by some professor—*Communism, Nationalism and Canadian Unions* by Irving Martin Abella, and he had a very dramatic description of how the Boilermakers Union was ripe for a communist "coup" and how the Party "marshalled its forces" starting off with Malcolm MacLeod and began "infiltrating" the union. It's worth repeating, the words he quotes to describe it: "By a process of strategy, relative terror and with a definite organization these adventurers sought to discredit the builders of the union by slander and ridicule, and union meetings became a nightmare where order disappeared and disorder took its place . . . as time went on the attendance at meetings of the union decreased to such an extent they were able to take virtual possession . . ."

Maybe this guy has a PhD., but I was there and I never seen any of that. Guys like this it seems to me don't realize how things a lot of the time just come together by happenstance. There was no goddamn crash effort to pluck the Boilermakers like a ripe plum and put it in the Party basket. It may look obvious to some guy trying to piece it together from letters and minutes years later, but it wasn't obvious before it happened that the Boilermakers was any more vulnerable than any other goddamn union. He forgets, the Party was working hard in established international unions like the IWA, even a lot of AF of L unions, at the same time. They were out to take any union they could get just like the CCF was and the Liberals were, and in Quebec even the Catholic Church was. The main place Abella gets his information for making this statement, if you look in the back of the book, is a Congress report bloody old Aaron Mosher had drawn up when he tried to throw Stewart out in '43. That report was just an attempt to justify the Congress action by its own officers, and it was later discredited both by six thousand union members who held a mass meeting in Athletic Park to reaffirm their support of Stewart, and by the BC Supreme Court who ruled Mosher's actions completely illegal.

The Party takeover of the Boilermakers was a fairly low-key, orderly process which was based on the workers' strong desire for improvement in their working conditions. The secret to its success, if you want to look for one, was the dictatorial attitude of the old-time bosses—of business and labour both. If they'd planned every move especially to antagonize and incense the workers, they couldn't have done better. They were the best organizers the Communist Party ever had. The only time there was any nightmare of disorder was when the Congress itself tried to interfere illegally with the union's democratic processes. There was a very "chaotic state of affairs" then. But I don't suppose anyone would take my word against a professor's.

MacLeod I think was one of the most popular of all the union leaders in Vancouver. He was always kind of joking with the guys, he'd slap them on the back and he was a great boozer, Jesus Christ he was drinking all the time. He was too easygoing, really, to be effective. He was good in that he'd always be right behind you if you waded into some ruckus and showed the way, but you couldn't leave it to him to go out and do it by himself. He was sort of a soft guy, and he was really split whenever it come to any disagreement between the union and the Party, but other than that I just told him what to do and he done it.

Stewart was a different matter. After he come out of purgatory there the Party let him get a part-time job as building manager of the Boilermakers' Hall and he started working his way back up in the union.

To put it in simple words, there wasn't room in that union for the both of us. I never had any open rows with Stewart and in fact on the surface of it we were good friends. He used to come out and stay with us at our summer cabin in Eagle Harbour, him and Barbara. But as soon as Bill started to get his foothold back in the union I could tell it. I could feel a resistance there that wasn't there before. It'd never be him, not his face on any of it, but things'd come up that didn't come up before and things'd go wrong that shouldn't have. And always I'd have the feeling his hand was somewhere in it. He was oh, just so devious and so scheming, you know. And he could never forget—not that he'd dare mention it but I knew damn well he thought of it every time he looked at me—I was the guy that turned him in that time he slugged the ballots.

It come out in little things. Mostly it was the hall. The Communist Party used to rent our hall which was all right—along with other parties, there was nothing wrong with that—but they ran up bills that they never paid and finally they got hundreds of dollars in arrears. I guess they didn't have the money, but it still burned me the way they took it as their right because they were communists they could use the hall whenever they wished. Anybody else welshed on rent we had a policy of reading their names out at the general meeting and putting them on the never-again list, but where it was the Party they had this goddamned attitude they were above the rules. They wanted to write off this debt without reading it out. Well, I wouldn't go for this. This isn't the Party's hall, this is the members' hall, I told them. The Party has no right to take money out of the members' pockets without even telling them. I said, put it to the members and let them decide. Ask for free rent for the Party and if they say yes, okay, I'll support the motion.

But the Party wouldn't do that, you see. This was beneath them. It was beneath them to ask the members for free rent but it wasn't beneath them to steal the rent.

They started another tactic then. They'd set up a committee and give it a special name—"The Committee for the Relief of Bunions"— or some such thing. They would book the hall in this name, hold their meeting, then you'd never hear from them again. I'd say to Stewart, "Here, what about this goddamn bill that's never been paid?" Oh well, that committee disbanded long ago. It doesn't exist and there's no one to bill, you see. This was worked over and over, and it was just a way of getting around me. So finally I said, alright, no more of these goddamn committees. Any group we don't have established credit for pays the full shot before they get in the door.

Well none of this here helped me with the Party, you see. I can see now how Stewart was probably planning it just to get me spatting with the Party more, and maybe I even knew it then, I don't know. All I can say is if the same thing come up all over again, I'd take exactly the same position. Because I was right. I knew damn well I was right.

The more I skirmished with the Party the more I got seeing a side of them I didn't like. They treated union property like it was their own. Like it was just a matter of capitalist mumbo-jumbo that things were in the union's name and everybody knew the real owner, the real force that created the union and all its property, was the Communist Party. And it was more important to do anything to advance Party interest than it was to honour any capitalist mumbo-jumbo.

The Party had its bookstore in there on the ground floor and there was always this godawful pile of old boxes and junk around, it looked like a goddamn garbage dump and it was a real bloody fire hazard too. Time and again I told them to clean the damn place out, but they just ignored me. Who the hell's he, you see, we can do what we want here. Finally I phoned the fire marshall to come down and he smartened them up right quick. But it pissed me off, to have to go to that length to get them to respect our wishes in our own building.

The next tactic the Party come up with was using the hall without booking in. They'd just come in and use it without putting their name in the book so unless you actually caught them at it there was no record they'd had the hall at all. What brought it to a head was the N-Fly. National Federation of Labour Youth, a bloody small communist youth club. Bunch of young kids all get together and scare hell out of each other with their own propaganda, and they took to using our hall for this. Old Ed Parkin, Al and Tom's father and a hell of a good guy, he was janitor and he'd get the hall set up for some group to come in and these goddamn young kids would wander in, push the chairs all around, fill the ashtrays up with butts, leave a hell of a mess, and Ed would have to come in and start his work all over again. He just done it and said nothing for a while, then he got mad and threw the buggers out. They got very indignant about this, important thinkers like them being ordered around by a mere janitor you see, and they told him they'd fix him, they'd tell Bill Stewart.

It happened Ed was in my office when Stewart found him, and he lit into the old guy like an angry god. He just got going and I lit into *him*. I went up one side of him and down the other. "This is not your goddamn hall," I said. "It's not up to you to decide who the hell gets to use this hall. This hall belongs to the members, and if anyone gets it free, it's for the members to decide. If those kids want it, you book them in and charge them regular rent. Either that or let them write in and request a free rental like anyone else would do."

And I said to Ed, "Any time you find them in here, you go look in the book and if they're not booked in, you kick them to hell and gone out." Well this was heresy, you see. There was real repercussions over this in the Party. And Stewart was very hurt that I had the temerity to dress him down in front of old Ed.

The corker though was the time the IWA decided they were going to take over the hall. I think it was in '46. They had that big strike and the men in the Charlottes all got shut out of the camps with no place to stay. Harold Pritchett turned up in my office one day and said to me, "We want the building."

"Whaddya mean," I said.

"Just that. We want the building."

"What the hell for?"

"We're going to bring the loggers into town, and we got to have a place to put them."

"Well, we'll make what space we got available to you."

There was three offices up in the mezzanine empty so I took him up there.

"This haymow?" he said. "We want more'n that."

"Well you can't have it."

"Why not?"

"We got tenants in here with signed leases."

"Break the leases."

"Like hell," I said. So away he went.

He was pretty sore. I thought a lot of the guy, but Jesus, I couldn't buy this kind of bullshit from anybody. This was when he was still riding high, and he had this secretary with him that he took everywhere, Jean McKenna. Just so damned important, you know.

After Pritch left, about half an hour later up come Nigel Morgan, who was the leader of the Party and also an officer of the IWA. He was quite steamed up too.

"We want the building."

"I told Harold we'd make available what space we have."

"Not enough. We want the whole thing."

"What about our leases?"

"Break them."

"Like hell we'll break them. We'd be sued out of our skins. We'll give you what we've got and that's it."

He give me a real hard look and says to me, "You've got a real bee in your bonnet about this hall, haven't you Bill? I'll tell you what we'll do. If you don't want to give it to us I'll lead a bunch of loggers up here and we'll *take* it," he said.

"Well bring your camera, because you'll get good action shots of a bunch of loggers being thrown out on their ass by a bunch of boiler-makers," I said.

Away he went—and that was the last I heard of it. It turned out they didn't need the damn hall anyway. They changed their mind about bringing the men down, and not because they couldn't get our hall—because they woke up to the fact of what an absolutely stupid idea it was. We'd have been in a hell of a nice fix if we'd broke the bloody leases and threw our tenants out in the street, then they come along and called it off.

This was a big turning point for me. I'd never had proof before that the likes of Morgan or Pritchett were behind any of the phoney goings on in the Party, but this time there was no mistake. For the first time it really come home to me that these messiahs who I thought were going to lead the people to the millennium had feet of clay. I got quite depressed. Ed Simpson, who was one of my strongest supporters, was really disgusted too.

III

It come to a head over this Rustproofing deal. Canada Rustproofing was a division of Western Bridge which was owned by Frank Ross and Colonel Victor Spencer, but it had a new manager by the name of Thormallen, a pipe-smoking Dutchman who'd come out from Massey-Ferguson back East, and Thormallen made the statement that employers on the West Coast didn't know how to deal with unions. He thought he was away ahead of us out here, but the fact was he was a throwback to the old no-good type of employer from the pre-war era. Frank Ross was a real heavyweight on the BC industrial scene of the '50's—he was a big philanthropist and a top shot-maker for the Liberals. His wife was Chancellor of the University of British Columbia—her son later became Prime Minister, and Ross himself did a stint as Lieutenant-Governor of BC.

Frank Ross (left), leading BC industrialist of postwar years and Liberal Party shotmaker, showed himself as one of the more enlightened Marine Workers employers during his years as head of Western Bridge (now Canron Western Constructors).

We'd been organizing at Western Bridge for some time, we got certified and we went into negotiations for a complete up-to-date package—wage increase, closed shop, benefits. This would be around '48 or '49. They wouldn't go for it so we took a strike vote and got a good vote. We were going out the next week and Ross called me in for a meeting with him and Colonel Spencer. The old Colonel didn't have much to say. He just sat there, he had a big red nose that if you give it a squeeze you'd get a quart of Scotch whisky, and every so often Ross would turn to him and yell, "Isn't that right Colonel?" "Yup!" the Colonel would say. Ross would go on talking then and a while after he'd turn to the Colonel again. "Isn't that right, Colonel?" "Yup!" This was the heir to the Spencer's Department Store chain, which later became Eaton's. "So you're going to take the guys out on Monday, are you?" Ross says to me.

"No," I says. "I'm not taking the guys out. *They* voted to strike, but I'm right behind them all the way. The only guy who has any control over it is you. You can call it off any time you decide to grant them their just demands."

"Well you go on strike then, White, but you be ready to stay on strike a good long time," he says. "You're a bull-headed son-of-a-bitch but this time you've run up against somebody just as bull-headed as you are."

The deadline come and the men went out. And they stayed out. Meanwhile we figured we might as well start negotiations with Rustproofing so we'd be in a position to bring in a settlement there as soon as we settled at the Bridge.

This Thormallen was something else. We'd only been in negotiations a few days before he announced he wasn't going to negotiate with me any more. He refused even to talk to me. I figured this was pretty rich, him telling us who he was going to negotiate with. I went back up to the hall and told Malcolm MacLeod and George Brown and the rest of them about it, and to my surprise they sided with Thormallen. They thought I was too hard on him. They hadn't been in on negotiations but this is what they thought. "Christ," I said, "we can't have the employer deciding who's going to do his own negotiating and ours both. He can say who'll represent the company but the members say who represents them and they chose me."

Oh, they weren't so sure. The next thing I know I'm summoned to the Kremlin and the Party orders me to lay off. MacLeod and Brown would do the negotiating with Thormallen. I had a mind to tell them where to put it, but I thought, well why don't I just let them go ahead and try it. I had a pretty good idea how far MacLeod and Brown would get.

They went down and talked with Thormallen and when they come back I said, how'd you make out? Oh fine, fine, they had no troubles with Thormallen at all, but there was really nothing they could do until the strike was settled at Western Bridge and the pattern was set.

Okay, I said. I knew what was happening. Thormallen had gone to the AF of L, got Roly Girvan to knock the dust off an old charter from some defunct local, Metal Polishers or something, called in his employees and told them to join this other union, or be fired. And a lot of them did.

This was completely illegal interference by an employer and I went down and raised hell at the Labour Relations Board, but of course I didn't get anywhere there. I told MacLeod and Brown all what was going on, but they stuck to this line that there was nothing they could do til the strike at Bridge was over. So Thormallen went merrily on and signed up everybody in the plant in this phoney AF of L union except six men in the polishing department. The phoney union applied for certification from the LRB, I objected, they got it, and a contract was signed.

The strike at the Bridge ended at about the end of the third week. We won hands down. Got a real contract, everything we wanted. I went down there in the yard the day they went back and the first guy I see is Frank Ross who comes waddling over with a hell of a big grin on his face.

"Well you won 'er, you bull-headed bastard," he says. "You won 'er fair and square. No hard feelings."

He stuck out his hand, just grinning that big grin of his. Frank Ross had a big round face that when he smiled it looked just like the full moon. Very good-natured, just a hell of a good guy. I never had any trouble dealing with him after that at all. Pretty near anything we wanted, if he could give it to us he would. And he done okay by us too. We had good relations with the Bridge. He even used to tell some of the other tycoons that a closed shop was a good thing and since he signed up with us his labour troubles had ended. I figured that was pretty good of him. He was one of the most enlightened employers I ever dealt with.

I called MacLeod and Brown in then and said to them, okay the Bridge strike's over now. Get cracking on Rustproofing.

"Oh," they said, "it's too late now."

"Too late? Whaddya mean?" I said.

"Well they've signed a contract with this other union and we can't come between an employer and another union," they said. "That's raiding."

I thought maybe they were joking, but they weren't.

"Well by Jesus, I'm going to do something," I said. I went down to see these guys in the polishing department who'd refused to sign with the AF of L and they told me Thormallen had given them til the next day to sign with this other union or he'd fire them. I said, "Don't sign. I'll go get a bunch of picket signs made up and as soon as you're fired you phone me and we'll shut the goddamn joint down."

He fired them the next day and we threw our picket line up. These other buggers had to go in through a little trap-door around back and Eli Lachance got a crayon and wrote a big sign over it, "Rat Hole." This went on about two weeks and they started to hurt. They weren't getting stuff in and out. Morale inside was shot all to hell and bolts were turning up between gears and this sort of thing.

Finally I got a call from Frank Ross one day.

"I don't like this that's going on. What's the score here?"

I told him.

"That's no good," he said. "I don't want that. What can I do to put things right?"

"All it'll take is one letter," I said. "The Labour Relations Board shouldn't've let this happen and I told them but they wouldn't take my word. What I want is a letter from Thormallen to the Labour Relations Board admitting the charges I made to the Board are correct."

"Come down tomorrow and you'll get it," he said. So I went down and here was Thormallen and Syd Hogg, Ross's general manager. Hogg was a good guy and he just sat there, watching. He never said a damn thing.

Thormallen puffed on his pipe and said, "Well Bill, I guess we gotta get this thing settled."

"Yeah, that's the general idea," I said.

"I understand you want some sort of a letter?" he said.

"Yeah," I said, and I told him what I wanted. He called his stenographer in and started to dictate a damn weasling bloody thing, you know.

I cut him off. "That's not what I want," I said. "Here, take this," I said to the stenographer. She looked at me, and him, and he didn't say anything, so she flipped up a new page and took down the letter I wanted. "Go type that up and bring it back," I said. She did, I read it over, handed it to Thormallen and said, "Sign it." It was a complete renunciation of everything he'd done and everything the LRB had done, and a complete vindication of everything I'd said against them. He read this, looked up at me, looked up at Syd Hogg who just stood there, then he signed.

The next day I demanded another meeting with the Labour Relations Board. I repeated my charges to the effect that Thormallen had improperly interfered in union activities and the LRB had improperly recognized this phoney union, reminded the Board as to how they'd previously dismissed them, and then read Thormallen's letter. They were flabbergasted. They didn't know what to do. Thormallen was sitting right there so they asked him to retire from the room.

"This is amazing," the chairman said. "In all my years I've never seen a document to match this! A complete admission of the same charges he denied when he last appeared before this Board. This guy must be absolutely stupid."

"I must disagree," I said. "What you got here Mr. Chairman, is something that's very rare, and that is an honest employer. He's so honest that when he finds out he's wrong he admits it."

"And because he's honest," I said, "you call him stupid."

Well they didn't know whether to go take a crap or send flowers to their mother. They were strapped. They stumbled and bumbled and hummed and hawed, and finally they revoked that bloody AF of L certification, washed out the contract, reinstated our union, and old Thormallen had to sign the same contract we'd been after when I'd first started in on negotiations with him. The next month he was fired.

For this I was rewarded with another Party trial. The charge was "adventurism." By going after Rustproofing I had risked the union and put its future in peril—true, I'd won it, but I was taking long chances and all this sort of thing.

That was it for me. I didn't wait to hear the verdict. I told them I'd had enough and I was leaving the Party.

They didn't quite know what to say. They threatened to put a piece in the *Trib* saying I was no longer a friend of the Party—I don't know if that was supposed to make me mad or glad—but I said, "You can do what you damnwell want."

So that's how I come to leave the Party.

17

Standing Alone

I

There was a time there, it must have been one of the last Party meetings I went to. I forget the exact date, it was in 1949. There was an account of it in this here union book by Sammy Jenkins that's a complete hallucination so I'd like to tell it the way it happened. It started when I picked Malcolm MacLeod up on my way to work. Malcolm didn't drive and he was on my way so I picked him up every day. I lived at 55th and Fraser and he lived down about 20th and Fraser. I picked MacLeod up that morning, I had lunch with him and I took him home that night. Jenkins says he had lunch with him in the boardroom, but it wasn't in the boardroom, it was across the street in the little cafe where we always had lunch. Again, Jenkins states Malcolm said he had indigestion so bad it was about knocking him off the chair. This is pure unadulterated bullshit. There was nothing wrong with MacLeod. MacLeod incidentally was one of the most healthy guys I ever met. He was one of these lean raw-boned Scotchmen, always just the picture of fitness and health. I never knew him to have even so much as a cold in all the years I knew him.

There was meetings that night, branch meetings of the Communist clubs, and one was in our hall and one was in the Holden Building.

We went home for dinner and I come down and stopped at MacLeod's place about seven. He wasn't quite ready, he was reading the paper. We sat and talked for ten minutes or so then he got on his hat and coat and we went down to the meeting. On the way down he was just as natural and normal as could be but when we got into the meeting about quarter to eight he complained of indigestion and went out for a Bromo Seltzer. He come back in and the meeting started but after about fifteen minutes he turned to me and said, "This damned indigestion is just about knocking me off the chair. I think I'll go home." This is where Jenkins gets the story, but Jenkins wasn't there at all. Jenkins and Stewart were down in the Holden Building.

About twenty minutes or half an hour later a Party member named Frank Flood came into the meeting to say they'd taken Malcolm off of the bus and he was quite sure he was dead.

I went and phoned the General Hospital and asked if he'd showed up. They said the ambulance had just brought a man in DOA but they hadn't identified him. I said, check his personal effects and I think you'll find that it's Malcolm MacLeod. I held for a few minutes while they checked and they said yeah, the effects were those of Malcolm MacLeod and they'd be sending him down to the morgue.

It was at that time I phoned Stewart at the Holden Building and told them Malcolm had dropped dead. This was the first they knew about it. The police came around next, two of them in a prowl car, they said they had to get information and go out and notify the widow. I told them where he lived and everything and they said are you acquainted with the widow and I said, "Very well."

"Would you be good enough to take her the news then?" they said. "It's a job we don't particularly enjoy." I took Bill Gee with me. Ina come to the door all smiles, "Come on in, come on in." So we come in and closed the door. "Where's Malcolm?" she said. She figured we were just stopping by after the meeting for a drink. "Well I've got some very bad news for you, Ina," I said. "Malcolm is dead." That right there was one of the most difficult things I ever had to say. "Bill, I can't believe you," she said. "Just an hour ago he walked out of here, he was fine."

"Well Ina, I'm afraid there's no doubt about it."

"Well I'll have to see him," she said. "If I see him I'll believe it, but I can't believe it unless I see him."

I took her down to the morgue, we went in, they hauled Malcolm out and pulled the sheet back. She stood looking at him for about a minute.

"Okay, you can take me home now," she said.

These are the true facts of the case of how Malcolm MacLeod died. His funeral was one of the biggest I ever was at. The hall auditorium was jam-packed—I guess there were two thousand people there.

A little aside to that, there was an old Greek, a derelict on the skid road down there named Jim Valallis. He owned a cafe during the Depression and went broke feeding the unemployed. He was a good-hearted guy and a left-winger, and quite well-educated. He could recite Byron and "The Isles of Greece" by the mile you know, when he got gassed up. To say he was eccentric would be putting it mildly. He come to the funeral and as they filed past the casket he took out this little Soviet flag the size kids have at a parade, you know, and he crossed himself and laid this flag on the casket.

So the headline on Malcolm's funeral read, "Hammer and Sickle Adorns Unionist's Bier." They couldn't miss a chance to get a spear into a guy even at his funeral, the bastards.

Apart from losing a good friend, the immediate effect for me in Malcolm's death was that Stewart pole-vaulted into his job as secretary of the union. Most of the union executive was on the other side of the Party fence now anyway, but this put the one guy who was most dedicated to fouling me up right at my right hand.

Actually on most things I got on with the Party okay. Matters of union policy and that, generally I could go along with them and they could go along with me. Where we fell out was where it came to pitting the interests of the Party against the interests of the union. Then it was pitched battle.

There was one time there it come up, Stewart wanted to borrow a thousand bucks to take a trip to Russia. I had a pretty good idea of what our chances were of ever seeing the money again, so I opposed it. Put it up to the members and if they support it I will too, I said. As usual, he didn't want to do that. Oh there was no worry, he said, soon's he got back he'd go around on a lecture tour and pay it all back, no problem. But I said, okay, tell that to the general meeting. What they done, he took it from the Shipyard and General Worker's Federation. And as long as I was in the union he never repaid it. I understand he made another trip after I left and I've no doubt but the members got stuck with the tab for that one, too.

For me it was a question of ethics plain and simple, but for them the ends justified the means, which meant anything they could get away with, they could go ahead and do it as long as they could show it as in some way being to the benefit of the Party. There was constant friction but mostly over small things. It wasn't until the per-capita business they really actively started trying to put the skids under me.

II

They come out with a plan to increase the per-capita contribution to the Shipyard and General Worker's Federation by ten cents. All the member unions would pay an extra ten cents per member, and that meant mainly the Marine Workers because we were the Federation to all intents and purposes. It was quite a husky boost, not quite double, but close.

The ostensible reason was to hire an organizer to organize members into the union, and they had a Party guy, Frank Flood, who'd already been on the payroll eighteen months, but they were finding they couldn't afford him. He'd broke the Federation. God knows how—he travelled all over hell, but he hadn't brought so much as one member into the union. What he was doing with his time is anybody's guess.

As I said earlier on, the Shipyard and General Worker's Federation, they were supposed to be the parent union of which the various shipyard unions were locals, but it really didn't amount to anything because all the members and all the power was in our union, the Marine Workers. It was set up by the Canadian Congress of Labour as one of the conditions of settlement when the Party had old Aaron Mosher with his pecker caught in the door over that court decision back in '43, so it was actually a Party tool from the start. It worked as a front for various activities, the main one being to take in money. The Party's supporting membership wasn't near as large as the other parties they were up against and it was pretty hard to pull off a Communist Party fund-raising bingo or anything like that, so they were always strapped for money to pay for their staff, rent, organizational programmes, and whatnot. Moscow may have chipped in a little to support the paper but it never amounted to much, I don't think. So I know they needed money and I know a hell of a lot of money disappeared into the Federation over the years so I always assumed somehow or another the Party was getting it. How it was worked I wouldn't know—whether a guy like Frank Flood would turn part of his salary over in a straight kick-back basis or whether he would keep it all but do Party work, I don't know. Considering the amount of travelling he did I assumed he was actually working as a Party organizer setting up Communist Party clubs. I could never prove it, I'm only speculating here.

The facts are the Federation was broke and Stewart brought a motion forward that the per-capita contributions made to the Federation by the member locals be increased a dime. This was at a meeting of the Federation executive, which I was on, and I objected, but the Party had a majority and I was voted down. Then it came to the Marine Worker's executive, a recommendation to the general meeting that we increase this per-capita. They had the majority there, too, and they recorded it as unanimous.

"No, it's not unanimous," I said. "I'm against it and I want to be recorded against it because I'm going to speak against it at the general meeting and explain to the members why I'm against it."

Naturally they didn't like that, and I caught hell.

"Save your arguments for the general meeting," I said. Well they knew the score, you see. They knew Flood hadn't one new union member to show for eighteen months work and no doubt they knew how he was really spending his time. Stewart was very uneasy about trying to defend this in front of the general membership, and about what I might say.

The next afternoon he said, "Will you come down and talk to Tom and Nigel about this?" I said, sure. I went down to the Kremlin and Nigel said, "Bill tells me you're opposed to this here increase."

"Yeah, you bet," I said.

"Well why?" So I told him why. "It's absolutely not justified. The worker's money over the last eighteen months was squandered. We got not one thing to show for it."

He asked Bill, "Is that right, Bill?" Bill had to say it was, but he tried to justify it like he was working on something big, you see. A bit more time and it would all unfold. Nigel knew as well as Bill what Flood was really up to, but they were testing me, you see, to see what kind of an argument I was going to come up against them with. To see how bad it was.

Old Tom MacEwen was holding his pipe and peering out at me under his eyebrows there through all this you know, and finally he speaks up, "You know, Bill is absolutely right. I think it would be the height of folly to increase the per-capita in the face of this." So they decided then and there that we *wouldn't* increase it.

There was a meeting that night and it was just about ready to get underway by the time we got back. The Party guys on the executive were all set to battle this thing through over my objections, and Stewart desperately wanted to get them aside and warn them off but I wouldn't let him. I kept right at his side so he couldn't say a damn thing. I called the meeting to order, the per-capita come up right off the bat, the Party guys started right in to fry my ass about it. "It's a sad day when a union man can't give a dime to support new organizing," and all this sort of thing.

I let them unload, then I stood up and I said, "I know you guys expect me to straighten you out on this now, but I'm not going to. I'm not going to speak at all. I'm going to let Brother Stewart here speak for me."

So Stewart had to get up and tell them it was off. And if you ever seen looks of absolute amazement on guys' mugs, well you should have seen them guys then. Here they were all geared up to steamroller it through and their own leader, the guy who put the motion in to begin with, stands in front of them and holds up his hand. They couldn't believe their goddamn ears. They had to retreat in disarray. I enjoyed watching it very much.

They can talk as they like about the Party not deciding policy in the union, but you couldn't have a better example of it than that there. Officially Tom and Nigel had no connection with our union at all, but there they were sending in orders just as obvious as hell—and this went on all the time.

18

How It Ended

I

Sometime after the per-capita affair the Party decided I'd become too much of an obstruction to its aims and I'd have to be liquidated. Simply, they would get me knocked out as president by someone who had a better talent for following Party orders. I never found out about this until later but I did notice this line of new faces started passing through that all seemed to be awful keen to get a knife into my ribs.

The first candidate was a fella named Fred Collins and he was about the best, too. He'd come over from Fur and Leather and he was one hell of a good trade unionist, but after they'd built him up for a year or so he double-crossed on them—he took a heart attack and died. The next one they brought in was Jack Scott, who was an organizer for Mine-Mill up in Yellowknife. He came into the union and went to work on the bull gang—which is quite a comedown for a union organizer. So they started to project him, but he went about it the wrong way. Here I was who'd helped build the union up and still had the respect of the general membership whatever the Party thought of me, and here he was an outsider who knew very little about the union, constantly attacking me in meetings over petty little things.

It come to a clash there one meeting, he accused me of making faces at him, of all goddamn things. I'd had enough damn nattering so I singled him out to the meeting and told the guys his history, how he'd left a well-paid organizing job to come in and work on the bloody bull gang, which is the lowest job in the yards. That made it so damn obvious that he'd been parachuted in by the Party, it finished him in the union. He come up after the meeting and told me that wasn't very nice and I said, "Well, when you start swinging a broadaxe you should be prepared to duck yourself." He kept on meowing so I said, "We can always go out in the alley and settle it there." That satisfied him. He kept out of my hair after that.

The next guy into the ring was Kenny Richards. I knew Ken and I knew he was one hell of a good trade unionist, too. He'd been in the Canadian Seaman's Union—in fact he's the guy who put the finger on McManus. There's a story that really deserves a book now—the busting of the CSU. There you had the government and the Congress openly working together with American thugs to break a good sound Canadian union and replace it with an American one that was rotten to the core.

Anyways the CSU were under a lot of pressure and their leaders kept phoneying up on them. First of all it was Pat Sullivan—he was president of the CSU and also secretary of the Trades and Labour Council in Ottawa, right up there next to Percy Bengough. This shows you the influence the Party had, with Pat Sullivan who was a long-time Party guy second in charge of what was supposed to be the reactionary side of Canadian labour.

Anyways Pat Sullivan went south and left the Seamen in the lurch, so Gerry McManus took over as president of the union. He was supposed to have turned down a one-hundred-thousand-dollar bribe from the Shipping Federation to sell out the union, and they advertised him as "Hundred-Thousand-Dollar McManus." On one of the May Day parades they had a big sign there.

Ken Richards was the guy that told the Party he was phoney, and Jesus Christ, they just about crucified him. They wouldn't believe it. But shit, it wasn't a few months before McManus went south too. He

Percy Bengough, circa 1942, long-time head of AFL-affiliated Canadian Trades and Labour Congress. CITY OF VANCOUVER ARCHIVES, 586-883

even wrote a book telling how his union had been captive of the red menace.

I knew Ken was sound, and when they proposed him for the executive of our union I was all for it. So they put him up for some position and he was elected. The first few meetings I thought, doggone, he's awful stiff, you know—I couldn't figure it out. I had no idea he was in on the plot.

Kenny wasn't there too long before an incident come up with Active Trading, one of the scrap metal yards. There was an old fella named Herman Pease that had been there for donkey's years. He was actually a complete non-entity who was not union-conscious at all but he lived right next door to the place and during one of the strikes we used it as a kind of picket headquarters, for guys to go in to phone, have a mug-up and one thing and another. We won the strike, everybody went back to work, and about a month later they fired old Herman. For incompetence.

Well, a guy that's worked there fifteen years, it don't take that long to find out he's incompetent. It was a case of being fired for union activity. That's illegal as hell. It was an open-and-shut case.

Sam Jenkins was supposed to be business agent for the small shops so I told him to go down and get Herman back on the job. He went down, come back, and said by God, they wouldn't take the old guy back. That was okay though, he told me, he could get Herman on as a welder's helper in the shipyards. I couldn't see why a man'd want to quit a job he was right next door to, but Sam claimed Herman wanted this shipyard job so I said alright.

Bygosh, he wasn't over the new job any length of time til he got fired there, too. And this was every bit as haywire as the first firing—all he had to do was pack rods to the welders. I was doing something and I couldn't go so I told Jenkins and Stewart, "Go put old Herman back on the job."

They went over and come back to me and said, "Oh no, the company, they won't take him back." I thought they were bullshitting. I said, "Whaddya mean?" but they stuck to it—"No, they won't take him back."

"They goddamn *will* take him back!" I said. And I quit whatever I was doing, jumped in the car, went over to Burrard, and by Jesus, ten minutes later I had the old bugger back on the job. It wasn't hard. They had no excuse. I think it was he chewed snoose and somebody thought it was unsanitary—some damn fool thing like that. So no time at all I was back and the two of them are there waiting.

"Did you get him back? Did they back down?"

"Well, Christ," I said, "There was nothing to that. They knew they were out a mile."

I could see it didn't sit too good with them and next executive meeting I be go to hell if they didn't both jump on me. For going over their heads and getting this old guy back on the job. "He made us look foolish," they said. I'll never forget the look on Ken Richards' face. He sat there like he couldn't believe his bloody ears. Finally he cut loose on them.

What the hell were they running, he wanted to know, a trade union or some goddamn ladies' aid. He said, "The union's function is to *protect* its members, not to protect the hurt feelings of its leaders when they make asses of themselves." Oh he give them a real blast. They had to back off, because they knew they couldn't put it over unless I was totally isolated. With one guy on my side they couldn't make it stick.

I didn't know what went on til later. Richards went down to the Party and told them they'd sent him in to get the wrong man. He said I was the guy who was doing the job, and the others were laying down on it. He told me later how he'd been brought in and they'd actually coached him how to attack me. He was supposed to keep nattering away at me and eventually he'd run against me for president, you see. They were working at it very deliberately. But as soon as Richards got his own ideas, well, that finished him. He became my staunchest ally on the executive, and they come to hate him worse than they hated me. The next election they were able to knock him out and then they set about to freeze him out of the trade.

Now there's something else that kind of backfired on me—union hall hiring. When I started in the yards hiring practice was one of the worst sources of abuse—they had the guys lining up outside the yards scrambling for brass tags, the boss's pets always got in first and all this sort of stuff. Well we made it one of our prime objectives to clean this up and install fair hiring practices through the union hall. Last off, first on, you see—seniority. I fought for it as hard as I ever fought for anything and oh Jesus, it was tough to pry that power over hiring loose from some of those old bosses.

I don't know how many times I took that one into negotiations or how many hours I spent arguing it before we finally broke them down. I don't mind saying it was me that did the arguing, either. Often Stewart or MacLeod or Brown would sit in with me on negotiations, but they didn't contribute. They'd let me go in with my jaw stuck out and try and hold our position, but neither of them had what it took to do it themselves. Other guys in the union, like Ed Simpson or Jack Klemola or Ken Richards did, but Stewart and Jenkins and Brown were useless in negotiations. They were great in the hall after though, announcing the gains we'd won. If it was some concession I'd won it would be *we* done it, but if it was something they'd done it'd be *I*. The union members wouldn't have any way of knowing the real score, and a guy couldn't stand up and start squabbling over who got credit, you'd look like a kid.

But finally we got our union hiring and I was proud of it for a long time, but you know in the end I come to realize all we'd done was trade one kind of abuse for another. Hiring instead of being a tool of the boss became a tool of the Party. The Fisherman's Union was a Party stronghold too, you see, and they'd have Party guys in there carrying two cards, one in their union and one in ours. Come to the end of the fishing, they'd put their Fisherman's card away, pull out their Marine Worker's card, and come over to be dispatched. This is absolutely haywire. To begin with, you're not supposed to carry two cards, and then to send guys out at the expense of full-time union members who've been on the list longer is just as rotten a type of abuse as anything the bosses ever did.

But this was that old communist thing of thinking they were on a holier plane, you see. They thought because a guy was in the Party he was automatically better than a guy who wasn't. As far as I can see the minute the communists started doing this any claim they got of representing a more just type of government goes out the window. They're supposed to eliminate privilege, not just take it from one group and give it to another.

After Ken's rupture with the Party he found he couldn't get dispatched. They just starved him right out. I tried what I could to help, but Sammy Jenkins, who was one dispatcher, would say, well I phoned him but he didn't answer and the job wouldn't wait. Ken finally had to leave the area. He went to New Zealand and became business agent of a union over there.

It went on for years like this. I never paid it too much attention, I was busy with the Kuzych case, the Compensation Commission, contract negotiations and settling beefs, but through it all I was aware that the Party was struggling along there sniping away carrying on a rear-guard action. None of their candidates lasted long enough to even get into an election against me, but it was making it harder to do my job and I was starting to be pretty fed up.

Their policies seemed to be getting harder to make sense of. They'd be for something one day and against it the next. There was a lot of funny noises coming out of Russia and they were having a hard time figuring out which propaganda to take as gospel. I told them, you guys went to bed one night and Stalin was the greatest thing since Christ was a pup and when you woke up the next morning he was a bloody chump. It's amazing the crap some otherwise intelligent people will swallow before they'll doubt their faith in a political party. I used to kid them about it, I'd say, it's twelve o'clock you guys, better go do your three bows to Moscow.

After the experience Ken had they couldn't get any more candidates outside the union so in desperation they turned to Sammy Jenkins, who'd been peeing his pants for the chance for some time.

II

I never give Sam Jenkins much credit but he had a cunning it was easy to underestimate. Take this piece he's got in that union book about his union card. He says he's proud to have been a member of our great union. "My number is one hundred and sixty-six in the union and I still pack my card today." This book was mainly for benefit of union members, present and retired and future, and the point of him saying his number, you see, is that it's so low. This is a big prestige item, to have a low number. He knows guys are going to be looking at that book with their own numbers up in the thousands and think, "Wow, this Jenkins is one of the founding members of the union. He's got seniority over everybody." What they don't know is that originally he had a high number too, and when he got on the union executive he went and switched it with some real founding member who'd been killed or died or left the union. My number was in the nine hundreds and I started in the yards two years before Jenkins. The point isn't that he switched his number because quite a few guys did that, but just the way he shows it off there. He doesn't actually lie, he just says "my number is one hundred and sixty-six," and creates a false impression.

When Jenkins come into the union he claimed to be a prizefighter, and it's a fact he had a few pro fights around Vancouver but he didn't last very long. He was very anxious to prove that he was one of the men and his language, early on, would've made a Missouri muleskinner blush.

He soon became an eager worker in the union, although it was never my impression that he was as interested in the problems of his fellow workers as he was in making himself important. And I was certainly not alone with this impression. Stewart and MacLeod regarded him with a kind of amused tolerance.

Still, no union is in a position to turn away a willing worker and it wasn't too long before Jenkins got to be a shop steward, then a business agent. I remember one time when he was new we went in to see about some beef with Syd Hogg, the general manager of Western Bridge, who was a guy I always had good relations with, and Jenkins swaggered in looking real defiant, flopped down in the best chair and propped his feet up on Hogg's desk. Hogg said, "You keep your goddamn feet on the floor, you're not home now." And you should have seen the wind go out of Sam's sails then, he was quiet as a boy.

I remember one of the bastards we always had trouble with, a guy named Izzy Stein at one of the scrapyards, Atlas Metals. He was one of those loudmouths, very profane and rough, you know. A big fella. We were organizing his place and he found out about it and fired our key guy. We weren't certified, we had no contract, but this was still just as illegal as could be so I went down and demanded he reinstate this fella. And oh, he was just wild. He wasn't going to do that even if he had to close up and put all the men out of work. I said, "Well alright, we don't have a contract here and we're not sure what we should do. We're going to have a study session to think it over. All the guys'll be coming off the job and it might take us quite a few days to figure out what to do."

"You're going to strike then!" he said.

"Oh no. No, no. That would be *illegal*. We're going to have a study session to try and see how to protect the workers against your anti-labour and blatantly discriminatory employment practices. We wouldn't do anything illegal like you done."

"You talk to my lawyer!" he said.

"No, I don't want to talk to your damn lawyer," I said, "You're the one that needs to talk to a lawyer."

Oh, Jesus Christ, he was screaming and piling on abuse, you know. He phoned his lawyer himself. I forget who this lawyer was—Bronfman or some such name, he ranted away at this lawyer as I sat there listening, then he said, "Here! He wants to talk to you." He shoved the phone over to me. I took it, this guy said, "What's going on up there?" So I told him, I said, "We're organizing this plant. We've got a majority now and we've applied for certification, and Stein here had fired our representative in the plant, which as you know is against the Labour Code. You can't fire a worker for union activity, and that's what I been trying to tell Stein but he seems to think he can get away with it." He asked me a bunch of questions then he says, "Okay. You put that guy back on the phone. I'll straighten him out but quick or he won't be a client of mine very damn long."

Stein was just about tearing the phone out of my hands anyways, pounding the desk and making faces, so I says, "Here. Listen good now." He starts screaming all his denials at this lawyer, but he starts dying down, dying down, talking quieter. Finally he's listening. "Oh," he says. "Alright," he says. "Yeah, I hear ya. I understand. Okay." He hangs up the phone without looking up. "Tell the son-of-a-bitch to go back to work," he growls.

Well now, this was supposed to be Sam's job you see, taking care of the small shops, but he hadn't been able to make a dint on Stein. When I come down Stein jumped onto me that Sam should be president of the Boilermakers instead of me, he was a fine man and a church man and all this. I guess Sam had been letting on to him about his ambitions you see, this guy made a pet of him. Any time an employer, especially one with anti-labour tendencies, starts praising a union man, it only means one thing to me—that he has him in his pocket. In the union book Sam has a piece there on what a fine man Isy Stein was. They had much in common.

Some time after he come into the union Sam stumbled into a revival meeting somewhere—I don't know just how it come about—but he found religion and started to go around putting the word to guys. Being tied up with the Pentecostal Church and the Communist Party at the same time is something you'd really have to know Sam to understand.

That being an evangelist can be a real narcissistic deal, there's quite an ego-jag in it for the type of guy who's looking for it. Sort of like being God for a day. And Sam's ego was driving him *all the time*. I suppose he might of been making a few bucks on it too, I don't know. Getting the extra buck was a big thing to him. One time there he got a compensation settlement, he got them to operate on a knuckle he jammed up years earlier in the yard, and while it was healing they paid him for work loss, not realizing he was drawing his full union salary at the same time. The union was right up against it at this time trying to raise money to fight Kuzych and I told him, I sure as hell wouldn't do that. Why don't you go off salary and donate your wages to the Kuzych fund while you're on compensation, I said. Because Christ, if he'd been caught it would have made us all look like a bunch of damn racketeers. But he said hell with that.

What gets me is how the Party was able to swallow this all, the way religion is supposed to be the opiate of the masses, you know. But this is where the cunning come in—Sam managed to work around so he was important to them. The big thing was this dispatching. It was a very, very powerful tool. Sam was running some kind of mission down on Skid Row then, trying to convert the alkies and hop heads and we started to notice quite a flock of these derelicts getting sent up on temporary work passes. Union guys would complain to me they were passed over for some goddamn bum from Pigeon Park and the girls in the office would tell me different times that these guys were getting first crack at jobs. It wasn't good for the union's relations with the companies or the members, but again, it was like chasing goddamn mirages to prove anything.

Jenkins gives his side of it in the union book. "I want to say a little about the union hiring and the dispatch system from the union because most of it centred around myself," he says. "Whether I was business agent or later on as president, I had my finger on the union hiring hall. But I can say with a completely honest conscience that I never discriminated against anyone in that union as far as jobs were concerned, and if I did, it was not a friend I sent to work, it was a so-called enemy that I would send to work. You know, if I had a choice between the two, I would rather do the favour to an enemy, rather than a friend, because I was overzealous of doing a good job and a fair job, as far as hiring was concerned. And another thing, I wouldn't even accept a cigar across that desk in my office, even in the days when I smoked cigars. But it's one of the things that's most gratifying, I think, that when I left that union, I could walk down the street and hold my head high. Not one soul in that union could I not look in the eye, and say, 'I dealt with you honestly.'" That's the gospel according to Sam.

When they decided to run him against me for the presidency they pulled out all the stops. They really campaigned. Guys come to me and told me they were told when they were sent out to work, "Don't forget who got you this job now, come the election." I got pretty bloody mad, but the guys wouldn't dare speak up you see, lest they'd end up frozen out like Ken Richards, and I didn't want to put them in a spot.

They really got the rumour-mill stoked up, too. That was Stewart's baby. He started off by saying I was an agent for the RCMP. It kind of fit you see, because guys knew there was friction between the Party and me, and this could be one explanation of it. Then once this got around they brought out about my having been in the force before I joined the union like it was a big revelation and I guess for a lot of guys that seemed to confirm the rumour. I made a complete disclosure of my police association, explained how I come to join and how I come to quit, but then they'd have a stooge there to say, "How come we're just getting to hear about this now?" Well I had told them all about it before I come into the union and I never tried to cover it up in any way—I talked about it all the time—but in the heat of the campaign, you know, it's very hard to get a point across. I pointed out that other labour leaders like Roly Gervin and George Harris of the UE had been policemen, but the more you talk in a situation like that the stickier it gets. They were able to raise doubts with a lot of the guys.

I was sitting on the North Van ferry one morning going over to check on some beef or other and this bloke come sit down beside me.

"You in the Boilermakers?" he said.

"Yeah. You?" I said.

"Yeah," he says, "I am, but I'm ashamed to admit it."

"Why is that? I said.

"Well, that goddamn crook we got for a president."

"Bill White, you mean?"

"Yeah, but that's not his real name, you know."

"No?"

"No, no, no. Everybody knows that. It's some foreign goddamn thing. Palooskachuck, I think. He changed it when he come out here. He had to change it."

"Is that so." I was just taking this in you see.

"He used to be in Montreal before he come here. He was a big name in the rackets and the cops run him out—that's when he come out and took over the union."

"How'd he do that?" I says.

"Infiltrated himself. You know that union hall we got there?"

"I guess I do."

"Well this White or Palooskachuck or whatever you want to call him, his wife used to own that, and when he took over he got the union to buy it off her for ten times what it was worth!"

"I didn't know that," I said.

"Well you should pay more attention to what's going on then," he said.

"You know this fella White, do you?" I said.

"I know him alright," he says.

"You'd recognize him?"

"Sure, anybody would. He looks just like Al Capony."

I had to laugh, you know. "Well, Buster," I said, "you better get yourself a pair of specs, because you're looking at him right now."

Well, he looked like he'd just seen a ghost. Before I could say another word, zip he was gone.

There were other things. At a meeting when you were speaking they'd have some guy stand up and say, "What about that thousand bucks, White, why don't you tell them about that?" You say, "What thousand bucks, I don't know what you're talking about." So then this stooge says, "Oh, you know what I'm talking about. You know." And he gets the hell out of sight. If you don't see it coming it can really throw you. Guys start saying, "Hey, what's this? What's he talking about? What thousand bucks? There must be *some*thing to it, *some* explanation." If you just deny it flatfooted, then they don't believe you. You're left there looking like a crook and a poor liar. Dirty tricks. Boy Tricky Dick had nothing on these guys.

One of the good ones was where they decided to unionize our office girls. This Jean McKenna, who Harold Pritchett married later after his first wife died, she turned up as business agent for the AF of L Office Workers and organized the two girls in our front office. Our girls were among the best-treated secretaries in the city but I said by all means, give them whatever seems right. I could see it was a Party caper so I figured they could just work it out among themselves. But they didn't want that. They wanted me to sit and negotiate with this woman. This seemed a complete waste of time but I said alright, we'll negotiate.

So she presented a demand that was so goddamned high it was more than the men in the yards were getting. I said, "Like hell!" and we had a bit of a set-to.

"I'm going to get Roly Gervin down here!" she said. I had to laugh out loud. Roly Gervin was about as scary as Santa Claus. "I wish to hell you would," I said. "What the hell are you trying to prove anyhow?"

"If we get a good contract here it'll make it easier dealing with the big companies," she said.

"They're not that stupid," I said. "In any case I'm tired of you people trying to loot this union for your damn schemes. You'll get a fair contract for a fair wage and that's all you get."

Well, then they had me in the bight, you see. Stewart and them took her side and they had me in the position of some damn skinflint employer. They threatened to bring in pickets and everything else. But can you imagine the bloody fuss there would have been, when our men found the office girls were getting more than they were? I gave them a good contract finally, but they took my damn terms.

But then you see, Stewart went in and told the girls it was me spoiled it for them and turned them against me. They'd be listening in on my phone calls and reporting everything to Stewart and Jenkins. A guy'd just have to get his neck bowed and tell them to layoff. They'd get this awful pained look, you know. It was a bugger.

There was a little fella named Taffy Pierce, a little Welshman who'd only weigh about a hundred and thirty pounds but just as tough as a keg of nails. He was always in the forefront of any ruckus. I seen him down at the *Province* strike that time, a cop tried to take him and Taffy nailed him in the knackers with his boot, just about crippled the guy, and got away into the crowd. Taffy was very dark, as you can gather from the name, and I remember the cop referred to him at the trial as "that dirty little Frenchman that kicked me." I got quite a laugh out of that.

Anyways Taffy was a Party member and he come in from a Party meeting where they'd really been putting the heat on me, really taking me apart, and he'd been defending me. They'd really give *him* shit then too and he come up to tell me what happened, and you know, the little bugger broke down crying. Because he was so upset what they were doing to me. It was getting really rough then.

Incidentally, his wife filleted him. I don't know just how it happened, Harry Rankin defended her and got her off. I think Taffy used to tamp up on her a bit, and they both drank, and I guess he made for her and she said he run on the bloody knife, and that fixed him. She was good with a knife because she worked in the cannery filleting fish. She was bigger than him too, but she'd be no match for Taffy.

I was getting very disgusted the way things were going. I give up trying to fight them off at all and withdrew from the campaign. I just did my job and went home. I told guys if they figured I was doing a good enough job, well they could vote for me and I'd keep doing it. Otherwise they could vote for Jenkins and the Party and I'd go do something else.

Now it's funny, but I forget whether I was in two elections with Jenkins or just the one. I asked Jack O'Kane recently and he thought it was two. It might have been. This last one was in December, 1954. Anyways, Jenkins' wires to heaven must have been crossed because in spite of his connections with the Maker and the full support of the Communist Party he never was able to beat me. The members kept on my side to the end.

Tommy Thompson, the old personnel manager for Burrard Drydock, hated my guts because I used to take the hide off him by the yard but there's one thing I agree with him on one hundred percent and that is the electricians' strike of 1955 "was one of the sad times for the labour climate in Burrard Drydock." It was one of the sad times for labour, period.

It was a contract year and we had joint negotiations that year, where for the first time all the unions in the Burrard Drydock sat down and negotiated with the company as one body. Jenkins claims I walked out on negotiations but I'm sure his memory isn't that bad. I headed those negotiations and I wound them up. It went to conciliation and the report we negotiated, our members accepted it by a vote of four hundred and eleven to thirty-eight.

What happened then is that one of the small unions in the yard, the Electrical Workers, pulled out of joint negotiations and demanded wage parity with the outside electrical workers. This was unfortunate, but they had every right in the world to do it if they wanted. They were a legitimate trade union chartered by the Congress and they were making a legitimate demand. I don't know what they wanted—about a dime more. Bert Adair was president and he come to our meeting, told us what he was planning, and asked for our support. "If you guys support us it won't go on too long," he said. So I said, "Well, I been president of the Marine Workers and Boilermakers Union eleven years and we've never gone through a picket line. And as long as I'm president we never will." Fine, okay. Figuring they had our backing to count on, they went ahead and struck.

It wasn't long before it come clear to me that I wasn't going to be able to keep my word. The Party went to work and decided to scab on Adair. Their plan was to break his little union and force its members into a union that was controlled by the Party, the IBEW. They were going to overrule me on the executive and take our members through Adair's picket line.

This time I could see there was no way I could stop them. This strike wasn't popular with our boys because they had nothing to gain. We had our contract, we were already working at our new rates and now it looked like we were going to have to go off anyway, for the sake of these electrical workers who'd broke out of our joint agreement. I could see how easy it would be to get our boys stirred up against them. If the leadership stood solid and appealed to the members to stand up for trade union principles I don't think there'd have been any problem, because we had the trade union consciousness and the discipline. But with all the rest of the executive egging the guys on to take the easy way out, telling them it was all okay and just me holding my hand up against it, I could see it was an impossible situation. Always before when I disagreed with the Party, I'd say alright, we'll put it to the membership and let them decide and they'd generally back off because they could see the rank and file would side with me. This time I couldn't do that because I could see plain as hell the membership would side with them. I'd said on other issues, if the members go against me, I'll accept their verdict. But here I'd given Adair my word we wouldn't cross a picket line while I was president and he had counted on this. I was in a box. I could have got out easy enough by going back on what I told Adair, and probably nobody would have blamed me. But I couldn't do it. I'd damn well know it was phoney, and I just wasn't going to let those bastards push me into it. I said, to hell with it, you guys go through if you want. But I won't be there.

That's how it ended. I ended it myself. I don't mean to say by that that I'd decided to end my period as head of the union for any other reason than the strike issue, because I didn't. Different guys have put it to me that way but that's not the way it was. I resigned for only one reason, and that was because I'd give my word the Marine Workers would never cross a picket line while I was president and it was a matter of keeping my word. It was one of the simplest decisions I ever had to make, and it was based on that issue alone. I had never thought of quitting before that and if that issue hadn't come up I might have gone on for a long time. I might still be there. Or I might have run into something else and resigned a week later. You can't say. The consequences were that my thirteen years as a labour leader came to an end as abruptly and unexpectedly as they'd begun.

January 5, 1955, was my last day. I cleaned out my office and went home. The *Vancouver Sun* reported it on the front page, "Well-known leftist Bill White resigns." The reporters wanted me to spill the beans but I wouldn't give them any satisfaction. Jenkins took over in a by-election the next week and the papers give him a big reception, "Pastor Sam takes over in surprise vote." He got one of his converts, Alex Livingstone in as vice-president and the papers played it as the Christians cleaning out the Communists. Sam claims he was out of the Party by this time, but in or out he suited their purposes fine.

I went to work in my brother's mill up at Quesnel and never had anything to do with the union again, except once or twice I sat in on a meeting. I don't even know exactly how the electricians' strike business worked out, except that the Marine Workers did cross the picket line and the IBEW did eventually take over the Electrical Worker's jurisdiction. I always thought they did it right off the bat but I'm told now they actually stayed out for a few weeks. They might have had to, because there were guys even at that who refused to cross and stayed out on their own, like Jack Klemola. There was a lot of guys in that union who took their trade union principles seriously.

But you see, the worst thing you can ever do is go out on strike half-heartedly. You're just laying your neck on the chopping block. My plan was that since we were in a spot where we couldn't avoid this strike, to throw the full force of the union behind it. Make a big issue of the principles and try and line the whole labour movement up behind us. If I'd been left to handle it my way, I've no doubt but the whole thing would of been settled clean and quick the way our strikes

The electrical shop at Burrard Drydock, 1945. NORTH VANCOUVER MUSEUM AND ARCHIVES, 27-75

always had been before. But once the bosses saw the union leadership was in dispute and no doubt heard about the Party plan to break the strike, they knew all they had to do was wait.

I think the whole West Coast labour movement was shocked when it happened. Because you have to remember, up to this time the Marine Workers and Boilermakers Union was always looked up to as being one of the outspoken champions of trade union principles in the country.

They were condemned by the Vancouver Labour Council and put on trial by the Canadian Congress of Labour. Jenkins made some lame goddamn excuse that he had to do it to save the Marine Workers from a raid by the AF of L International Boilermakers, but the AF of L didn't have a single member in the yards he could point to. They tried to say the Electrical Workers wasn't a real picket line either, but it was. The courts would have folded it up quick enough if it wasn't. They just didn't want to admit they were scab herders. But it just goes to show you how the goddamn Party would compromise the most fundamental trade union principles if they figured it was an asset politically. This is the thing that was so bitter to me. I figured with that one move they'd destroyed the reputation and the militant spirit our union had build up over the years, and subsequent history bears me out on this. The Marine Workers has never been a force of any consequence on the West Coast labour scene since. You hardly ever hear of it anymore.

19

Old Labour Leaders

I

Right now, in 1983, the Party still exists and it's still got a few of the smaller unions but it's what you might call a "closed shop." The leadership has barely changed for thirty years and there's very little youth coming in. It's an old men's club where most of the members are life members. It's at a dead end and the whole militant tradition is at a dead end.

Whenever any of us old radical bastards get together it's usually not too long before the conversation gets around to the theme of "what did we do wrong?" Mostly it seems to me we blame the wrong things. We dwell on the goofs like Murphy's Underwear Speech or Pritchett's bad arithmetic at the '48 convention or the IWA pullout. This Professor Abella makes a big thing of the folding of the Worker's Unity League back in 1935.

There's no question that the Party made a lot of bad mistakes which hurt them over the short haul, but there was mistakes on all sides and the Party had its share of victories, too. Looking back now, you can see there was more to it than the mistakes. You can see now that history was moving away from us.

As I said before, it was the Depression that made the Party. These real solid old Party warhorses I keep mentioning got their start in the Depression with the unemployed and the Unity League, and it was them built the Party base in the labour movement. The opportunists and the cranks and fellow travellers jumped onto the bandwagon later after they saw how the organizing was going. But the further they got away from the Depression, the weaker its influence became. Generations grew up that knew nothing but fat times—lots of jobs, big money, good conditions. As much as the Party built the unions that brought those fat times in, it authored its own destruction. There's no doubt the Cold War took its toll but the progressive spirit survives a hard go better than an easy one. Only another Depression could bring the left back like it was in this country.

As far as labour goes, it appears to be in great shape—on the outside. It's got more members, more coverage than ever before. It's got closed shop with compulsory checkoff. The TLC and CCL merged to form the Canadian Labour Congress (CLC) in 1956, so it's got unity. It's got things in the Labour Code that we didn't even dream about in the old days. According to the establishment all this has made labour too big and powerful.

I'm not so damn sure about that. It might be big, but it looks awful flabby to me. Most fellas in a union today, they hardly know they're in it except for the nick in their paycheque, and half of them don't notice that. There are exceptions, but the typical union today has very little presence in the workplace, and much as I hate to say it the closed shop has a lot to do with this. When you had to go out and sell your union to every member you worked harder to prove it was worth it and you kept more men in the field. Now the leadership can lay back in the head office and pay themselves big salaries because they know the dues are going to come rolling in anyway. I doubt there's a union in the country that has a shop stewards' movement like the one we had.

When I see the face of a labour leader on the TV now it's always fat. All jowls like hogs ready for the knife, it's hard to imagine the sight of any of them striking fear in the capitalists' hearts. It's bad enough not being able to tell the bosses from the labour leaders by looking at them but the worst of it is half the time you can't tell when they talk either. They talk about workers out of work like some abstract thing, like so many head of livestock. You have the CLC getting the government to set up a ten-million-dollar programme to train labour leaders, and there's all these sweetheart deals between big unions like the Teamsters and big business.

Still, trade unionism is such a powerful tool even bum leadership can't stop it doing its work. The unionized worker in Canada today has reached a level in the economic scale where he is challenging the professional classes. He has won a degree of security and self-respect that before was known only to the exploiting classes. These are gains Marx preached that only a shooting revolution could bring, and if you don't think unions had anything to do with it you only have to look at the rich countries where there aren't any, like Venezuela. There's all kinds of money there, but the peasants live in packing-crate shanties. Or Japan. I was talking to a guy who worked in Tokyo for a few years and he said a place of your own to live is something the ordinary worker there can't even think about. He was stuck all the time in subsidized company housing where it was no girls and lights out at eleven. So what's the use of supporting one of the biggest economies in the industrialized world? There's no strong unions in Japan, it's all worked on the paternalistic system.

There is quite a campaign going on today to make Canadian workers feel guilty because of the standard of living they've achieved, with everyone from the Prime Minister on down ordering us to "tighten our belts"—the phrase Herbert Hoover made famous. The thrust of the argument is that Canadian wages are so high they've made industry lose its competitive edge in the world market. This pitch is old as the hills. We heard it all through the years I was negotiating and I've no doubt that the first bunch of factory slaves who demanded an end to sixteen-hour days back in the 1700s heard it too. "If you drive my costs up I'll lose all my business to the sweatshop down the road and you'll starve." The answer then was the same as it is now, and that is to organize the sweatshop down the road at the same time. That way the boss's costs stay in line and workers get ahead in both plants. Today we have multinationals appealing to the better side of their workers to keep wage costs down so as not to force them to send more business down to their Latin American branches where wages are still at the 18th-century level. I guess if the union appealed to the corporation's better side to raise their Latin American employees' wages to the 20th-century level and even up the balance that way it would be ruled out of order. But it's too bad labour hasn't expanded at the same rate as business so they could force this to happen. This is one of the frontiers labour should be looking at, following business into the multinational sphere. If it doesn't it'll wish it did.

Even if Canadian workers had the best deal in the world, which they don't, there would be no shame in it. There's nothing to be ashamed of in leading the way out of the bloody pits and giving everyone else something to shoot for. We always figured if we could get some gain established in one plant, well, that was the biggest part of the battle because it was the strongest argument you could have if you could go to the next place and say. "We got it over there, why can't we have it here?" Getting people to realize things *can* be different is often the hardest thing.

What I see coming now is an all-out campaign in Canada to push the working stiff back. Like this doctor was saying in the election "put things back in perspective." In fact it's already well underway. There's campaigns going against pensions and others against Medicare, unemployment insurance and welfare. Workers' Compensation is back to its old tricks. The IWA is complaining about the upsurge of accidental deaths and calling for better safety standards, while the employers' council is saying the companies can't afford to keep up the standards they got now. There's pressure on for another Royal Commission. When you add it up there's not one gain the labour movement has won since the Depression that isn't under attack on some quarter. I can see it coming. The change they want isn't a financial one but a philosphical one, and their philosophy is Robin Hood in reverse: 'take from the poor and give to the rich.' This is supposed to be the very latest thing handed down from on high by the new-look economists, but I can tell you, it's the same broken record they've been playing for the forty years that I've listened to them, and they must be just peeing their pants at the way today's public is falling for it. This is the chance they've been waiting for ever since the war, and they're going to push it just as far as they can.

I just hope some the things I've said here about the way it used to be and the things us oldtimers went through will get some of the younger ones thinking and maybe be of use in the battles to come. They call it the new conservatism but it's the same old conservatism to me. It's like I said before, the battle for the working stiff is never over. The bastards are always in there keeping the pressure on, and the minute they see a chance to gain some ground they put on a drive. Right now they can see people are mixed up and disorganized so they're going to bag it to them for all they're worth.

II

The last official contact I had from the Party was Murphy come over to see me once when I was still in Vancouver. He wanted to join me up again as a member-at-large. This was a deal where you'd be in the Party but you wouldn't pay regular dues or go to regular meetings, you'd just kind of float in the stratosphere with no identifying marks. But I said, ah, the hell with it. I still agree with the philosophy, but like I always say, the only thing wrong with communism is the communists.

I wasn't the only one to throw my hands up over their damn shenanigans, either. There was Charlie Caron, who originally signed me into the Party. He left and joined the Maoists. Jack Scott, the fella they brought in to replace me, he ended up leaving them for the Maoists too. And I think he was at one time quite high up in the Party organization. Far as that goes, Fergie McKeen quit them, and he was *leader* of the provincial Party. *And* Malcolm Bruce. But the big one was Joe Salzberg. The backbone of their whole trade union movement. It was well after I left and I don't know the details, but they finally drove him away. There were hundreds like that. It's harder to think of guys who stayed in than it is guys who got out.

There was one time there some of the fellas down at the union tried to get a draft going to put me back in, they come up and said, "Jesus, things is in a terrible mess, you gotta come back," and so I went down and sat in on a few meetings. When I'd resigned they gave me an Honourary Life Membership that was supposed to allow me to sit in on meetings and take whatever hand I pleased in the running of the union, but when I showed up I found the executive put through a motion removing most of the privileges that went with Honourary Life Membership. I could speak but not vote. That would be Stewart's doing, I guess. He had things pretty well to himself from then on. I don't think that was a good thing for the union either. I don't know, I could be all wrong, but I always had a suspicion that if anybody was an agent it was Stewart himself. The main reason I suspect that is he never done anything all the years he was in the union. He was no good at negotiations, he was no good at beefs—the minute he got away from the men in the yard closed up with a boss, he'd give. Just fold. His favourite expression was, "We'll bring the boss to 'ees knees." He'd yodel it out and slam down his fist. But when you got thinking about it the only time he ever used that expression was when he was trying to call a confrontation off. It was invariably always followed by a great big BUT: "*But we have to wait for just that right opportunity. Now is not the time.*" The time never come.

Different times fellas in management said things about Stewart. Old Claude Thicke who was general manager of Burrard and a real tough old rooster, he was just about as direct as a bolt of lightning, I guess everybody hated him except me, he said to me once, "You know, you're not like these other guys. These other guys aren't the same guy here in the office that they are down in the yard with the men. They sound mean as hell as long as they're in the mens' hearing but it's an altogether different story once they're in here with me."

Old Geordie Matthews was another one. He was general superintendent at Burrard and he was a master shipbuilder, too. Geordie and I always got along good—we had awful arguments, don't think we didn't, but he was what you'd call a fair guy. I respected him. He'd come up the hard way, and you could talk to him. I seen Geordie at Christmas-time, oh a few years ago, and he greeted me like a long-lost friend. We got talking old times, and he said, "Stewart's still in there calling the shots I guess." Geordie was out of the yards by this time, and it was just before Stewart died. "Yeah," I said, "I guess he is."

"I don't know what you think about that guy," he said, "But I'll tell you something. He's no good, and he never was any good, all the time he's bin in there." And he meant for us, for the men.

This was the management view of Stewart. I've put it to guys, I've said, name me one thing Stewart ever did. Well, they can't do it. Generally the way they get out of it is they say he provided "leadership." Great leadership. But that's pretty damn vague. Leadership isn't sounding off at meetings once a month then going home and doing nothing, leadership is going into negotiations and holding the line, standing firm when the chips are down, and that's just the thing Stewart never did.

You can't spot an agent by listening to him talk, or checking his credentials because agents always talk up a storm and carry the best of credentials. Christ, in the thirties there it turned out one of the highest officers in the Party's national organization was an RCMP agent. Esselman was the name he was known by in the Party, and I think his right name was Leopold. The only way you can spot an agent is by analysing how he behaves over the years, in critical times, and you'd find with an agent whenever there's bullets in the air he won't be there. I might be all wrong, I don't know. The Party still thinks Stewart's a hundred percent. All I know is, if he had been hired to go in and pull that union's teeth, he couldn't have done a better job.

Stewart died in 1974. He wasn't that old, sixty-two I think. He drank himself to death. He had it bad towards the end. Jack O'Kane said one time there Stewart was supposed to be away somewhere but he got a suspicion and went out and found him in the Crease Clinic. Saw him in a ward, and his wife Barbara was with him. He was just in a kind of a coma. They tried to make him stop drinking but he couldn't.

III

Old labour leaders don't fade away, they vanish the minute they're out of office. Politicians complain about this same thing, but they're nothing compared to labour leaders. They can go on all their lives saying they were an MP once, and it means something, but it means nothing to say you were once head of some union most people have never heard of to begin with.

One day you're a power to be reckoned with, reporters are banging on your door, the next day they're walking past and not seeing you. It's like a con getting out of the pen—suddenly it's ten years later and you're back at square one again. The only guys who still wanted to talk to me after I left were the cops. I got a call at my home from the Mounted Police one day, very shortly after I resigned. They said, "We'd like to talk to you."

I said, "Well, I'm not hard to talk to."

They said, "Alright, where would you like to meet?"

"Well, you know where I live," I said.

"Oh, would that be alright?" they said.

"Why not? I've got nothing to hide." So out they come. They said they understood I was no longer with the union and I said yes, and they wanted to know why. I said, well, that's personal. Alright, they said, now we know you're not in the Party, and we'd like to talk about some guys that are. So I said, "You might as well get one thing straight. I'm no damn stool pigeon. If you come out for that you've wasted a buck's worth of the taxpayer's gas."

"But you are familiar with most of the Party members?" they said.

"I know 'em from Halifax to Victoria, the main ones," I said. "But I'll tell you something, you know them too, and I'm pretty damn sure you can tell me more about the Party than I can tell you."

"Whaddya mean?" they said.

"Christ," I said, "do you think I don't know about the damn spies you got in the union movement?"

"Do you know any specifically?"

"Yeah, I figure I do."

"Who?" they said. So I named off a few.

"Why don't you get rid of them?" they said.

"You might put a son-of-a-bitch in we *didn't* know," I said.

That was as far as it went then. They left and I never heard from them again.

Fred Smelts was another one. He come out to see me with a proposition. Fred Smelts was on the Labour Relations Board representing the employers and oh Jesus, did he and I ever used to go at it hammer and tongs now. He come from the BC Electric, he was manager of the gas division, and he was about the best thing the employers ever had going for them. He was just as hard and smart as any guy I ever locked horns with. And he was one of the roughest talking guys I ever seen. His language would curl the hair on a hedgehog. Right in formal hearings—"Wot the fock is wrong with you ya sick-lookin son-of-a-bitch?"—he'd talk like that. A great big guy too, he weighed over two hundred forty pounds.

He had this here dog. Big dumb dog, he took it everywhere and during settings of the LRB often you'd see it asleep under the table. I come there one time and just him and Harry Strange, another LRB member, were there with his dog under the table. Smelts introduced me to Strange, and then he points to the dog and says, "And this is the third member of the board, here."

I looked down at this dog and said, "Well, I'm mighty pleased to know you. I've never met you before but I've read quite a few of your decisions." I guess I spent more time fighting Smelts than just about anybody else.

When Smelts left the LRB he went labour-faking—he went into business taking care of union negotiating for various businesses and as soon as he heard I was out of the union he come down and tried to get me in with him. He said, "I'll guarantee you ten thousand a year, but I'm telling you Bill, that's chicken-feed to what you *will* make."

He said, "You come in and we'll get all the damn negotiations on the coast."

I said, "No, nothing doing. I've been too damn long on the other side."

That's one thing I'll never be able to forgive about Harvey Murphy. He let the bastards get to him. He took Mine-Mill into Steel. After all the goddamn time we spent fighting those phoney bastards, he went and delivered the union up to them. They give him $500 a month for life. I guess that'd be pretty nice you know, on top of the old age pension. Still, a guy'd know inside, wouldn't he?

What made me sick about that whole Mine-Mill deal was a speech Murphy give for Pen Baskin when the merger took place. Pen Baskin was the West Coast rep for Steel and one of the left wing's oldest enemies. When Mahoney was cleaning out the reds at that famous BC Fed convention in '48, Pen Baskin was the guy the right-wing put up to knock off Stewart for vice-president, and Murphy worked as hard against him as anybody did. And then to see old Murph up there giving this phoney a real "man-who" speech. This is the man who done this, this is the man who done that. It was just about enough to make a guy puke.

The last time I seen Murphy was at Robbie Robson's funeral, he had his arm in a goddamn cast. Said he fell down the stairs.

"Drunk again, eh," I said.

"I knew you'd say that," he said.

"Well it's too bad you didn't break your goddamn neck."

"Why do you say that?"

"Taking Mine-Mill into Steel!"

"Well," he said. "At least I took it in all in one piece." But I don't know what the hell kind of an excuse that was. If they were going to smash him, better to let them smash, I say. Better than letting them get it easy. At least that way the idea keeps going.

I was talking to a guy who was back in Toronto talking to Murph in 1976 just before he died. He said he'd kind of gone soft in the head, couldn't talk about anything except excuses for taking Mine-Mill into Steel. He died making excuses, poor bastard, after fighting for all those years.

In a job like I had there in the union you never had time to look left or right, your both hands were tied up dealing with all the things that kept coming up in front of you. I know I haven't made much mention here of any type of personal life or family life, but the damn truth is, I didn't have enough to mention. As Ivy is very fond of saying, I was married to the union. I'd sometimes get a minute to myself to think, though, and I thought of a lot of things a guy could do if he ever got off the hook and had a bit of time. Going back to school there like Sloan suggested was probably the most attractive one, and taking lawyer training. Jesus how I would of loved to do that!

But you know when the chance finally come I never give it a thought. The first thing I did was get the hell out of town and away from all the damn bullshit I'd been going through in the union, up where I wouldn't hear the name of Jenkins or Stewart or any of these guys, and they wouldn't hear mine. And you know, it felt so damn good. I got up there working with my hands, going to bed tired and getting a good night's sleep—well hell, it was all I could do to go back to town to see Ivy and Marilyn and Shirley, my two daughters.

I stayed with my brother a few months and I could see there was money in the sawmill business and you could still get timber in those days, so I mortgaged our house and started up a little mill of my own near Lac La Hache. It would have worked out real well but every time I'd be just over the hump my luck would run out on me. I got to cutting half a million board feet a month when I slipped driving logs down a crick and messed my back up. Then just as I was getting over that one the goddamn mill burnt up. Lost every stick of it.

I went down to the Compensation Board to see if I couldn't get something out of them for my back injury—I was quite crippled up and had to have two operations—and who should turn up for the examination but one of the old doctors I'd battled with back in the union days. He got me up on the examining table and lifted my leg up and just cranked it sideways with all his weight. I thought I'd pass right out. It was worse than the original fall. I had to be helped out of the room.

I called up Doc Inglis and told him what happened and he couldn't believe it. There's nothing the son-of-a-bitch could have done what would have hurt more or been worse for my injury. But what he was doing you see, he was teaching me a lesson. It wasn't just a matter of hurting me, it was that he could do that to me now and get away with it. It made me realize how damn powerless I was. That hurt more than my back.

I had to cut my losses and give up on the mill so as soon as my back got good enough I went out on construction. My first job who should I get as foreman but this Maxamento, the riveter whose job I saved back in the days when Bill Jordan was running Pacific Drydock. And by Jesus, you know, he was as ornery as any foreman I ever run into. I come up to him once and reminded him how we'd looked after him in the yards but I got no response at all. It might of never happened as far as he was concerned.

Smelts, the bugger, made another stab at getting me to go in with him later on. He was doing quite good, so he upped the ante and made a special trip from Vancouver up to Quesnel. To see if he could talk me into changing my mind, but Christ, I couldn't even think about it. How the hell could a guy spend half his life fighting for something then turn around and fight against it? The bastards never did accept it that the reason I fought them so hard was I believed in the damn thing.

Index